# Innovative Approaches and Explorations in Ceramic Studies

edited by

Sandra L. López Varela

Archaeopress Archaeology

ARCHAEOPRESS PUBLISHING LTD

Summertown Pavilion
18-24 Middle Way
Oxford OX2 7LG

www.archaeopress.com

ISBN 978 1 78491 736 4
ISBN 978 1 78491 737 1 (e-Pdf)

© Archaeopress and the authors 2017

Cover: Jaina figurines (Photographs courtesy of Centro INAH Campeche, México)

All rights reserved. No part of this book may be reproduced, in any form or
by any means, electronic, mechanical, photocopying or otherwise,
without the prior written permission of the copyright owners.

This book is available direct from Archaeopress or from our website www.archaeopress.com

# Contents

List of Figures and Tables ..................................................................................................................................... iii

**Chapter 1**
Innovative Approaches and Explorations in Ceramic Studies ................................................................................. 1
Sandra L. López Varela and Philip J. Arnold III

**Chapter 2**
What is a Ceramic Assemblage: Chronology and Belongings of the Late Classic Maya ........................................ 11
Sherman Horn III and Anabel Ford

**Chapter 3**
Investigating Maya Ceramic Figurines: challenges to the use of non-invasive portable technologies
    in archived collections ..................................................................................................................................... 25
Sandra L. López Varela

**Chapter 4**
Documenting Accommodation and Change in the Tarascan Ceramic Economy .................................................. 41
Amy J. Hirshman

**Chapter 5**
Forming Pots and Community: Pottery Production and Potter Interaction in
    an Ancestral Wendat Village ............................................................................................................................ 53
Sarah Striker, Linda Howie and Ronald Williamson

**Chapter 6**
Clay Choice: the Impacts of Ceramic Formation Methods and Cultural Behavior .............................................. 71
Mary F. Ownby

**Chapter 7**
Complementary Approaches for Understanding Mazapan Pottery ..................................................................... 89
Destiny L. Crider

**Chapter 8**
Sherds of Spartans Past: Ceramics from the Michigan State University Campus Archaeology Program ..... 107
Lynne Goldstein, Lisa Bright and Jeffrey Painter

**Chapter 9**
The Ethnoarchaeology of an Abandoned Potter's Workshop in Ticul, Yucatán, México .................................. 119
Dean E. Arnold

**Chapter 10**
Making Traditional Pottery Sustainable Today: Three Case Studies in Akita Prefecture, Japan .................... 129
Cara L. Reedy and Chandra L. Reedy

# List of Figures and Tables

### Chapter 1. Innovative Approaches and Explorations in Ceramic Studies
*Sandra L. López Varela and Philip J. Arnold III*

Table 1. Ceramic Ecology Sessions. Papers by Area of Studies and Topic presented in between 1986 and 2016 at the American Anthropological Association ................................................................................................................................................................ 2

### Chapter 2. What is a Ceramic Assemblage: Chronology and Belongings of the Late Classic Maya
*Sherman Horn III and Anabel Ford*

Figure 1. El Pilar and the Maya Lowlands .................................................................................................................................................. 11
Figure 2. Jars from Uaxactun .................................................................................................................................................................... 13
Figure 3. Bowls from Uaxactun ................................................................................................................................................................. 13
Figure 4. Plates from Uaxactun ................................................................................................................................................................. 14
Figure 5. Belize Red:Belize Red variety vessels from Barton Ramie .......................................................................................................... 14
Figure 6. Survey Transects and Settlement in the El Pilar Area ................................................................................................................. 16
Figure 7. Basic Vessel Forms in the El Pilar Area ....................................................................................................................................... 17
Figure 8. Common Shapes in Late Classic Assemblages in the El Pilar Area ............................................................................................ 18
Figure 9. Common Bowl Shapes in Late Classic Assemblages .................................................................................................................. 18
Figure 10. Common Jar Shapes in the Late Classic Assemblages .............................................................................................................. 19
Figure 11. Common Plate Shapes in Late Classic Assemblages ................................................................................................................ 19
Figure 12. Common Vase Shapes in Late Classic Assemblages ................................................................................................................. 20
Table 1. El Pilar Area Ceramic Attribute Assessment ................................................................................................................................. 17
Table 2. Diagnostic Late Classic Vessel Forms from the El Pilar Area ....................................................................................................... 17
Table 3. Late Classic General Form and Common Shape Diagnostics from Full-Scale Excavations .......................................................... 18
Table 4. Diagnostic Late Classic Vessel Shapes by Geographic Zones ...................................................................................................... 21

### Chapter 3. Investigating Maya Ceramic Figurines: challenges to the use of non-invasive portable technologies in archived collections
*Sandra L. López Varela*

Figure 1. Map showing location of Jaina, off the coast of Campeche, Mexico ........................................................................................... 26
Figure 2. On-site analysis of the ceramic figurines at the Centro INAH Campeche: (A) use of a Thermo Scientific Niton® XL3t GOLDD- handheld XRF spectrometer; (B) Use of a FieldSpec3® spectrometer from Analytical Spectral Devices Inc. (ASD) ................................................................................................................................................................................ 29
Figure 3. Bivariate plot of $Log_{10}$ Ti (ppm) versus Cr/Rb (ppm) showing the separation of groups based on the abundances of trace elements Ti, Cr and Rb ................................................................................................................................................. 29
Figure 4. Bivariate plot of $log_{10}$ Zr (ppm) versus $Log_{10}$ Cr (ppm) showing the separation of groups based on the abundances of trace elements Zr and Cr .................................................................................................................................................................. 30
Figure 5. Figurines depicting elements of power and war: (A) A ruler wearing a fan-shaped headdress depicting two zoomorphic figures (SM 10-342651); (B) A ruler holds a war related object and a fan shaped War Serpent headdress (SM 10-339781); (C) A masked ruler holding an ax on his left hand, wears a fan-shaped War Serpent headdress and a mantle (BCC-10-343434) similar to those represented at Stelae 13 of Tikal .............................................................................. 32
Figure 6. Representation of seated Maya rulers. (A) A male portrayed on his ruling seat, with a very elaborate headdress (HKAN 10-343413); (B) A ruler portrayed on a platform, inscribed with hieroglyphs, wearing a tunic and a zoomorphic fan-shaped headdress (HKAN 10-343413); (C) A ruler wearing a bird shaped headdress on his ruling seat (SM 10-342652) ..... 32
Figure 7. (A) Male figurine wearing a cylinder pixom (HKAN 10-343354); (B) Male figurine wearing a complex cloth headdress and a spondylus shell identifying him maybe as a *saha* (HKAN 10-343415); (C) Male figurine wearing a rough application covering the chin and the cheek (SM 10-223510); (D) Male figurine wearing big ear spools and a complex design on his face, as well as a necklace formed by oliva snails (SM 10-342819) ............................................................ 33
Figure 8. (A) Male wearing a shield and a shell necklace (SM 10-397874); (B) A male warrior with a complex headdress, commonly, found among warriors at Chichen Itzá (HKAN 10-342655); (C) Male wearing a fan and a warrior suit (SM 10-339782) ......................................................................................................................................................................................... 33
Figure 9. (A) A musical instrument with one resonator chamber portrays an owl (SM 10-339778); (B) A male ruler wearing an owl headdress and a thick necklace with an ahau representation at the center (HKAN 10-343435); (C) Ball player wearing a protruding thick yoke around his waist and a wavy headdress still exhibiting traces of Maya blue (HKAN 10-343380) ............................................................................................................................................................................. 34
Figure 10. (A) Elderly male with a female figurine (SM 10-342814); (B) A female figurine with a young adult male (SM 10-343125); (C) A female figurine holding a beaded strand (SM 10-522662); (D) A female figurine with a double necklace formed by thick beads (BBC 10-343340) ................................................................................................................... 34

Figure 11. (A) A female figurine with a child placed on her lap (SM 10-398036); (B) A female figurine carries a child behind her back (SM 10-339983); (C) A female figurine with a red rounded bowl (SM 10-342637); (D) The same female figurine carries a child on her back (SM 10-342637) ............................................................................................................... 35

Figure 12. (A) A musical instrument portraying a female figurine wearing a large hollow broad-brimmed hat over a complex hairdo exhibits three dots on her face (SM 10-290541); (B) A fragmented flute displaying a male with a bloated belly (SM 10-398032); (C) A mold made ocarina with one resonator chamber, recovered from the 1964 field season of excavations (SM 10-342828), represents a male wearing a mask representing a howler monkey .................... 36

Figure 13. (A) A female figurine with bent arms and outward hand palms served as a rattle (BBC 10-398097); (B) A similar rattle depicts a woman with one bent arm showing her outward hand palm, while the left arm rests on her left flank (SM 10-339983); (C) Another rattle depicts a woman with arms to her side and showing both outward hand palms (SM 10-49613); (D) A female articulated figurine exhibits a Tlaloc motive (BBC 10-398075 0/3) ...................................................... 36

## Chapter 4. Documenting Accommodation and Change in the Tarascan Ceramic Economy
### Amy J. Hirshman

Figure 1. Map of the Lake Pátzcuaro Basin showing sites named in the text................................................................. 42
Table 1. Chronology for the Lake Pátzcuaro Basin ........................................................................................................ 42
Table 2. Rim Sherd Within cluster Error Sum of Squares (ESS) One-Way ANOVA .................................................... 44
Table 3. Alphabetical Listing of Paste Categories Identified by Pollard ...................................................................... 45
Table 4. Compositional group by time and by site.......................................................................................................... 46

## Chapter 5. Forming Pots and Community:
## Pottery Production and Potter Interaction in an Ancestral Wendat Village
### Sarah Striker, Linda Howie and Ronald Williamson

Figure 1. Surficial geology of south-central Ontario........................................................................................................ 57
Figure 2. Soil parent material composition of south-central Ontario............................................................................ 62
Figure 3. Learner vessel fabrics showing range of compositional variation observed................................................ 64
Table 1. Distinguishing characteristics of Group A ceramic fabrics groups that include learner vessels ................ 60
Table 2. Distinguishing characteristics of Group B ceramic fabrics groups that include learner vessels ................ 61

## Chapter 6. Clay Choice: the Impacts of Ceramic Formation Methods and Cultural Behavior
### Mary F. Ownby

Figure 1. Map showing locations where clay was collected for the experimental vessels. Cultural group areas are also shown .... 72
Figure 2. Experimental pots made from several different clays using paddle and anvil (vessels on the left) and coil and scrape (vessels on the right) forming methods ............................................................................................. 74
Figure 3. Petrographic thin section images of the coil and scrape pots made from several different clays ................... 75
Figure 4. Map showing areas for case studies on clay choice and mobility highlighting the mountains where pottery was made ...................................................................................................................................................... 79
Table 1. Experimental pottery samples............................................................................................................................. 73
Table 2. Ceramic samples from Utah sites in Beaver Valley ......................................................................................... 80
Table 3. Ceramic samples from northern Colorado sites. EP=Early Proterozoic; MP=Middle Proterozoic................ 81
Table 4. Ceramic samples from northwest New Mexico sites along US-491 ............................................................... 82
Table 5. Plain ware samples from southeastern Arizona sites on the eastern side of the Tohono O'odham Reservation ................ 84
Table 6. Sells Red ware samples from southeastern Arizona sites on the eastern side of the Tohono O'odham Reservation ........ 84

## Chapter 7. Complementary Approaches for Understanding Mazapan Pottery
### Destiny L. Crider

Figure 1. The distribution of Mazapan Wavy Line pottery within the Basin of Mexico ............................................. 90
Figure 2. Schematic of associated pottery types by chronological periods and phases for Tula and parts of the Basin of Mexico, as used in study of Mazapan Wavy Line pottery. Wavy Line pottery spans the end of the Epiclassic to the early part of the Early Postclassic ............................................................................................................. 90
Figure 3. Vessel examples of Mazapan Wavy Line pottery from Vaillant's 1930s excavations at Teotihuacan San Francisco Mazapan (part of the collections at the American Museum of Natural History). Vessels are not shown to same scale, but to highlight the view of interior designs ................................................................................. 91
Figure 4. Categories of information collected as part of the attribute study of Epiclassic and Early Postclassic pottery, including Mazapan Wavy Line ........................................................................................................................ 93
Figure 5. Schematic of the hierarchical organization of the Basin compositional groups by quadrant and the subgroups........... 94
Figure 6. Cross-tabulation of the results of compositional group assignments for Mazapan Wavy Line pottery selected for Instrumental Neutron Activation Analysis as compared to the Collection Blocks. For example, three defined variants of Mazapan Wavy Line were collected from the Tula region and nearly all of those samples were assigned to either the Tula or Tula G2 compositional groups, indicating a strong pattern of consuming locally produced pottery ................... 95
Figure 7. Mazapan Wavy Line, Matte Variant, Tula compositional group, interior decorated: A) MURR ID DLC026, B) MURR ID DLC027, C) MURR ID DLC039, D) MURR ID DLC035, E) MURR ID DLC038, F) MURR ID DLC032, G) MURR ID

DLC037, H) MURR ID DLC028, I) MURR ID DLC032, J) MURR ID DLC030. These examples demonstrate a range of motifs that vary from straight, curved, and interlocking design panels .................................................................................................. 95

Figure 8. Mazapan Wavy Line, Matte Variant, collected from Cerro Portezuelo and assigned to the Teotihuacan compositional group, interior decorated: A) MURR ID AZC214, B) MURR ID AZC216, C) MURR ID AZC217, D) MURR ID AZC218, E) MURR ID AZC231, F) MURR ID AZC234, G) MURR ID AZC242, H) MURR ID AZC243. These examples have technological and design similarities to those in the Tula compositional group. However, the Teotihuacan produced pottery tends to be less complex in design layout ................................................................................................................. 96

Figure 9. Mazapan Wavy Line, Burnished Variant, CPZ compositional group, interior decorated: A) MURR ID AZC219, B) MURR ID AZC222, C) MURR ID AZC237, D) MURR ID AZC229, E) MURR ID AZC240, F) MURR ID AZC238, G) MURR ID AZC239, H) MURR ID AZC241, I) MURR ID AZC225, J) MURR ID AZC233, K) MURR ID AZC227. Most of these examples are painted with a single brush to create parallel lines, those that might have implemented a multi-prong brush (e.g., D) are not as even and separated of lines as compared to those typical of Matte Variant. The surface is sloppily burnished and streaky, an attribute more typical of Epiclassic pottery, especially low-quality Coyotlatelco Red-on-natural .................. 97

Figure 10. Selected examples of variety Mazapan Wavy Line from attribute study and the list of goals and parameters set for experiment to replicate brush technology for multi-prong brush ............................................................................................. 99

Figure 11. Selected materials used in creating bristles and paint. On the top row, agave leaves are stripped of outer layer and fibers cleaned and tried for bristles and binding cordage. Center row includes hair for brush fibers: deer fur on left, and donated human hair on right. Bottom row includes mixing and testing consistency of red paint after mineral powder and water mixed .............................................................................................................................................. 100

Figure 12. Differing media are prepared for testing. Top panels include Jayne Cole preparing bisque bowl forms made in molds, dried, and brush tests on interior and exterior of the bowl forms by Benjamin Moore. Center left panel is a Mazapan Wavy Line sherd with undulating lines in a horizontal design panel, while center right panel is resulting test on texted art paper using stylus brush to replicate common design patterns. Bottom left panel is set of clay test tiles set out to dry, and bottom right panel is Jayne Cole measuring ingredients for paint recipe ........................................... 101

Figure 13. Examples of selected brush prototypes and selected paint tests. Left column from top to bottom: wooden comb stylus cut from balsa wood, Comb style 'split handle with agave fibers, comb style with split stick holder and attached handle with human hair fiber brush bristles, and com raft with five agave fiber brushes. Center column shows clay test tiles to compare results on clay media. Each brush used is set next to results test run. Right column shows additional tests of varying brush prototypes. Top image is a stylus comb on paper, which shows the intensity of paint changes from dark to light as brush releases less paint by end. Center image is a complex brush prototype with a large number of hair bristles in a split comb. Bottom image compares large hair brush (single) with a split comb with hair and a stylus style using toothpicks rather than balsa ......................................................................................................... 102

Figure 14. Comparison of three brush fibers. The top brush is agave fiber, which readily absorbs the paint into the coarse fiber, but does not easily release the paint evenly and consistently for duration of a long line. The center brush is human hair that had difficulty absorbing the paint, but readily releases the paint to the surface medium. Best for more 'scriptive' designs for single brush decoration because the fibers bend easily and do not keep narrow and separate lines. The bottom brush is deer hair, which readily absorbed paint, easily released paint to clay medium ........... 103

Figure 15. Methods for holding and using different style brushes. The top row includes the comb split handle which was difficult to dip in paint and not leave paint drips and fingers interfere with motion needed to produce complex motifs. The center row includes the comb raft brush, which is easy to handle and keeps fingers away from paint and clay surface. The bottom row shows handling a single brush, which requires moving both the hand and the bowl to get long line of paint. Finally, the stylus wooden comb requires dipping the entire surface of the stylus in paint and fingers become covered in paint ..................................................................................................................................... 103

## Chapter 8. Sherds of Spartans Past: Ceramics from the Michigan State University Campus Archaeology Program
*Lynne Goldstein, Lisa Bright and Jeffrey Painter*

Figure 1. Early campus maps. (A) – upper map. State Agricultural College map, 1870; map by Professor Beal. (B) – lower map. Campus map 1927, showing extent that the college had grown ............................................................................... 109

Figure 2. Phase 1 (1855-1870) ceramics. (A) Example of Wedgwood fig pattern. One plate bares a registered design mark indicating a production date of November 27th, 1856; (B) Plate in the 'Berlin Swirl' pattern. Ceramics with this pattern have been recovered produced by Liddle Elliot & Sons (1862-1869), and J. & G. Meakin (Denton 1998); A registered design mark indicates a production date of December 18th, 1856; (C) A wheat pattern plate produced by J. & G. Meakin. J. & G. Meakin produced the wheat pattern from 1860-1930 (Sussman 1985, 8); (D) The scalloped decagon, or Cambridge shape, design (Bev and Ernie 1998) was produced by Davenport. Unfortunately the registered design mark is illegible. We have recovered this pattern in several shapes and sizes ........................................... 110

Figure 3. Phase 2 (1870-1900) ceramics. (A) Soup tureen fragment with handle in the Delphi pattern. The W.T. Copeland maker's mark (1867-1890) was found on a Delphi pattern plate fragment; (B) W. Adams Company stone china plate in the Fairy Villa pattern, produced 1891-early 1900s; (C) Mercer Potter's New Jersey 'Bordeaux' pattern ........................... 113

Figure 4. Phase 3 (1900-1925) ceramics. (A) Undecorated whiteware 'Ramona' style bowl produced by Knowles Taylor & Knowles company, circa 1907-1915; (B) Partial 'Montana' pattern saucer produced by Johnson Brothers post 1913; (C) Onondaga Pottery Company hotelware cup and saucer, white with three green stripes. The maker's mark and date stamp found on one fragment indicate a 1914 production; (D) Partial gold-leafed shamrock patterned plate produced by Homer Laughlin between 1900-1960 ............................................................................................................. 114

## Chapter 9. The Ethnoarchaeology of an Abandoned Potter's Workshop in Ticul, Yucatán, México
*Dean E. Arnold*

Figure 1. Structural remains of an abandoned pottery workshop May-June, 2008 looking Southeast, noting the location of the principal features .................................................................................................................................................. 120

Figure 2. Piles of raw materials at the site and their comparison with an image of piles of raw materials for building and repairing a kiln in a potter's house lot in 2008 (*upper left*). The tongue of marl from the pile towards the *lower right* is likely the detritus falling from moving the marl to the kiln to add its cement facing (Figure 5). It could, however, have resulted from the unloading the marl from the vehicle that brought it to the workshop ................................................. 121

Figure 3. The area in front (*north*) of the pole structure (see Figure 1) showing the oval foundation of a structure in the shape of a traditional Maya house. The remains of white material within this foundation appears to be screenings from temper preparation, and indicates that the structure was a location where potters sifted and perhaps stored temper and mixed temper and clay. Insets show raw temper stored inside a house (*upper right*), mixing temper with clay inside a house (*upper left*), and a workshop, (*lower left*), and kneading the mixture outside when weather permits (*lower right*) ........................................................................................................................................................................... 122

Figure 4. *In situ* remains of discarded vertical-half molds at the abandoned workshop site (*upper right*) compared with the outdoor storage of molds covered with a roof (*upper left and lower left*) in 2008, and with uncovered discarded molds at the same household (1997) in the *lower right*. When molds are discarded they are not protected from rainfall, absorb moisture, are subject to the growth of moss, and therefore are difficult or impossible to use again. Molds in active use thus are sheltered from the rain by a roof or stored inside a structure ............................................. 123

Figure 5. The kiln at the abandoned workshop site (*below*) showing the lack of wasters around it compared with abandoned kilns in Ticul in the *upper left* (in 1984) and *upper right* (in 2008). Compare the lack of wasters in these images with four active kilns from 1984 (Figure 6) that show wasters on the sides and front of the kilns ................... 124

Figure 6. Active kilns in 1984 that show wasters beside them. These kilns use branches of *huano* palm (*upper right*), tar impregnated cardboard (*upper left and upper right*), sheet metal (*upper left*) and boards (*upper left and upper right*) to protect the kiln from rainfall and keep it from deteriorating. Facing the exterior of the kiln with cement prevents this problem ............................................................................................................................................................................ 125

Figure 7. Charcoal scatters around the abandoned workshop site in 2008 (*bottom and upper right*) compared with charcoal scatters in front of active kilns in Ticul in 1984 (*upper left*) and 2008 (*upper middle*) ............................................................. 126

## Chapter 10. Making Traditional Pottery Sustainable Today: Three Case Studies in Akita Prefecture, Japan
*Cara L. Reedy and Chandra L. Reedy*

Figure 1. Map showing location of Akita Prefecture in the northeast of Japan. The three pottery sites are found in the central part of Akita Prefecture ................................................................................................................................. 132

Figure 2. (A) Shop at Naraoka kiln; (B) Naraoka's original 1863 four-chambered climbing kiln, still used once per year ............ 133

Figure 3. (A) Fabricated objects drying on wooden shelves in the workshop, with enhanced air circulation to facilitate drying; (B) Burnt rice straw for glaze being prepared for elutriation on the workshop patio ............................................. 134

Figure 4. (A) The shop highlights the kiln's signature mottled blue 'sea cucumber' glaze (namako-yu); (B) Signage accompanying this 'three-colored delicacy holder' suggests uses for it ....................................................................... 135

Figure 5. (A) This grouping of objects displays how they could be used together, encouraging more purchases; (B) A sign informs potential customers that these plates are in the shape of Akita's prefectural flower, the giant butterbur, and provides local lore about the plants .................................................................................................................................. 136

Figure 6. (A) The main specialty of Waheegama kiln is Shiraiwa ware, a graduated blue and white speckled/mottled glaze over a brown iron-rich body; (B) The kiln sells many variations on Shiraiwa ware, as well as a white-glazed ware ............ 137

Figure 7. (A) Traditional four-chambered climbing kiln at Waheegama that was reconstructed in 1992-1993; wood fuel is stacked alongside it; (B) Zigzag-shaped white paper streamers on and above the kiln are used in Shinto ceremonies to bless the kiln and its operation; (C) Netting over kiln openings prevents entry by birds, since there are ventilation openings below the rafters .................................................................................................................................................. 137

Figure 8. (A) For fire safety, the kiln is housed in a separate building, with ventilation openings between the walls and rafters; (B) Many customers travel to the shop located at the kiln site to make their purchases ..................................... 138

Figure 9. (A) A second specialty of Waheegama kiln is a white glaze over brown iron-rich clay; (B) A traditional Waheegama kiln product is a portable stove used to heat water during a tea ceremony. C. Chopstick rests are another traditional product .................................................................................................................................................. 139

Figure 10. (A) Ojizou-sama statues commemorate deceased children and are usually made of stone; ceramic versions are a specialty of Waheegama kiln; (B) In addition to its traditional products, the kiln also sells some modern art pottery ...... 139

Figure 11. (A) Kurashi no Utsuwa Mike pottery shop is located in a residential neighborhood, and sells a variety of inexpensive handmade utilitarian products; (B) This table in the back of the store is used for craft workshops; the owner himself made most of the objects displayed here ................................................................................................ 141

# Chapter 1

# Innovative Approaches and Explorations in Ceramic Studies

## Sandra L. López Varela
Universidad Nacional Autónoma de México ; slvarela@comunidad.unam.mx

## Philip J. Arnold III
Loyola University Chicago; parnold@luc.edu

**Abstract**
*Ceramic Ecology is an international and interdisciplinary symposium initiated at the 1986 American Anthropological Association (AAA) meeting. Ceramic Ecology has provided an open venue for the presentation of research and insight on all aspects of ceramic production, consumption, trade and their economic, political, social, aesthetic, cosmological, and phenomenological implications. The 30th in the annual series brings together scholars working all over the world to discuss multiple theoretical and methodological approaches related to environmental parameters, raw materials, technological choices and abilities, and sociocultural variables to the manufacture, distribution, and use of pottery. Through a wide range of methods and instrumental techniques, the following contributions discover how potters transform raw materials into meaningful objects to approach the societies we dedicate our studies to. Interpretation of these data and explanations of the ceramic materials utilize methods and paradigms derived from the social sciences, humanities, and the arts to approach fundamental anthropological questions, such as the socio-economic context of production, social systems of learning, communities of practice, or the formation of identity. By fostering interdisciplinary interactions, Ceramic Ecology has pushed the boundaries of what can be understood about the human experience through the creative and systematic study of ceramics.*

**Keywords**
*Ceramic Ecology, Ceramics, Instrumental Studies, Experimental archaeology*

## Introduction

*Innovative Approaches and Explorations in Ceramic Studies* is a volume that continues to celebrate the critical role of Charles C. Kolb in fostering an international and interdisciplinary climate of interaction at the Ceramic Ecology symposia at the annual meetings of the American Anthropological Association (AAA). In 1986, Charles C. Kolb and Louana Lackey organized the first ceramic ecology symposium at the AAA meetings to honor Frederick R. Matson, who was retiring from Pennsylvania State University. Kolb and Lackey had many reasons to honor Matson.

When Matson organized the Viking Fund Conference in 1961, Anna O. Shepard (1956) had published her seminal work *Ceramics for the Archaeologist*, demonstrating the value of incorporating instrumental analyses into ceramic studies. Frederick R. Matson was the first scholar to continue the legacy of Anna O Shepard and to move beyond the earlier research goal of building cultural historical sequences by ordering potsherds in a sequence of formal characteristics and styles and to interpret past cultures (López Varela 2008). Placing ceramic studies in this context, Matson's (1965) intentions behind the publication of *Ceramics and Man* were to embrace the role of humans in the making of pottery. After the publication of *Archaeology and the Study of Gender* (Conkey and Spector 1984), Matson's major work may appear very sexist (López Varela, Arnold, and Pool 2014, 6), especially now, that ceramic studies recognize the role of women in pottery making. Matson (1965) coined the term 'ceramic ecology' to incorporate environmental studies to understand pottery production.

Ceramic Ecology became a theoretical reference to understand the ecological and sociocultural context in which pottery is made (Rice 1987). Ceramic Ecology has been criticized for its alleged deterministic approach and reductionist explanations (Santacreu 2014, 142-145). Influenced by systems theory, Kolb (1989a, 338, Table 1) revisited the term 'Ceramic Ecology' and introduced a complex of seven variables or subsystems (behavioral, production, distribution, socioeconomic, sociocultural, socio-political, and socio-religious) related to the production of ceramic objects. Kolb's model expressed the complexity of the relationship between ceramics and their sociocultural environment. The model was criticized for its environmental determinism in structuring pottery production (e.g., Gosselain 1998; Livingstone Smith 2000).

With all of the seeming incongruity behind the term today (Arnold 2011, 63), the Ceramic Ecology symposium has become an annual AAA tradition. Indeed, it might be the time to revisit the title of the symposium and to express strongly its anthropological approach to the making of pottery and how Ceramic Ecology goes hand in hand with current theoretical and methodological approaches. The Ceramic Ecology symposium, therefore, is much more than what is embraced in its name; it is a friendly space to discuss and learn about ceramics under rigorous theoretical and methodological approaches, involving the creation and perpetuation of a professional network that investigates ceramic studies in the past and the present.

By the end of 2016, three decades of Ceramic Ecology symposia had gathered together at least 210 scholars and students from fourteen nations, to discuss multiple theoretical and methodological approaches to analyze ceramics (Table 1). These scholars have presented 336 papers, placing potters and their products into both an environmental and anthropological frame of reference. Many of these papers were published in *A Pot for All Reasons: Ceramic Ecology Revisited* (Kolb and Lackey 1988); *Ceramic Ecology Revisited, 1987: The Technology and Socioeconomics of Pottery* (Kolb 1988); *Ceramic Ecology 1988: Current Research on Ceramic Materials* (Kolb 1989b). The compilation, *Social Dynamics of Ceramic Analysis: New Techniques and Interpretations* (López Varela 2014a), joins these publications in honor of Charles C. Kolb, who retired from the National Endowment for the Humanities and from his long-running role as organizer of Ceramic Ecology symposia in 2013.

| Area of Studies | | Topic | |
|---|---|---|---|
| Mesoamerica | 147 | Theoretical | 12 |
| North America | 36 | Introductions | 26 |
| South America | 23 | News from the Field | 13 |
| Asia | 40 | Panel | 4 |
| Europe | 19 | Comparative Studies | 3 |
| Africa | 8 | Honoring Louana Lackey | 1 |
| Oceania | 3 | | |
| **Total** | **277** | **Total** | **59** |

Table 1. Ceramic Ecology Sessions. Papers by Area of Studies and Topic presented in between 1986 and 2016 at the American Anthropological Association. (Data by Charles C. Kolb and Sandra L. López Varela)

To a certain extent, these publications testify to the history of ceramic analysis and archaeological advances. In the 1980s, the theoretical challenge, inspired by the growing ethnoarchaeological literature (Ascher 1961; Arnold 1971, 1985; Gould 1978; Kramer 1985; Nelson 1985; Tringham 1978), was to investigate the 'reasons' behind the making of pots by testing the significance of the patterning observed in the archaeological record through the formulation of hypotheses and experimental studies (Sheehy 1988). It is an interesting period in which the scientific investigation of the production and social organization of pottery making was crucial to ceramic studies. Scientific studies aimed to approach archaeological interpretation and explanation to explore pottery making in the present as a way to connect with the past by establishing analogies (Deal 1988). Under the influence of positivism, ethnographies of pottery making around the world were powerful deductive tools to learn about the past (Hagstrum 1988). Experimental studies were crucial to meet this research quest by analyzing the selection of raw materials and preparation of the clay body to achieve specific technological and functional properties that incorporated petrographic studies and residue analysis (Arnold 1989; Beaudry 1988; Childs 1988; Deal and Silk 1988).

The Ceramic Ecology symposium, in the organizing hands of Sandra L. López Varela and Kostalena Michelaki since 2013, has published a series of contributions that leapfrog the early theoretical and methodological approaches that led to its original criticism. The participants of *Social Dynamics of Ceramic Analysis: New Techniques and Interpretations* (López Varela 2014a) have moved beyond the conventional limits of anthropology to research the socio-economic context of production, social systems of learning, communities of practice, the formation of identity, or the effects of economic development in local technologies.

Scholars have examined the spatial relationship of ceramic production and distribution by using instrumental neutron activation analysis (INAA), XRF (X-ray Fluorescence) or Inductively Coupled Plasma-Mass Spectrometry (ICP-MS) in the study of archaeological ceramics studies and supported these studies with geographical information systems (GIS). The use of material sciences is now fundamental to our learning about the physical and chemical characteristics of the ceramics. INAA has long stood as the golden standard of ceramic chemical analysis, thanks to its high precision and accuracy for determining trace element concentrations (Ford 2014; Galaty, Bey III, and Ward 2014; Straight 2014). Now, we are in a position to appreciate its limitations and the potential of other techniques to investigate the chemical composition and technological properties of many different kinds of archaeological materials (McCormick and Wells 2014). With the use of instrumental techniques, ceramicists are reconstructing the step-by-step process in the making of ceramics and the choices potters have to make to address environmental and social variables. This is not the sole interest of applying instrumental studies to pottery analysis. These studies demonstrate how the production of robust trace-elemental data that can be analyzed by multiple forms of multivariate statistical analysis and geological studies contribute to our understanding of regional economies and politics (Arnold III 2014; Galaty, Bey III, and Ward 2014).

Ethnoarchaeological studies have modified their goals and have moved beyond inductive inferences that implicitly assume the existence of an underlying relationship with the past (Ascher 1961). The introduction of philosophy of science in archaeological studies is questioning the ways we create knowledge from ethnoarchaeological research and historic documents (López Varela and Aguilar Escobar 2014). Currently, ethnoarchaeological researchers are often concerned about the disappearance or the replacement of pottery technologies with crafts in the face of economic growth and development (López Varela 2014b). Analyzing the effects of economic development policies to combat poverty on local technologies is creating the space to introduce an ethnoarchaeology of poverty. These new approaches to the present have encouraged studies discussing the formation of collective memories and identities (López Varela 2014a, 2014b; Wierucka and Sacha 2014). These studies have extended their analysis to discuss institutional visions of cultural heritage against peoples' heritage. Broadly defined, the 'ceramic ecological approach' in all of these studies seeks to understand the making and use of pottery by peoples in the present and the past. Therefore, the current volume celebrates thirty years of Ceramic Ecology's advancing the field of ceramic studies and maintaining the most significant network of scholars of ceramic studies in anthropological archaeology.

**Innovative Approaches and Explorations in Ceramic Studies**

Ceramic Ecology is a holistic enterprise. It involves all aspects of ceramic studies and is devoted to both deeper and more recent time periods. As long as the goal is to understand better the relationships between human activity and ceramics, a perspective that emphasizes Ceramic Ecology is appropriate and valuable. The contributors to this volume make ample use of that broad discretion.

The chapters within this volume highlight the use of instrumentation and other innovative approaches with respect to the anthropological study of ceramics. Instrumental explorations, involving such areas as trace elements and mineralogy, have become commonplace in the literature. But instrumentation is merely a means to an end, whereby these compositional data become the foundation on which to build various behavioral models. Other non-technological analyses seek to break down the temporal barriers between the present and the past. These inferential approaches are innovative in their use of historical documents or participant observations to evaluate archaeologically based assumptions that would otherwise go untested.

Consequently, the following chapters could be grouped in myriad ways. Their reliance on various analyses frequently overlaps, as does their emphases on the archaeological record, experimental approaches, and/or more contemporary material culture studies. Thus, no single matrix does service to their analytical breadth. Nonetheless, and mindful of these intersections, we have selected three main themes as axes of organization: 1) Formal/Stylistic Analysis; 2) Physico-Chemical/Stylistic Analysis; and 3) Analyses of Documented Behavior. The first and second group involves archaeological data, while the third group comprises studies that move from the more recent past into the present day.

*Formal/Stylistic Analysis*

Variables such as shape, size, and means of decoration undergird the archaeological analysis of ceramics. While not always as 'high-tech' as the more recent interests in elemental and mineralogical studies noted below, formal and decorative attributes constitute the stepping off point for most studies that adopt a Ceramic Ecology perspective.

Horn III and Ford address the role of ceramics in understanding Late Classic (AD 600-900) lowland Maya domestic occupation. They argue that the type-variety system commonly used by Mayanists works well for chronological considerations, but fails to provide much information regarding residential activities and the household economy.

Toward that latter goal, they suggest that greater attention be paid to the formal/functional characteristics of Maya ceramics.

Using data obtained via archaeological research within the El Pilar region of western Belize, the authors compare ceramic vessel forms and shapes from residences within three different environmental zones. Basic forms include bowls, plates, jars, and vases, while shapes reflect different sizes within these formal categories. The authors note that the domestic assemblage found within valley and uphill residences are most similar, diverging from the houses within their ridgeland zone. They also observe that vases, often associated with upper-status residences, may be more widely available than previously thought.

*Physico-Chemical/Stylistic Analysis*

Increased access to high-precision elemental and mineralogical analyses has proven to be a boon to Ceramic Ecology. The ability to identify the physico-chemical fingerprint of particular combinations of clay and temper—the ceramic paste 'recipe'—enables researchers to investigate issues of production location, trade, and exchange. More recent advances in these technologies have not only made them more cost effective, but have also allowed researchers to bring the instrumentation to the artifact, rather than the reverse. Consequently, items that would otherwise not be candidates for analysis, such as museum pieces or unwieldy artifacts in the field, are now contributing to a growing dataset.

In her contribution, López Varela marshals a host of portable, non-destructive/non-invasive analytical techniques (e.g., XRF, UV-vis, FORS, UV/UNIR) to investigate the elemental and mineralogical composition of a sample of Jaina figurines from Campeche, Mexico. Few New World ceramic figurines are more celebrated than these famous miniature Mayan sculptures. The non-destructive/non-invasive character of this analysis is especially significant, as these pieces derive primarily from museum collections. Such portable and low-impact technologies afford access to a much wider range of samples than might otherwise be available.

Through these analyses López Varela isolates several production groups, including possible foreign imports and provides information on the use of Maya blue and red ocher as pigments. Moreover, her research suggests a productive avenue for evaluating the authenticity of supposed Jaina figurine examples, based on characteristics resulting from digenetic processes.

At the same time, identifying behavioral patterning is made difficult by the general lack of contextual information. However, a few tendencies appear: for example, the association of standing female figurines with children and sub-adults. Moreover, many of these female figurines appear to be mold-made, rather than the hand-modeled, male gendered forms. Mold-made figurines also served as ocarinas and other musical instruments and are strongly associated with child burials. As several scholars have noted, those mold-made figurines have stylistic ties to southern Veracruz; moreover, their outlying chromium levels relative to other samples also identifies them as possible imports.

Of course, why these figurines might be imported from outside the Campeche area remains an important question to consider. López Varela appears to suggest that figurines in this 'orant' stance (following Goldstein 1979) may be associated with rain petitions; certainly the association of infants and children with later Tlaloc sacrifices is well documented.

Hirshman evaluates the evidence for 1500 years of economic organization spanning the development of the Tarascan empire. Her point of departure is Hirth's (1998) 'Distributional Approach' which theorizes that market economies should leave a relatively homogeneous fingerprint of household access to goods across social strata. Instead of households, per se, Hirshman investigates patterning in ceramic characteristics across the Lake Pátzcuaro Basin, both before and after state formation.

Hirshman's study incorporates INAA ceramic paste information, as well as data involving stylistic and morphometric traits. She compares data from three settlements: Urichu, a formerly independent polity that becomes a tertiary Tarascan center; Erongarícuaro, a secondary Tarascan center that oversaw Urichu; and Tzintzuntzan, the Tarascan capital.

Ultimately, Hirshman finds that commoners and several levels of elites all had access to a similar suite of ceramics, both in terms of paste recipes as well as surface treatments. At the same time, a few forms and decorative techniques were reserved for the highest echelon of Tarascan society. These patterns result in several important conclusions. First, it does not appear that the Tarascan state co-opted ceramic production, instead allowing the craft activity to remain relatively decentralized and conducted at the household level. Second, the relative equality of access supports the market economy model, based on Hirth's (1998) expectations. Finally, the patterning within status-specific elite goods is best understood via reference to a system of elite gifting and patronage.

Striker *et al.* extend the use of petrographic analysis to explore learning frameworks among sixteenth-century Wendant (Iroquian) potters. Petrography is most often employed to assess production provenience, determining if clay and tempers were locally available. Striker *et al.* not only provide information on local clay and temper resources, but also consider the degree to which poorly made 'juvenile' vessels reflect the different learning contexts of novice potters.

The authors divide a sample of 62 rim sherds into two groups: a less-standardized ('novice' or 'juvenile' producer) and a more standardized ('expert' or 'adult') version. They then evaluate the petrographic characteristics within each group. These patterns are also compared to the mineralogical data from a local sample of clays and possible tempers.

Striker *et al.* identify a wide range of paste fabric combinations. They note that the sample of novice vessels includes unique mineralogical combinations, examples of the more standard paste, and finally versions of the standard paste that lack temper or include minor amounts of temper. They suggest that these differences may reflect distinct learning contexts; for example a novice experimenting on her own versus having access to and using already mixed material. Each of these possibilities affords additional insight into the community of practice exhibited among the Wendant potters.

In her chapter, Ownby similarly extends the application of petrographic analysis beyond simply documenting the provenience of ceramics on an archaeological site. She begins by comparing formation techniques from the southern and northern southwestern US. She notes that paddle and anvil formation frequently associates with the southern region, while coiling and scraping is more commonly found within the northern portion of the Southwest. Drawing upon her own experimental work, and by considering the characteristics of the available clay/temper combinations, she is able to demonstrate the logic of these practices. She also makes the important observation that ceramic formation can be water intensive, an important consideration for potters in the arid Southwest.

The second half of Ownby's discussion involves vessel formation and mobility patterns. Again, she shows how the temper/clay characteristics reveal production in different locales, thereby providing information on the seasonal rounds of southwestern groups. She also considers how such activities may be embedded within other activities, such as chert extraction, and how certain ideological notions may imbue vessel with additional desirable qualities. Taken together, Ownby's two examples situate petrography within a ceramic ecological perspective, thereby significantly expanding the utility of such analyses.

Crider's contribution involves Mazapan Wavy Line ceramics, a diagnostic pottery of Central Mexico that spans the Classic-to-Postclassic transition (e.g., AD 850-1150). Her study combines Neutron Activation Analysis and Proton Induced X-ray Emission (PIXE), and also makes use of replicative studies and experimental archaeology.

The geochemical component of Crider's study demonstrates that there were multiple centers of Mazapan Wavy Line pottery production associated with the increased ruralization that took place during the Epiclassic to the Early Postclassic transition in the Basin of Mexico. Her compositional analysis also indicates that the Matte version of Mazapan pottery, produced in the Northeastern Basin, occurs disproportionately in the East Central Basin, particularly around the site of Cerro Portezuelo.

The fact that portions of the East Central Basin were importing Mazapan Wavy Line pottery led Crider to consider the manner in which their eponymous design was created. Crider and her assistants make several attempts to replicate these designs using different materials to create the brushes. Adopting something akin to a 'Goldilocks investigative strategy', they perform several iterations of production, in which some lines are too broad and others leave a paint trail that is too faint. Crider's 'Just-right' solution employs deer fur and multiple aligned stiles to achieve the final product.

Of course, it's almost impossible to verify that Mazapan potters actually employed the techniques identified during the replicative studies. But, we are not sure such verification is really the point. Rather, we are talking about a kind of investigative possibilism in which more-or-less likely scenarios are played out. Knowledge acquisition is as much about eliminating possibilities as it is identifying likelihoods; moreover, like the unintended offshoots of a NASA space program, one never knows what collateral insights can be gained from such experimental activities.

*Analyses of Documented Behavior*

Most archaeological analysis is conducted in the absence of data independent of the archaeological record itself. Not surprisingly, resulting explanations may suffer from circular reasoning or may be self-fulfilling. In the face of such pitfalls, researchers are constantly seeking ways to improve their inferential strategies (e.g., Wylie 2002).

The use of historical documents and/or contemporary observations to evaluate our archaeological assumptions affords such learning opportunities. This approach is well reflected in several of the volume's contributions, via historical archaeology, ethnoarchaeology, and more general participant observation.

Goldstein *et al.* chart the ceramic changes associated with the development of Michigan State University and its main campus. The authors identify four general phases of MSU's expansion from its pre-Civil War origins through the next one-hundred years. The ceramic record associated with this trajectory is understandable, albeit at times surprising. For example, the earliest dish sets reflect a catch-as-catch-can emphasis on sturdy, embossed ironstone, although it is noteworthy that these ceramics were generally imported from England. It is only during the second phase of occupation, supported by the Morrill Land-Grant Act of 1862, that pottery from the United States appears in any frequency. It remains to be seen if this difference was strictly a financial issue, or if some form of post-Civil War nationalism flavored the acquisition of these US produced ceramics.

Historical documents provide additional information regarding the excavation context. Data from the fourth phase of occupation derive primarily from laboratory classrooms that produced few—and very small—sherds. But, while the lack of ceramics is certainly a drawback given our particular focus, one might broaden the emphasis and consider container assemblages. It is useful to remember that pottery is ultimately a container, and we can certainly benefit by understanding the circumstances under which different sets of containers are adopted or discarded.

In his ethnoarchaeological contribution, Dean Arnold revisits a ceramic workshop on the outskirts of Ticul, Mexico, a locale that he had seen just six years earlier in 2002. The workshop is now abandoned, and, with an archaeologist's eye, Arnold notes the location and contextual relationships of several production markers, including discarded molds, ash dumps, left-over clay/temper piles, several partial foundations, and the kiln itself. Based on his ethnographic understanding of how these elements function in unison, Arnold is able to identify and reconstruct the patterns of behavior that likely took place within this production facility. His cautionary conclusion is somewhat sobering: 'The most puzzling aspect of the material remains of this workshop is that there is so little evidence of pottery production.'

Nonetheless, Arnold also makes the important observation that separate workshops like the one he documented tend to have a much shorter 'use life' than smaller scale production facilities associated with households. Researchers often emphasize the scale of production as an important aspect of economic reconstructions. Arnold's observations indicate that, like the tortoise and hare, the slow, steady production of the household may ultimately 'win the race' and leave a more enduring archaeological mark.

Reedy and Reedy explore attempts to preserve traditional Japanese ceramic production techniques by the potters themselves, rather than rely on national and/or NGO initiatives. Their focus is the Akita Prefecture, located in northeastern Japan. The authors document pottery manufacture within three contexts: two (Naraoka and Waheegama) utilize the famous updraft 'climbing kilns' while the third is a small workshop (Kurashi no Utsuwa Mike) in a residential area.

The Naraoka facility includes five potters whose training results from formal art education, rather than apprenticeship. Clays are mined and mixed on-site and the majority of firing involves gas and electric kilns. Once a year, the original climbing kiln (in use since 1863) is fired up. In contrast, Waheegam is a family-run workshop that employs a more recently constructed climbing kiln (ca. 1990), although one of their specialties is a Shiraiwa ware that dates back to the late 1700s. One of their goals is to produce pottery for contemporary use via traditional techniques. Finally, the Kurashi no Utsuwa Mike pottery shop is a small enterprise, run by a husband/wife and their daughter and emphasizes utilitarian items. Much of their business involves pottery not made on-site and their merchandise also includes many non-ceramic items, such as lacquer ware, jewelry, and other hand crafted items.

The sustainability reflected in these three examples emphasizes addressing contemporary consumer populations, even when traditional potting techniques are invoked. Nonetheless, a blending of these techniques ensures that they remain cost-effective in their execution. And while the Naraoka and Waheegam production units are geared toward a larger tourist market, the small residential shop emphasizes local consumption of handmade pottery. Taken together, all three production facilities seek to maintain the value of traditional Japanese pottery.

*Closing Thoughts*

Ceramic Ecology has come far since its maiden voyage originally captained by Frederick Matson (1965). Charlie Kolb subsequently assumed command of that helm and charted Ceramic Ecology's course for thirty years. With the 2013 transfer of stewardship to Sandra L. López Varela and Kostalena Michelaki, we see Ceramic Ecology steaming ahead well into the future.

That future represents brave, new worlds of exploration that continue to produce innovative research and results. Technology and instrumentation are important components of that exploration; they are increasingly more sophisticated, yet at the same time more readily accessible. Moreover, increased sophistication often yields increased portability, affording researchers access to data sets that were off limits just a few years prior.

Nonetheless, technology and instrumentation are but one tool in the operation of a holistic Ceramic Ecology. Ceramic Ecology is fundamentally an anthropological endeavor, so datasets, however generated, must ultimately address questions of human behavior. When dealing with an unknown archaeological past, research still begins by constructing a framework of observations, commonly built upon trestles of ceramic form and decorative attributes. It is with the bracing support of such information that further studies, usually involving instrumentation, can move ahead.

The archaeological record, however, usually reflects undocumented behaviors. Thus, it is always necessary to consider the strategies of inference by which those data are turned into anthropological assessments. Since we cannot 'test' models and/or expectations with the archaeological record itself, our methods are vastly improved by using historically documented contexts, experimental research, and ethnographically informed studies to shore up our inferences. The cause-and-effect 'controls' provided by these approaches provide the necessary behavioral arguments that allow us to build bridges of inference between the present and the past.

Working in the present, scholars dedicated to the study of ceramics continue to investigate how potters transform raw materials into meaningful objects. Increasingly, these studies analyze the entwined relationship between people and their ceramics, and how this relationship constitutes part of who they are, of their identity, and collectiveness. By fostering interdisciplinary interactions, the Ceramic Ecology symposia continue to push the boundaries of what can be understood about the human experience through the creative and systematic study of ceramics.

**References Cited**

Arnold, Dean E. 1971. 'Ethnomineralogy of Ticul, Yucatan Potters: Etics and Emics.' *American Antiquity* 36 (1): 20-40.
Arnold, Dean E. 1985. *Ceramic theory and cultural process, New Studies in Archaeology*. New York: Cambridge University Press.
Arnold, Dean E. 1989. 'Technological diversity and evolutionary variability: A comparison of contemporary pottery-making technologies in Guatemala, Peru, and Mexico.' In *Ceramic Ecology, 1988: Current Research on Ceramic Materials*, edited by Charles C. Kolb, 29-59. BAR International Series 513. Oxford: British Archaeological Reports.
Arnold, Dean E. 2011. 'Ceramic Theory and Cultural Processes after 25 Years.' *Ethnoarchaeology* 3 (1): 63-98.
Arnold III, Philip J. 2014. 'Of Polychrome and Politics in Southern Veracruz, Mexico.' In *Social Dynamics of Ceramic Analysis: new Techniques and Interpretations, Papers in Honour of Charles C. Kolb*, edited by Sandra L. Lopez, 64-74. BAR International Series 2683. Oxford, England: Archaeopress.
Ascher, Robert. 1961. 'Analogy in Archaeological Interpretation.' Southwestern *Journal of Anthropology* 17 (4): 317-325.
Beaudry, Marilyn P. 1988. 'The Function of Nonfunctional Ceramics.' In *A Pot for all Reasons: Ceramic Ecology revisited. Papers Dedicated to Frederick R. Matson*, edited by Charles C. Kolb and Louana M. Lackey, 23-37. Philadelphia: A special Publication of Ceramica de Cultura Maya.
Childs, S. Terry. 1988. 'Clay resource specialization in ancient Tanzania: Implications for cultural process.' In *Ceramic Ecology Revisited 1987: the technology and socioeconomics of pottery*, edited by Charles C. Kolb, 1-31. BAR International Series 436. Oxford: British Archaeological Reports.

Conkey, Margaret W., and Janet D. Spector. 1984. 'Archaeology and the Study of Gender.' In *Advances in Archaeological Method and Theory*, edited by Michael B. Schiffer, 1-38. New York: Academic Press.

Deal, Michael. 1988. 'An Ethnoarchaeological Approach to the Identification of Maya Domestic Pottery Production.' In *The Technology and Socioeconomics of Pottery*, edited by Charles C. Kolb, 111-141. BAR International Series 436. Oxford: British Archaeological Reports.

Deal, Michael, and Peter Silk. 1988. 'Absorption Residues and Vessel Function: a Case Study from the Maine-Maritimes Region.' In *A Pot for all Reasons: Ceramic Ecology revisited. Papers Dedicated to Frederick R. Matson*, edited by Charles C. Kolb and Louana M. Lackey, 105-125. Philadelphia: A special Publication of Ceramica de Cultura Maya.

Ford, Anabel. 2014. 'The Conundrum of Volcanic Ash in the Maya Lowlands, an Essay in Honour of Charlie Kolb and International and Interdisciplinary Ceramic Ecology.' In *Social Dynamics of Ceramic Analysis: new Techniques and Interpretations, Papers in Honour of Charles C. Kolb*, edited by Sandra L. Lopez Varela, 36-49. BAR International Series 2683. Oxford, England: Archaeopress.

Galaty, Michael L., George J. Bey III, and Timothy J. Ward. 2014. 'Cross-Cultural Ceramic Analysis: Albania and Yucatan in the Keck Lab at Millsaps College.' In *Social Dynamics of Ceramic Analysis: new Techniques and Interpretations. Papers in Honour of Charles C. Kolb*, edited by Sandra L. Lopez Varela, 13-21. BAR International Series 2683. Oxford, England: Archaeopress.

Goldstein, Mary M. 1979. 'Maya Figurines from Campeche, Mexico: Classification on the Basis of Clay Chemistry, Style and Iconography.' PhD Diss., Faculty of Philosophy, Columbia University.

Gosselain, Olivier P. 1998. 'Social and Technical Identity in a Clay Crystal Ball.' In *The Archaeology of Social Boundaries*, edited by Miriam T. Stark, 78-106. Washington, DC: Smithsonian Institution.

Gould, Richard A. 1978. 'Beyond Analogy in Ethnoarchaeology.' In *Explorations in Ethnoarchaeology*, edited by Richard A. Gould, 249-293. Albuquerque: University of New Mexico Press.

Hagstrum, Melissa B. 1988. 'Ceramic Production in the Central Andes, Peru: An Archaeological and Ethnographic Comparison.' In *A Pot for all Reasons: Ceramic Ecology revisited. Papers Dedicated to Frederick R. Matson*, edited by Charles C. Kolb and Louana M. Lackey, 127-145. Philadelphia: A special Publication of Ceramica de Cultura Maya.

Hirth, Kenneth G. 1998. 'The Distributional Approach: A New Way to Identify Marketplace Exchange in the Archaeological Record.' *Current Anthropology* 39 (4): 451-476.

Kolb, Charles C., ed. 1988. *Ceramic Ecology Revisited 1987: the Technology and Socioeconomics of Pottery*. BAR International Series 436. Oxford: British Archaeological Reports.

Kolb, Charles C. 1989a. 'Ceramic ecology in retrospect: a critical review of 1989 methodology and results.' In *Ceramic Ecology 1988: Current Research on Ceramic Materials*, edited by Charles C. Kolb, 261-375. BAR International Series 513. Oxford: British Archaeological Reports.

Kolb, Charles C. 1989b. *Ceramic Ecology 1988: Current Research on Ceramic Materials*. BAR International Series 513. Oxford: British Archaeological Reports.

Kolb, Charles C., and Louana M. Lackey. 1988. *A Pot for all Reasons: Ceramic Ecology revisited. Papers Dedicated to Frederick R. Matson*. Philadelphia: A special Publication of Ceramica de Cultura Maya.

Kramer, Carol. 1985. *Ceramic Ethnoarchaeology*. Annual Review of Anthropology 14:77-102.

Livingstone Smith, A. 2000. 'Processing Clay for Pottery in Northern Cameroon: Social and Technical Requirements.' *Archaeometry* 42 (1): 21-42.

López Varela, Sandra L. 2008. 'Maya Ceramics.' In *Encyclopaedia of the History of Science, Technology, and Medicine in Non-Western Cultures*, edited by Helaine Selin, 496-503. New York: Springer.

López Varela, Sandra L. 2014a. *Social Dynamics of Ceramic Analysis: New Techniques and Interpretations, Papers in Honour of Charles C. Kolb*. BAR International Series 2683. Oxford: Archaeopress.

López Varela, Sandra L. 2014b. 'Clay griddles, analytical techniques, and heritage: an ethnoarchaeological perspective of economic development policies in Mexico.' In *Social Dynamics of Ceramic Analysis: new Techniques and Interpretations, Papers in Honour of Charles C. Kolb*, edited by Sandra L. Lopez Varela, 95-107. BAR International Series 2683. Oxford, England: Archaeopress.

López Varela, Sandra L., and Daniel Aguilar Escobar. 2014. 'Building Landscapes of Memory with Pots: Hermeneutic Expressions of Tlaloc in a Festivity of the Valley of Morelos, México.' In *Social Dynamics of Ceramic Analysis: new Techniques and Interpretations, Papers in Honour of Charles C. Kolb*, edited by Sandra L. Lopez Varela, 75-86. BAR International Series 2683. Oxford, England: Archaeopress.

López Varela, Sandra L., Dean E. Arnold, and Christopher A. Pool. 2014. 'Ceramic Ecology XXVII: Celebrating more than a Quarter Centruy of Ceramic Ecology.' In *Social Dynamics of Ceramic Analysis: New Techniques and Interpretations, Papers in Honour of Charles C. Kolb*, edited by Sandra L. López Varela, 4-12. BAR International Series 2683. Oxford: Archaeopress.

Matson, Frederick R., ed. 1965. *Ceramics and Man*. Chicago: Aldine Publishing Company.

McCormick, David Rafael, and Christian Wells. 2014. Pottery, People, and pXRF, Toward the Development of Compositional Profiles for Southeast Mesoamerican Ceramics. In *Social Dynamics of Ceramic Analysis: new Techniques and Interpretations, Papers in Honour of Charles C. Kolb*, edited by Sandra L. Lopez Varela, 22-35. BAR International Series 2683. Oxford, England: Archaeopress.

Nelson, Ben A., ed. 1985. *Decoding Prehistoric Ceramics.* Center for Archaeological Investigations Publications in Archaeology. Carbondale: Southern Illinois University Press.

Rice, Prudence M. 1987. *Pottery Analysis: A Sourcebook.* Chicago: University of Chicago Press.

Santacreu, Albero Daniel. 2014. *Materiality, Techniques and Society in Pottery Production, the Technological Study of Archaeological Ceramics through Paste Analysis.* Warsaw/Berlin: De Gruyter Open Ltd.

Sheehy, James J. 1988. 'Ceramic ecology and the clay/fuel ratio: Modeling fuel consumption in Tlajinga 33, Teotihuacan, Mexico.' In *Ceramic Ecology Revisited 1987: the technology and socioeconomics of pottery*, edited by Charles C. Kolb, 199-226. Oxford: British Archaeological Reports.

Shepard, Anna O. 1956. *Ceramics for the Archaeologist.* Washington, D.C.: Carnegie Institution of Washington, Publication 609.

Straight, Kirk Damon. 2014. 'Investigating the Production and Circulation of Pottery Vessels in Peripheral Tikal during the Classic Period.' In *Social Dynamics of Ceramic Analysis: new Techniques and Interpretations, Papers in Honour of Charles C. Kolb*, edited by Sandra L. Lopez Varela, 50-63. BAR International Series 2683. Oxford, England: Archaeopress.

Tringham, Ruth. 1978. 'Experimentation, Ethnoarchaeology, and the Leapfrogs in Archaeological Methodology.' In *Explorations in Ethnoarchaeology*, edited by Richard A. Gould, 169-199. Albuquerque: University of New Mexico Press.

Wierucka, Aleksandra, and Magdalena Sacha. 2014. 'Using Traditional Pottery as a Tool for Strenghtening Local Cultural Identity in Poland.' In *Social Dynamics of Ceramic Analysis: New Techniques and Interpretations, Papers in Honour of Charles C. Kolb*, edited by Sandra L. Lopez Varela, 87-94. BAR International Series 2683. Oxford, England: Archaeopress.

Wylie, Alison. 2002. *Thinking From Things: Essays in the Philosophy of Archaeology.* Berkeley: University of California Press.

# Chapter 2
# What is a Ceramic Assemblage: Chronology and Belongings of the Late Classic Maya

## Sherman Horn III
HD Analytical Solutions, Inc.; sherman.w.horn.iii@gmail.com

## Anabel Ford
University of California Santa Barbara; anabel.ford@ucsb.edu

### Abstract
*Ceramics in archaeology have traditionally served as chronological markers, critical as a relative dating technique. This is the case for the Central Lowland Maya area, where the ceramic chronology was established in the 1930s with the Uaxactun project, expanded for the Barton Ramie project, and detailed for Tikal as the type:variety system was refined. As useful as this chronology has been for studies of the ancient Maya, with all our understanding of the chronological distribution, we know precious little of the distribution of vessel form that is a critical component of function. Our chapter examines Late Classic vessel form and shape, in an effort to define the vessel diversity from Maya residential units. By describing the Late Classic Maya assemblage of vessel forms and shapes, we can begin to understand common and variable features of Maya residential unit belongings as they relate to the settlement patterns and the Maya forest landscape.*

### Key words
*Maya Household Archaeology, Maya Ceramics, Ceramic chronology, Type:Variety System, Ceramic Assemblage Diversity, Vessel Form and Function*

## Introduction

Households comprise the basic units of socioeconomic production and reproduction in communities (Netting et al. 1984), and archaeologists have recognized the importance of studying ancient Maya household remains for nearly a century (Wauchope 1938). Household artifact inventories, which reflect an incomplete range of household possessions and activities, provide productive avenues to study daily life in ancient communities. Descriptions and analysis of household possessions are integral to comparative studies of wealth inequality (Smith 1987), and recent studies of lowland Maya household assemblages document variability in access to items that may reflect differences in wealth or status (e.g., Blackmore 2012; Ford 2010; Ford and Olsen 1989; Keller 2012; Robin 2013).

Ceramics are largely absent from these discussions of Maya household inventories, despite a long history of ceramic analysis in the area. Traditional Maya ceramic analyses

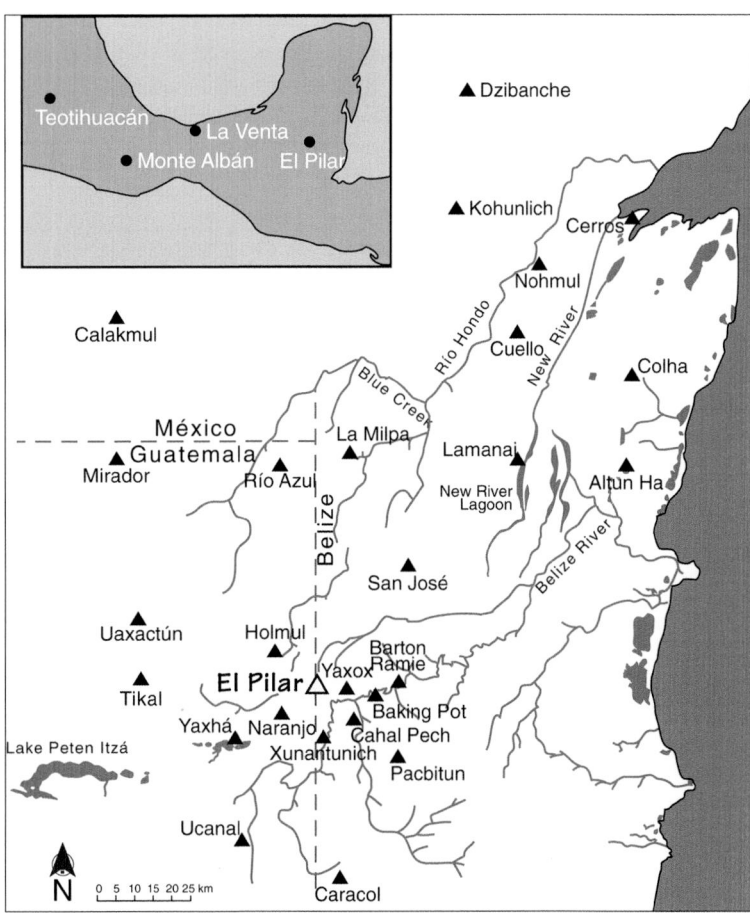

Figure 1. El Pilar and the Maya Lowlands. (Figure by Ford)

focus on constructing architectural and occupation chronologies (e.g., Gifford 1976; Smith 1955), interpreting iconographic and epigraphic elements (e.g., Grube 1992; Reents-Budet and Ball 1994), and identifying imported vessels and trade-wares, but few studies expand beyond this scope to explore how pottery functioned in daily life (but see Howie 2012). Diversity and complexity in domestic pottery assemblages have been hinted at but not fully explored (Ford 1991, 1992), and ceramics remain an underexploited resource for answering essential questions in Maya household archaeology due to the lack of comparative assemblage studies.

To address this shortfall, we present an approach that elevates formal, functional, and technological analyses to characterize the ceramic inventories of Late Classic Maya (c. AD 600-900) households. Different vessel forms served different functions and were potentially acquired from different producers, and analysis of assemblage variability can elucidate important differences in household practice. Assemblage description is an essential step in comparing ceramic consumption patterns and investigating how households used pottery to meet daily needs. Our data derive from several households, representing a range of environmental and social contexts in the El Pilar area of the upper Belize River (Figure 1), which provide a broad baseline for comparing the socioeconomic relationships encoded in ancient pottery.

## Maya Household Archaeology and the Potential of Ceramics

Maya household archaeology developed from a long tradition of studies focused on defining settlement patterns and site-rank hierarchies (e.g., Ashmore 1981; Arnold and Ford 1980; Robin 2012; Webster and Gonlin 1988, among others). Surveys reveal numerous small structures surrounding monumental city centers that were interpreted as redundant and comparable residential units. Maya settlements represent composites of domestic spaces, and this context provides opportunities to compare household wealth, access to resources, and relative degrees of social status (see Ford 1990, 1991). Members of households acquired resources for survival, and the acquisition and passing of wealth and resources through inheritance promoted social reproduction at the most basic level in ancient Maya society (Wilk and Rathje 1982).

Households also represent the essential contexts of daily life for elite and non-elite members of preindustrial communities. Ancient Maya households were the settings for a variety of domestic activities – the storage, preparation, and serving of food prominent among them – that are reflected in the material record by the equipment used to accomplish specific tasks. Although Maya households certainly possessed a variety of tools, ornaments, and ceremonial accoutrements made from different materials, the remnants of ancient household belongings are dominated by pottery and stone-tool fragments.

Investigations of ancient Maya households have tended to focus on relationships between the size of structures and the frequencies of associated specialty items and/or exotic artifacts (see Robin 2012). Data suggest that the size of Late Classic Maya residential units relates to material consumption, as larger residences use more stone and frequently contain more exotic artifacts than smaller ones (Abrams 1994; Ford 1991, 1992; Ford and Fedick 1992; Ford and Olson 1989). Other lines of evidence indicate that domestic artifact inventories were more diverse than previously thought, and that small households could access what archaeologists assumed were sumptuary items (Ford 2010; Ford and Olson 1989; LeCount 1996; Robin 2012, 2013; Wiewall and Howie 2010).

Household inventory studies have produced tantalizing hints of material diversity among common Maya farmers. Such studies, typically, focus on household procurement of non-local resources such as obsidian or green stone (e.g., Asaro *et al.* 1978; Ford *et al.* 1997; Horn 2015, among others), production of chert tools or marine shell ornaments (e.g., Hohmann 2002; Shafer and Hester 1983), and the distributions of these objects and other rare materials (e.g., granite, slate) across different household contexts (see chapters in Robin 2012). Detailed descriptions of ceramic household inventories are notably absent from these comparisons, however, leaving a significant portion of the material record unexplored.

Ceramic assemblages are archives of data on resource procurement, production, distribution, and consumption that can shed valuable light on socioeconomic interactions. Macroscopic analysis of paste attributes can document variability in materials and manufacturing methods, allowing the partial reconstruction of socioeconomic interaction networks that linked producers and consumers (Horn 2015). More detailed petrographic and compositional analyses can identify production zones and technological traditions of potting groups (e.g., Ford and Spera 2007; Howie 2012; López Varela 2005; Shepard 1955). We can employ these analyses to investigate household resource use, participation in economic systems, and knowledge of local environments.

## Chapter 2  What is a Ceramic Assemblage: Chronology and Belongings of the Late Classic Maya

Ceramics are ubiquitous at Maya sites, providing a largely untapped reservoir of data for comparing daily household practices. Excavations in the El Pilar area have recovered 236,388 ceramic artifacts weighing 3,418 kilograms. The majority comprised vessel fragments (e.g., rims, bodies, bases, jar necks, handles, and pods), with ornamental and utilitarian items (e.g., figurines, spindle whorls) and amorphous baked clay objects (e.g., briquettes, daub) making up smaller fractions. There are 1.8 ceramic objects for every recovered item of chert, and the total weights of these two different materials are nearly identical. Ceramics were clearly as important as other materials for fulfilling everyday needs, and yet their functions in Classic Maya households have been widely ignored. The remains of ceramic belongings reflect the basic domestic activities essential to the daily lives of household members, and formal/functional assemblage descriptions allow the comparison of these activities at different households.

### From Chronology to Possessions – A New Direction for Maya Ceramic Studies

Early work on lowland Maya ceramics focused on establishing chronological markers to date construction episodes at monumental centers (e.g., Thompson 1939). Detailed ceramic analysis from the Carnegie Institution of Washington's excavations at Uaxactun, Guatemala, produced a sequence of stylistic horizons (Mamom, Chicanel, Tzakol, Tepeu) that has been essential to temporal comparisons in the central Maya lowlands (Smith 1955). The Uaxactun analysis considered vessel form as an important taxonomic attribute and recognized relationships between form and function. Jars were important for food preparation, storage and transport, food was served and consumed in bowls and plates, and the rarer vases were used exclusively for drinking. These functional categories would have provided a solid basis for comparing assemblages across different household contexts, but comparative household studies would not become prominent in Maya archaeology until decades after the Carnegie project (Figures 2-4 ).

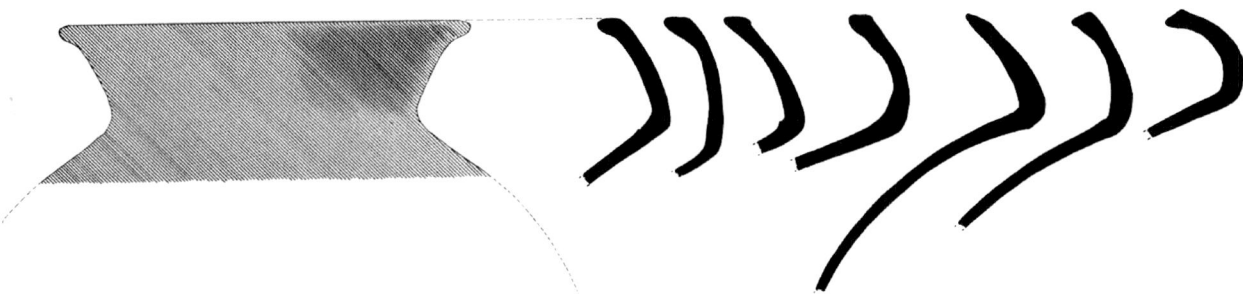

Figure 2. Jars from Uaxactun (Figure by Ford, after Smith 1955: Figure 47b)

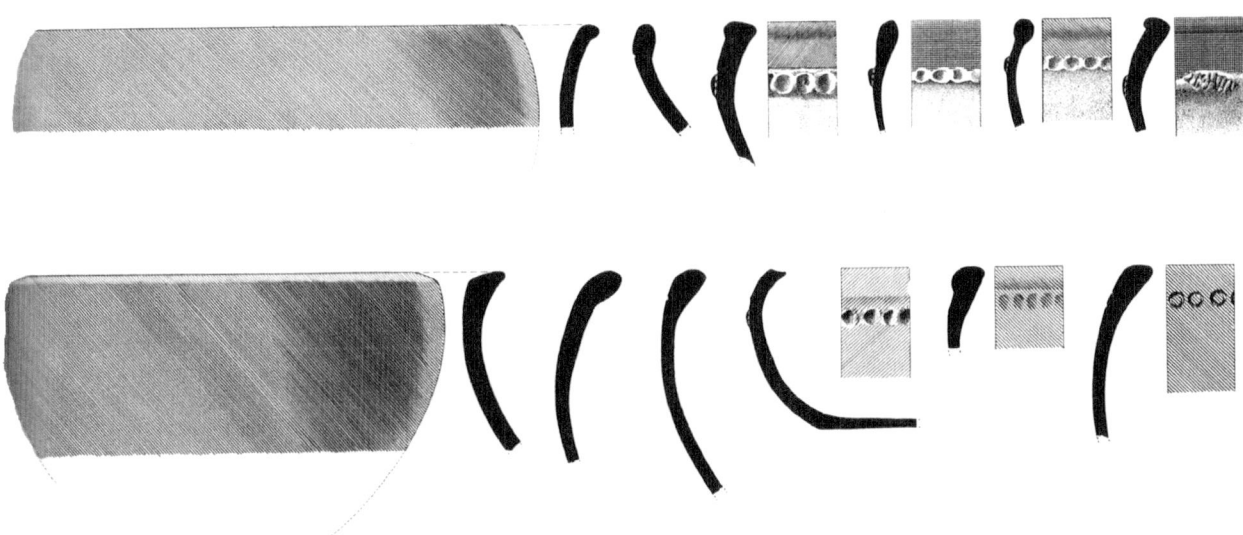

Figure 3. Bowls from Uaxactun (Figure by Ford, after Smith 1955: Figure 48a, 48b)

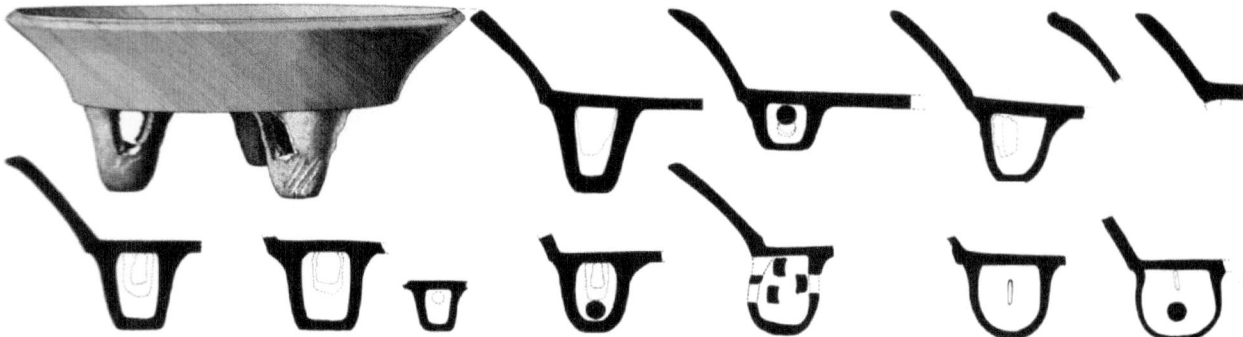

Figure 4. Plates from Uaxactun (Figure by Ford, after Smith 1955:51b)

Subsequent research at Barton Ramie, a domestic settlement along the Belize River, led to the development of type-variety analysis that dominates Maya ceramic studies to this day (Gifford 1976). Initially created to classify pottery in the Southwest United States (Colton 1953; Wheat et al. 1958), type-variety analysis in the Maya area elevates surface treatments (e.g., slips, washes, burnishing) and other stylistic attributes above vessel form – an attribute more closely related to function – in classification schemes. This method privileges the most elaborately decorated vessels and largely ignores formal and functional characteristics (but see LeCount 1996). Numerous vessel forms and rim shapes can be subsumed in types defined primarily by a distinctive surface treatment, as is the case with Late Classic Belize Red:Belize Red variety pottery, which is common in the eastern Maya lowlands. This ceramic type contains comprises multiple vessel forms that were likely used for different functions in different social contexts (Figure 5).

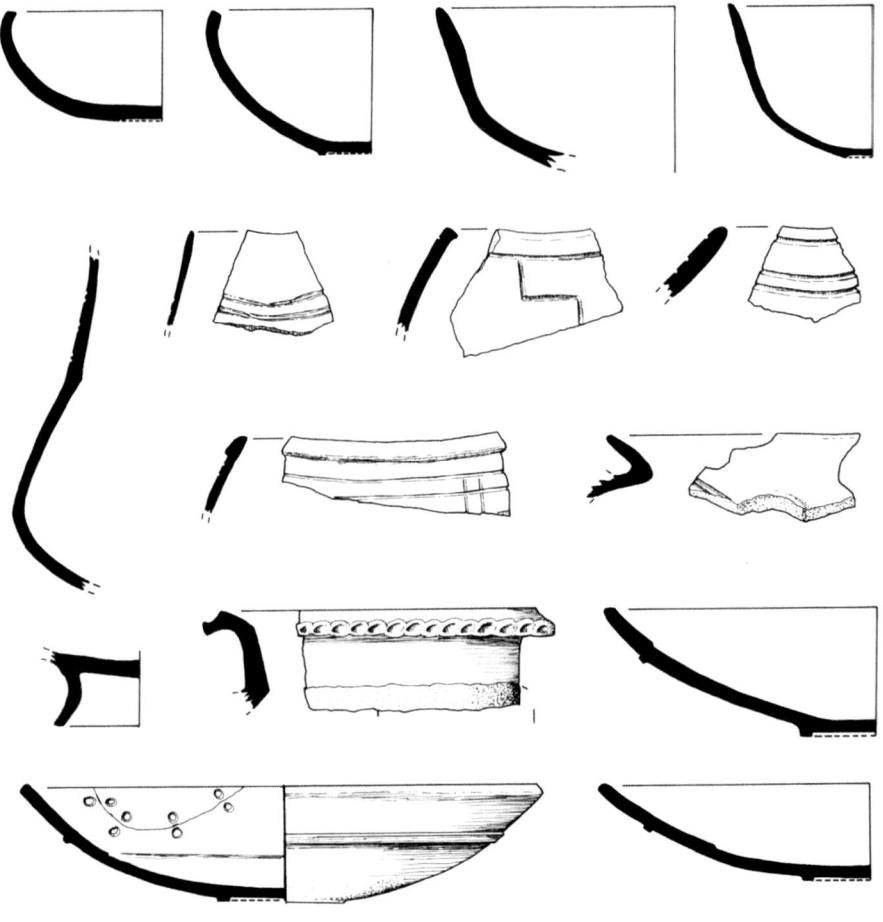

Figure 5. Belize Red:Belize Red variety vessels from Barton Ramie (Gifford 1976: Figure 162)

Type-variety analyses generate descriptions of new types and/or report frequencies of established types (e.g., Ball 1977; Kosakowsky 2012). Attention to surface treatment, a temporally dynamic stylistic attribute in Maya pottery, makes type-variety effective for assessing occupation sequences at sites, and type-variety assessments provide a common terminology to construct chronologies at the regional scale. Tabulations of type frequencies facilitate temporal comparisons and are a useful first step in assessing information exchange, but this approach minimizes functional data essential to comparing household activities. Standard procedures record frequencies of types and varieties present in an assemblage based on raw sherd counts, but these tabulations may include multiple sherds from the same vessels. An approach that calculates the minimum number of vessels present from diagnostic sherds – such as rims, bases, necks, shoulders, feet, and handles that allow original vessel shapes to be identified – is necessary to define household ceramic inventories (Howie 2012). We must construct new frames of reference, contextualized within ceramic ecology and reflecting local resource use, that view vessels as finished products that were circulated and used by ancient Maya households.

We can begin to move beyond chronology and into an investigation of daily life in the Late Classic by building formal and functional descriptions of Maya household ceramic assemblages. Vessel forms and shapes provide essential clues to domestic activities, and we can generate expectations for variability among household inventories for testing with archaeological data. For example, we might expect similarities among cooking and storage vessels if different households cooked similar meals and stored food in the same ways. We might also expect the quality and size of serving vessels to vary with household wealth and status, reflecting the ability of wealthier households to access pottery needed for special events or social occasions. A final hypothesis concerns the size and content of household assemblages: elite households would be expected to possess larger and more diverse ceramic inventories than their lower-status contemporaries. Despite the long history of research on Maya pottery, however, we do not yet know what constitutes a 'typical' household ceramic inventory. In this paper, we construct a comparative baseline through the detailed description of household assemblages from the El Pilar area.

Variability in Maya ceramic inventories can reveal socioeconomic relationships at different geographic scales. Once we have defined the pottery assemblages associated with different households, we can compare these to traditional wealth indicators – such as exotic artifacts and house size – to explore the effects of relative status on household ceramic belongings. Were higher-status families able to access better quality pottery in more diverse forms, or were assemblages essentially the same in kind, regardless of wealth? Were certain kinds of vessels – perhaps analogous to service sets – common to all households in an area? Did ceramic possessions vary among communities as the result of different economic systems, social conventions, or political relationships? Ceramic assemblage descriptions that consider the frequency and diversity of different functional vessel categories put the answers to these questions within our grasp.

**Ceramic Assemblages from the El Pilar Area**

Our data derive from survey and excavations in the El Pilar area of western Belize, which occupies an ecotone between the limestone ridges of the western interior and the coastal plains to the east. It comprises three environmental zones – the valley, foothills, and ridgelands – that are marked by distinctive landforms, geologies, and biotic communities. Differences in soil quality and agricultural potential in each of these zones, which likely affected household subsistence strategies and relative wealth, is discussed elsewhere (Fedick 1995; Ford and Fedick 1992). Research conducted by Ford and colleagues from 1983-1999 mapped over 600 hectares of settled area and 400 residential units (Ford 1990, 1991, 1992). One-eighth of the residential units (n = 48) identified in survey transects were selected for testing in a stratified random sample based on their distance from the river, and eleven of these households were selected for full-scale excavation. Excavations targeted large, medium, and small residential units, along with specialized production areas, in all three environmental zones, representing the range of social and environmental contexts in the El Pilar survey area (Figure 6).

Our objective in this chapter is to investigate the composition of ceramic inventories that reflect the household belongings of the Late Classic Maya. We focus on Late Classic ceramic assemblages only, although earlier (e.g., Late Preclassic) and later (Terminal Classic) ceramics were recovered at several residential units. Structures occupied during Late Classic times were associated with refuse dominated by Late Classic pottery, however, which provided the largest samples for reconstructing household ceramic inventories. Work to correlate this assemblage data with Late Classic residential unit architectural sequences is ongoing and has potential to explain some morphological variability within vessel forms and shapes.

Detailed microscopic and technological studies – necessary to define the economic networks that connected producers and consumers and to investigate household resource use – are planned as a later stage of research. We

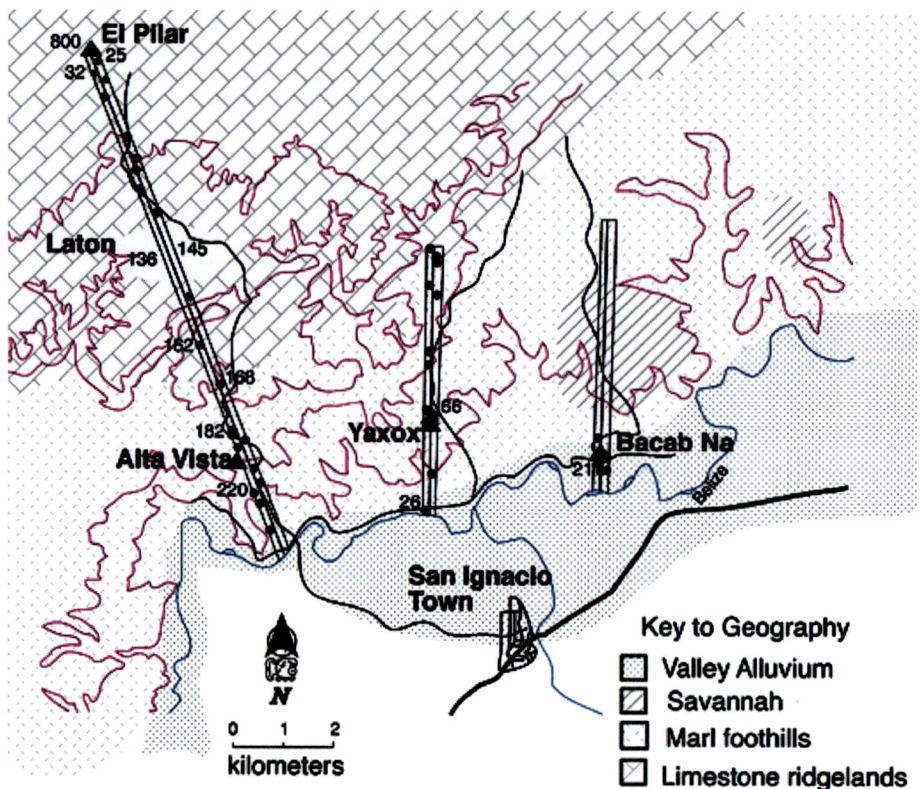

Figure 6. Survey Transects and Settlement in the El Pilar Area. (Figure by Ford)

espouse a functional perspective, focusing on basic vessel form categories and variation in vessel shape and size, to compare ceramic assemblages at different scales. In describing the merits of functional analyses, the pioneering ceramicist Anna O. Shepard (1956, 224) once said:

> 'The study of vessel shape can be approached from the standpoint of function, esthetics or taxonomy. Function has the appeal of human interest; the purpose of the vessel tells us something of the activities and customs of the people who used them.'

With this perspective in mind, we turn to the household ceramic assemblages from the El Pilar area and ask a straightforward question: what can these remains tell us about household belongings and daily life in the Late Classic?

**Late Classic Vessel Forms and Maya Ceramic Belongings**

Maya residential units provide the data for exploring Late Classic household ceramic assemblages. We analyzed all sherds collected from residential unit excavations and identified 9,651 diagnostic samples for our assessment of household inventories. Given our analytical focus, we considered sherds diagnostic if they provided information on basic vessel form. Late Classic vessel form categories can be further divided into common shapes through analyses of rim and profile characteristics, and we have classified diagnostic sherds by form and shape whenever possible. Classification by shape allows us to examine variability within form categories and to compare this variation across residential units. Recognizing this variability is an important first step toward identifying pottery consumption patterns, which reflect economic relationships and household activities. This more detailed classification permits the reconstruction of assemblage components in three-dimensional drawings, which are important tools for visualizing the ceramic inventories of the Late Classic Maya.

All diagnostic sherds were further subjected to an attribute analysis to delineate variation among the assemblages. Twelve distinct attributes were measured for diagnostic sherds and were tabulated for analysis. These attributes provide the basic descriptions for comparisons within the El Pilar collection and among collections analyzed with other classification systems such as type-variety. We work to ensure comparability with other systems by using objective and standardized attribute descriptors, including Munsell colors or Udden-Wentworth grain sizes (Table 1).

## Chapter 2  What is a Ceramic Assemblage: Chronology and Belongings of the Late Classic Maya

| Catalog Number and Suffix | HCl Reaction (identify carbonate-bearing ceramic bodies) |
|---|---|
| **Period Assessment** | Temper Uniformity (evenness, spatial/size distribution) |
| Ceramic Form | Temper Percent (relative abundance) |
| Shape (profile characteristics) | Firing Description (color; presence/absence firing horizons) |
| Group (profile/rim shape/rim diameter) | Surface Description (presence/absences of slips/paints/washes) |
| Rim Diameter | Design Elements (nature/type decorative embellishments) |
| Munsell Slip Color | Wall Thickness |
| Munsell Paste Color | Weight |
| Pocking (spalling; removal of carbonate inclusions from surface) | |

Table 1. El Pilar Area Ceramic Attribute Assessment. (Table by Ford)

We use the attributes of vessel form, shape, and size to examine assemblages for patterns related to daily activities and pottery consumption. Our comparative analyses are ongoing, and we present preliminary results below along with descriptions of common Late Classic vessel shapes. We aim to demonstrate the utility of this approach to characterizing Maya ceramic possessions as well as its potential for comparative analyses at multiple scales.

The basic forms of the Late Classic assemblages include bowls, jars, plates, and vases. These formal categories reflect how vessels functioned in a range of activities by the inhabitants of the El Pilar area. Table 2 and Figure 7 illustrate the relative frequencies of different vessel forms. The formal categories occur in differing proportions, suggesting that assemblage variation relates to function and use. The low percentage of vases (5%), for example, suggests they served more restricted functions or saw more restricted use than bowls (40%), although small bowls were also likely used for drinking. We can compare this composite picture to assemblages across the Maya lowlands to look for differences in activities, and it serves as a baseline for comparing individual household assemblages in the El Pilar area (Table 2, Figure 7).

| Form | Frequency | Percent |
|---|---|---|
| Bowls | 3813 | 40% |
| Wide Jar | 2122 | 22% |
| Narrow Jar | 1452 | 15% |
| Plates | 1747 | 18% |
| Vases | 517 | 5% |
| **Grand Total** | **9651** | **100%** |

Table 2. Diagnostic Late Classic Vessel Forms from the El Pilar Area. (Table by Ford)

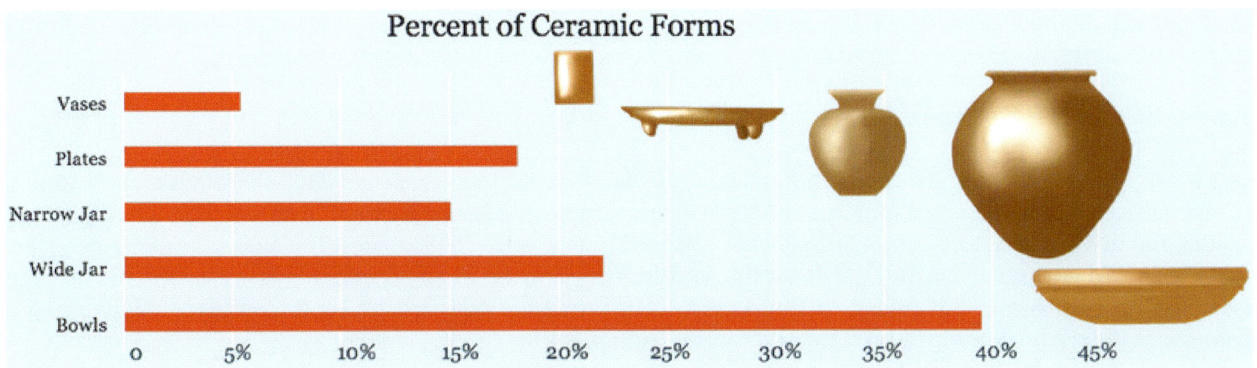

Figure 7. Basic Vessel Forms in the El Pilar Area. (Figure by Ford)

Using the attributes discussed above, we have identified and defined common Late Classic shapes within our broader form categories. We were able to assign about 60% (n = 5040) of our diagnostic sherds to one of these shape classes, which we describe below (Table 3, Figure 8).

17

| Residential Unit | Geographic Zone | Household Size | Form Diagnostics | Shape Diagnostics |
|---|---|---|---|---|
| 281-21 | Valley | Medium | 2254 | 1288 |
| 278-26 | Valley | Small | 862 | 397 |
| 278-66 | Foothills | Small | 190 | 104 |
| 272-220 | Foothills | Medium | 553 | 344 |
| 272-182 | Foothills | Medium | 512 | 280 |
| 272-168 | Ridgelands | Small | 72 | 35 |
| 272-162 | Ridgelands | Medium | 3 | 0 |
| 272-145 | Ridgelands | Large | 1098 | 593 |
| 272-136 | Ridgelands | Large | 403 | 230 |
| 272-032 | Ridgelands | Small | 1 | 1 |
| 272-025 | Ridgelands | Large | 2864 | 1768 |
| **Total** | | | **8812** | **5040** |

Table 3. Late Classic General Form and Common Shape Diagnostics from Full-Scale Excavations. (Table by Ford)

Figure 8. Common Shapes in Late Classic Assemblages in the El Pilar Area. (Figure by Ford)

### Late Classic Common Bowl Shapes

Bowls were serving containers that varied from incurving to everted rim shapes. Late Classic common bowls made up 34% (n = 1692) of our collections from the El Pilar area and were made in four basic shapes. Rim diameters ranged from individual-sized, small bowls (12 cm diameter) to large communal serving containers or basins (55 cm in diameter or more). Bowls were everyday food containers and serve multiple purposes (Figure 9).

### Late Classic Common Jar Shapes

Jars were generally used for storage & cooking. Common Late Classic jars comprised 2108 sherds and made up 42% of the collection. We identified four common rim shapes that include complex and everted rims for containing liquids and dry goods. Liquid containers generally had narrow or restricted orifices. The average rim diameter for narrow-necked jars was 19 cm. Dry-goods storage and cooking jars had wider mouths for easier access and average rim diameters of 26 cm. This robust collection of vessels presented an opportunity to consider how household belongings differed according to residential activities (Figure 10).

### Late Classic Common Plate Shapes

Plates were open food-service vessels produced in individual and larger sizes. We identified four common shape groups among the 830 plate sherds, which constituted only 16% of the whole collection. The sizes ranged from smaller plates (15 cm in diameter) to larger ones (50 cm in diameter) that were likely used to feed larger groups of people. Variations in plate sizes likely reflected different functions and may be related to residential unit size and location (Figure 11).

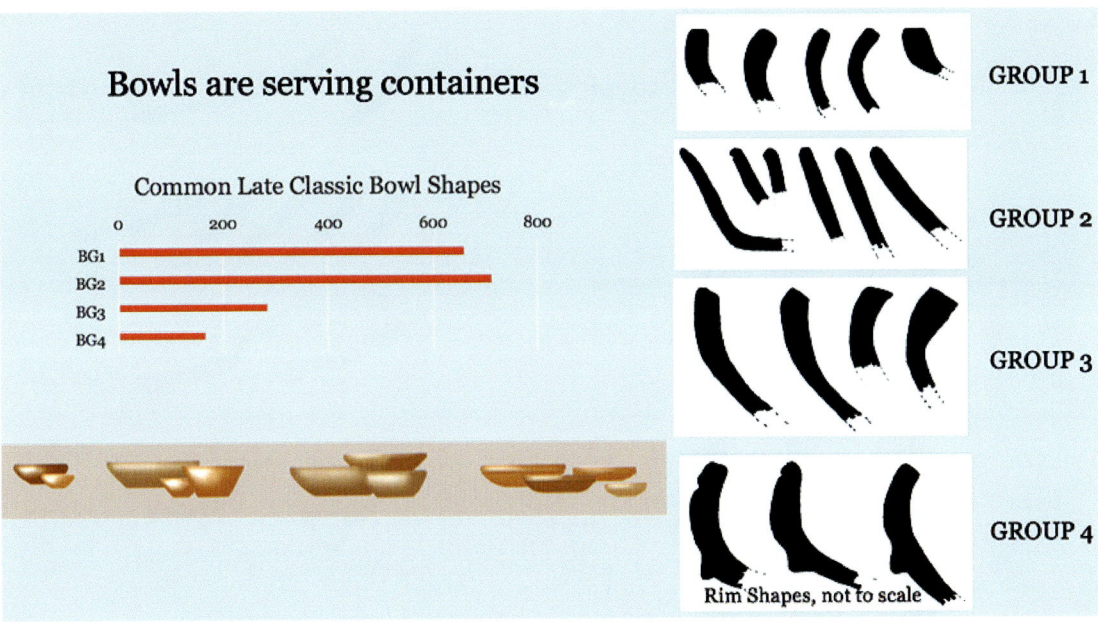

Figure 9. Common Bowl Shapes in Late Classic Assemblages. (Figure by Ford)

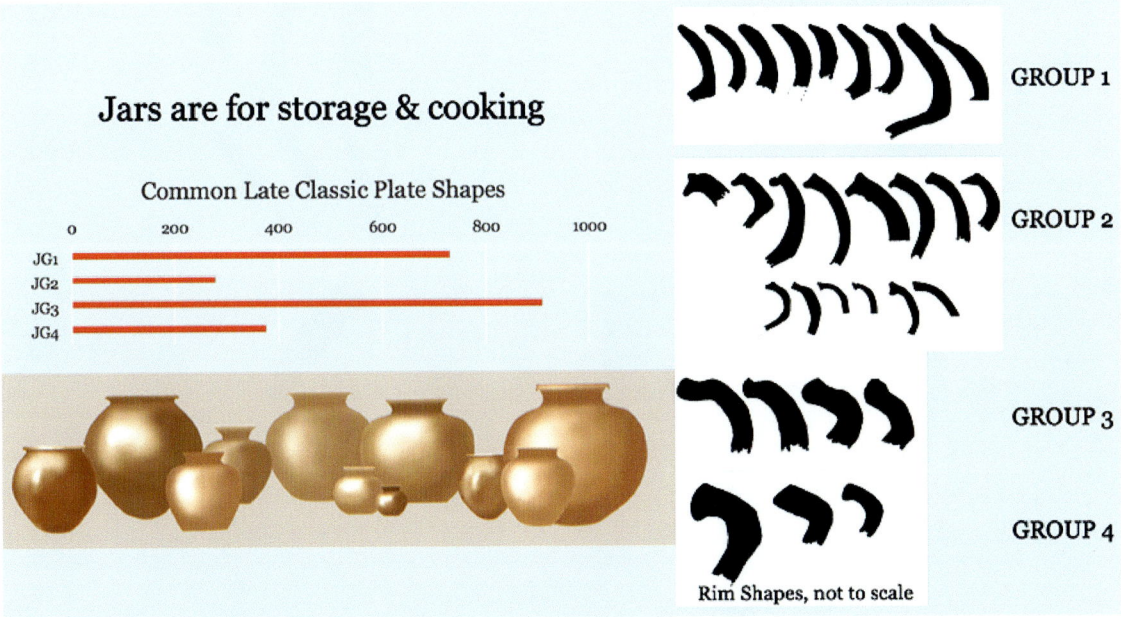

Figure 10. Common Jar Shapes in the Late Classic Assemblages. (Figure by Ford)

*Late Classic Common Vase Shapes*

Largely considered drinking vessels, vases made up the smallest number of the total forms of our Late Classic assemblage. We identified two common vase shapes among 410 diagnostic sherds (8% of assemblage), with an additional minor variant forming a third group. The smallest vases had 8 cm rim diameters, and the average rim diameter was 16 cm. This size variation suggests that vases functioned in a variety of settings and may have been used for more than simply drinking (Figure 12).

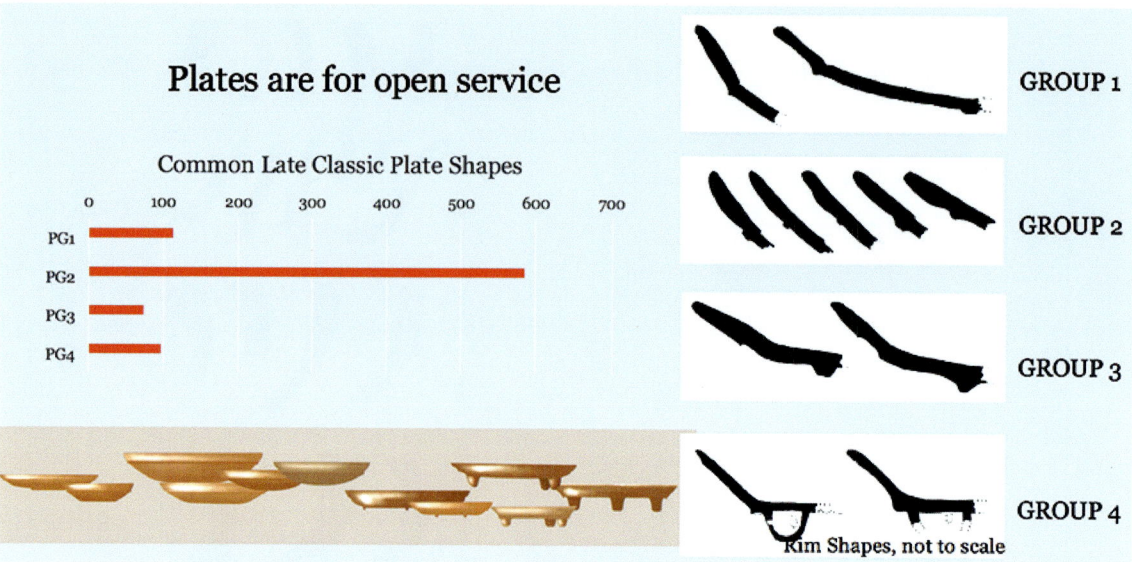

Figure 11. Common Plate Shapes in Late Classic Assemblages. (Figure by Ford)

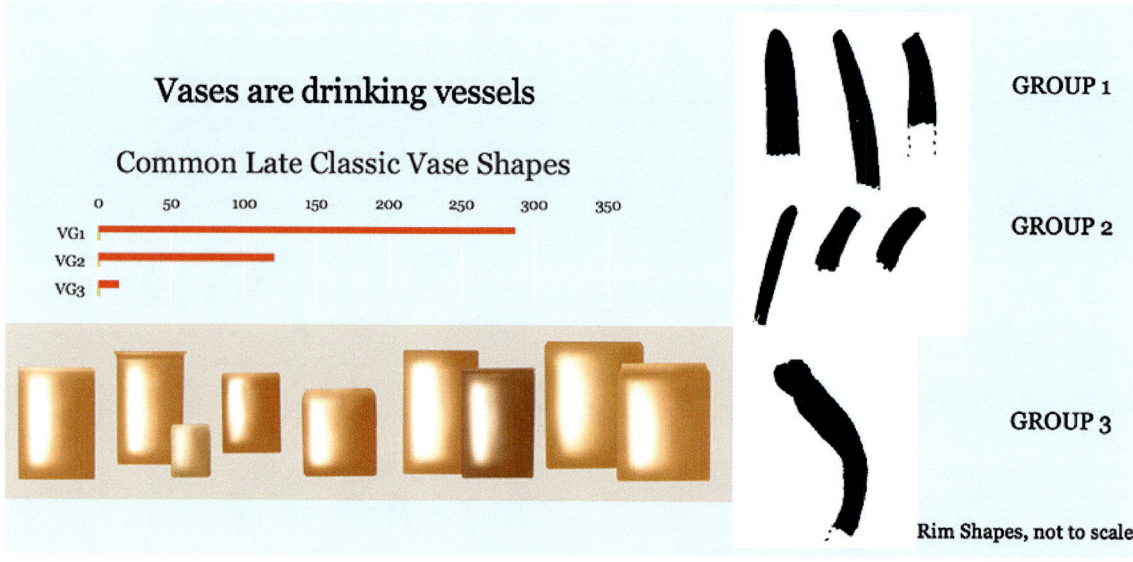

Figure 12. Common Vase Shapes in Late Classic Assemblages. (Figure by Ford)

**Preliminary Household Comparisons**

The ceramic assemblages varied in size by residential unit across the El Pilar area. Some of this variation related to the period of occupation, as can be seen in units 272-162 and 272-032 in Table 3, which yielded almost no Late Classic sherds. We can attribute additional variation in assemblage size to sampling bias at different sites, although the data suggest patterns in pottery consumption related to geographic zone. Residential units in the valley, for example, yielded relatively larger quantities of diagnostic sherds than comparably sized households in the foothills, indicating higher levels of pottery consumption. This suggests that valley households maintained access to pottery producers over extended periods of time and were relatively wealthier than households in the foothills, which correlates with lithic consumption patterns across the two environmental zones (Sponagle 2017). The larger sample of residential units from the ridgelands shows more variability in pottery consumption that requires additional investigation (Table 4).

CHAPTER 2   WHAT IS A CERAMIC ASSEMBLAGE: CHRONOLOGY AND BELONGINGS OF THE LATE CLASSIC MAYA

| Residential Unit | Household Size | Bowls | | Jars | | Plates | | Vases | | Total |
|---|---|---|---|---|---|---|---|---|---|---|
| | | N | % | N | % | N | % | N | % | |
| 281-021 | Medium | 433 | 34 | 429 | 33 | 297 | 23 | 129 | 10 | 1288 |
| 278-026 | Small | 176 | 44 | 117 | 30 | 76 | 19 | 28 | 7 | 397 |
| *Valley Totals* | | **612** | **36** | **546** | **33** | **373** | **22** | **157** | **9** | **1685** |
| 278-066 | Small | 29 | 28 | 59 | 57 | 6 | 6 | 10 | 9 | 104 |
| 272-220 | Medium | 174 | 50 | 77 | 22 | 43 | 13 | 50 | 15 | 344 |
| 272-182 | Medium | 78 | 28 | 67 | 24 | 106 | 38 | 29 | 10 | 280 |
| *Foothills Totals* | | **281** | **39** | **203** | **28** | **155** | **21** | **89** | **12** | **728** |
| 272-168 | Small | 16 | 46 | 16 | 46 | 0 | 0 | 3 | 8 | 35 |
| 272-162 | Medium | 0 | 0 | 0 | 0 | 0 | 0 | 0 | 0 | 0 |
| 272-145 | Large | 142 | 24 | 303 | 51 | 78 | 13 | 70 | 12 | 593 |
| 272-136 | Large | 77 | 33 | 119 | 52 | 19 | 8 | 15 | 7 | 230 |
| 272-032 | Small | 0 | 0 | 1 | 100 | 0 | 0 | 0 | 0 | 1 |
| 272-025 | Large | 567 | 32 | 920 | 52 | 205 | 12 | 76 | 4 | 1768 |
| *Ridgelands Totals* | | **802** | **31** | **1359** | **52** | **302** | **11** | **164** | **6** | **2627** |
| *Total* | | *1692* | *34* | *2108* | *42* | *830* | *16* | *410* | *8* | *5040* |

Table 4. Diagnostic Late Classic Vessel Shapes by Geographic Zones. (Table by Ford)

Examining the distributions of basic vessel shapes reveals additional patterns of pottery consumption and activities that vary among households and across geographic zones. At the highest level of comparison – that of the geographic zone – we see broad similarities in the percentages of bowls that make up household assemblages. This likely reflects the many roles bowls can play in cooking and serving food as well as their probable use for drinking. Bowls were an important component of Late Classic ceramic inventories regardless of relative household wealth or environmental zone because of their utility. Jars varied more by environmental zone and made up about half of ridgeland household assemblages, which may reflect the abilities of those households to acquire and store food.

Interestingly, plates and vases accounted for more of the assemblages among valley and foothills households than those in the ridgelands. We might expect these types of vessels, which are exclusively associated with food service, to be more prevalent in the assemblages of larger households such as those located in the ridgelands. This suggests different access to service vessels or participation in specific food-service activities may have characterized households in the different geographic zones. The presence of vases at households of all sizes and in every geographic zone suggests these vessels, often thought to be wealth indicators, were not restricted to specific segments of society. Finally, at the aggregate level, household assemblages in the valley and foothills more closely resemble each other than those from the ridgelands.

Variation among household inventories from the same environmental zone was most pronounced in the foothills and ridgelands, although the smaller sample from the valley may skew this interpretation. The two valley households differed in size and presumably in wealth, but the proportions of different vessel shapes were remarkably similar. This suggests that each household engaged in similar activities related to food preparation, storage, and service, and that each had similar abilities to access pottery producers to meet household needs.

Residential units in the foothills showed the greatest variability in assemblage composition. The small household 278-066, for example, possessed relatively more jars and fewer plates than other households in the foothills. This may reflect its smaller size and the possibility that it was a secondary residence, although the remaining medium-sized households also showed variability in ceramic possessions. Household 272-182 yielded more than three times as many plates as 272-220, which suggests a preference for open-service vessels and possible participation in different social events.

Late Classic ridgeland household assemblages varied more in scale than in kind, although some differences in ceramic belongings are apparent. Three of four residential inventories contained significantly higher than expected proportions of jars compared to the total collection, but the assemblage associated with residence 272-168 was less diverse than the other ridgeland households. This assemblage contained equal, but small, numbers of jar and bowls, yet no plates, suggesting a limited range of cooking and serving activities occurred there. Despite the lack of plates, 272-168 yielded three vase fragments, which might not be expected at a small household with a limited ceramic inventory. More diverse assemblages from the larger residences 272-136 and 272-025 contained lower percentages of vase fragments, further complicating interpretations of the role vases played in Late Classic daily life.

**Conclusions and Directions for Future Research**

Decades of ceramic analyses have focused on chronology building to understand the extent and development of Maya civilization. This puts us in a good position to move toward more nuanced understandings of household activities and the impacts of Late Classic societies on the Maya lowland landscape. Our vessel descriptions and preliminary comparisons show the utility of functional ceramic analyses to address the questions of household archaeology and ceramic ecology, although much work remains to be done. We have recognized functional variability among the ceramic belongings of different households, which suggests detailed analyses of residential assemblages will produce information on the resource use, economic systems, and daily activities that characterized life in the Late Classic period.

Variability in assemblage composition indicates differences in food storage, cooking, and service practices among the different households we examined. Some of this variability may have related to household wealth, although traditional wealth indicators, such as vases and serving plates, were not disproportionately concentrated in the larger household assemblages. Functional variability also seems to vary with environmental zone, which may reflect participation in different social events or economic strategies by households in different areas. Additional comparative study, incorporating stylistic and technological attributes collected during ceramic analysis, will refine investigations of assemblage variability and the Late Classic activities that produced it.

Future microscopic analyses and geological survey will allow us to link household belongings to the landscape of the El Pilar area. Connecting ceramic assemblages to Late Classic environmental zones is essential to understanding ancient Maya resource use, which certainly impacted how household members lived on a day-to-day basis. The resources available within the ten-kilometer radius traditional potters will travel to obtain them were diverse (Arnold 1985:54-55), and identification of different geologic materials will shed light on economic networks that connected pottery producers and consumers. This line of inquiry holds great potential for explaining the assemblage variability documented in different environmental zones. Only by investigating this variability, rather than subsuming it in classificatory schemes designed to answer different questions, will we gain a fuller picture of the importance of ceramics to Late Classic daily life.

**References Cited**

Abrams, Elliot M. 1994. *How the Maya Built Their World: Energetics and Ancient Architecture.* Austin: University of Texas Press.
Arnold, Dean E. 1985 *Ceramic Theory and Culture Process.* Cambridge, UK: Cambridge University Press.
Arnold, Jeanne E. and Anabel Ford. 1980. 'A Statistical Examination of Settlement Patterns at Tikal, Guatemala.' *American Antiquity* 45 (4): 713-726.
Asaro, Frank, H. V. Michel, R. Sidrys, and F. Stross. 1978. 'High-precision chemical characterization of major obsidian sources in Guatemala.' *American Antiquity* 43 (3): 436-443.
Ashmore, Wendy, ed. 1981. *Lowland Maya Settlement Patterns.* 1st ed. Albuquerque: University of New Mexico Press.
Ball, Joseph W. 1977. *The Archaeological Ceramics of Becan, Campeche, Mexico.* Middle American Research Institute Pub. 43. New Orleans: Tulane University.
Blackmore, Chelsea. 2012. 'Recognizing Difference in Small Scale Settings: An Examination of Social Identity Formation at the Northeast Group, Chan.' In *Chan: An Ancient Maya Farming Community,* edited by Cynthia Robin, 173-191. Gainseville: University of Florida Press.
Colton, Harold S. 1953. *Potsherds: An Introduction to the Study of Prehistoric Southwestern Ceramics and Their Use in Historic Reconstruction.* Flagstaff: The Northern Arizona Society of Science and Art.
Fedick, Scott L. 1995. 'Land Evaluation and Ancient Maya Land Use in the Upper Belize River Area, Belize, Central America.' *Latin American Antiquity* 6 (1): 16-34.
Ford, Anabel. 1990. 'Maya Settlement in the Belize River Area: Variations in Residence Patterns of the Central Maya Lowlands.' In *Prehistoric Population History in the Maya Lowlands,* edited by T. P. Culbert and D. S. Rice, 167-181. Albuquerque: University of New Mexico Press.

Ford, Anabel. 1991. 'Economic variation of ancient Maya residential settlement in the upper Belize River area.' *Ancient Mesoamerica* 2 (1): 35-46.

Ford, Anabel. 1992. 'The Ancient Maya Domestic Economy: An Examination of Settlement in the Upper Belize River Area.' Memorias del Primer Congreso Internacional de Mayistas, San Cristobal de las Casas, México, 57-86. México: Universidad Nacional Autónoma de México.

Ford, Anabel. 2010. 'Conspicuous Production of Exotics among the Maya: The Organization of Obsidian Procurement, Production, and Distribution at El Pilar.' In *Producción de bienes de prestigio ornamentales y votivos de la América Antigua*, edited by E. M. Tisoc, R. S. Ciriaco and E. G. Licón, 111-130. Doral: Syllaba Press.

Ford, Anabel and Scott L. Fedick. 1992. 'Prehistoric Maya Settlement Patterns in the Upper Belize River Area: Initial Results of the Belize River Archaeological Settlement Survey.' *Journal of Field Archaeology* 19 (1): 35-49.

Ford, Anabel and Kirsten Olson. 1989. 'Aspects of Ancient Maya Household Economy: Variation in Chipped Stone Production and Consumption.' In *Prehistoric Maya Economies of Belize*, edited by P. A. McAnany and B. L. Isaac, 185-211. Research in Economic Anthropology Supplement 4. Vol. 4. Greenwich: JAI Press.

Ford, Anabel and Frank Spera. 2007. 'Fresh Volcanic Glass Shards in the Pottery Sherds of the Maya Lowlands.' *Research Reports in Belizean Archaeology* 4: 111-118.

Ford, Anabel, Fred Stross, Frank Asaro and Helen V. Michel. 1997. 'Obsidian Procurement and Distribution in the Tikal-Yaxha Intersite Area of the Central Maya Lowlands.' *Ancient Mesoamerica* 8 (1): 101-110.

Gifford, James C. 1976 *Prehistoric Pottery Analysis and the Ceramics of Barton Ramie in the Belize Valley*. Memoirs of the Peabody Museum of Archaeology and Ethnology 18. Cambridge, MA: Peabody Museum, Harvard University.

Grube, Nikolai. 1992 'Classic Maya dance: evidence from hieroglyphs and iconography.' *Ancient Mesoamerica* 3 (2): 201-218.

Howie, Linda A. 2012. *Ceramic Change and the Maya Collapse: A Study of Pottery Technology, Manufacture and Consumption at Lamanai, Belize*. BAR International Series 2373. Oxford: Archaeopress.

Hohmann, Bobbi M. 2002. Preclassic Maya Shell Ornament Production in the Belize Valley, Belize. PhD Diss., Department of Anthropology, University of New Mexico, Albuquerque. University Microfilms, Ann Arbor.

Horn III, Sherman W. 2015. The Web of Complexity: Socioeconomic Networks in the Middle Preclassic Belize Valley. PhD Diss., Department of Anthropology, Tulane University, New Orleans. University Microfilms, Ann Arbor.

Keller, Angela H. 2012. 'Creating Community with Shell.' In *Chan: An Ancient Maya Farming Community*, edited by C. Robin, 253-270. Gainesville: University of Florida Press.

Kosakowsky, Laura J. 2012. 'Ceramics and Chronology at Chan.' In *Chan: An Ancient Maya Farming Community*, edited by C. Robin, 42-70. Gainesville: University Press of Florida.

LeCount, Lisa Jeanne. 1996. Pottery and Power: Feasting, Gifting, and Displaying Wealth among the Late and Terminal Classic Lowland Maya. PhD Diss., Anthropology, University of California, Los Angeles.

López Varela, Sandra L. 2005. 'The Microcosmos of Formative Pottery from K'axob, Belize.' In *New Perspectives on Formative Mesoamerican Cultures*, edited by T.G. Powis, 159-170. BAR International Series 1377. Oxford: Archaeopress.

Netting, Robert McC., Richard R. Wilk and Eric J. Arnould. 1984. 'Introduction.' In *Household: Comparative and Historical Studies of the Domestic Group*, edited by R. M. Netting, R. R. Wilk and E. J. Arnould, xiii-xxxviii. Berkeley: University of California Press.

Reents-Budet, Dorie, and Joseph W. Ball. 1994. *Painting the Maya universe: royal ceramics of the Classic period*. Durham, NC: Duke University Press.

Robin, Cynthia, ed. 2012 *Chan: An Ancient Maya Farming Community*. Gainesville: University Press of Florida.

Robin, Cynthia. 2013. *Everyday Life Matters: Maya Farmers at Chan*. Gainesville: University Press of Florida.

Shafer, Harry J. and Thomas R. Hester. 1983. 'Ancient Maya Chert Workshops in Northern Belize, Central America.' *American Antiquity* 48 (3): 519-543.

Shepard, Anna O. 1955. 'Technological Analysis.' In *Ceramic Sequence at Uaxactun, Guatemala, Volume 1*, pp. 32-36. Middle American Research Institute Pub. 20. New Orleans: Tulane University.

Shepard, Anna O. 1956. *Ceramics for the Archaeologist*. Carnegie Institution of Washington Publication 609. Washington, D.C.: Carnegie Institution of Washington.

Smith, Michael E. 1987. 'Household Possession and Wealth in Agrarian States: Implications for Archaeology.' *Journal of Anthropological Archaeology* 6 (4): 297-335.

Smith, Robert E. 1955. *Ceramic Sequence at Uaxactun, Guatemala, Volume 1*. Middle American Research Institute Pub. 20. New Orleans: Tulane University.

Sponagle, Samuel. 2017. Chert Lithic Production and Consumption from Late Classic Maya Households. Senior Honors Thesis, Anthropology, University of California, Santa Barbara.

Thompson, J. Eric. 1939. *Excavations at San Jose, British Honduras*. Carnegie Institution of Washington Publication 506. Washington, D.C: Carnegie Institution of Washington.

Wauchope, Robert. 1938. *Modern Maya Houses: A Study of their Archaeological Significance.* 1st ed. Washington, D.C.: Carnegie Institution of Washington.

Webster, David L., and Nancy Gonlin. 1988. 'Household Remains of the Humblest Maya.' *Journal of Field Archaeology* 15 (2): 169-190.

Wheat, Joe Ben, James C. Gifford, and William W. Wasley. 'Ceramic variety, type cluster, and ceramic system in Southwestern pottery analysis.' *American Antiquity* 24 (1): 34-47.

Wiewall, Darcy and Linda Howie. 2010. 'A Synthesis of Ceramic Production and Consumption at Lamanai, Belize, during the Postclassic to Spanish Colonial Periods.' *Research Reports in Belizean Archaeology* 7: 201-217.

Wilk, Richard R. and William L. Rathje. 1982. 'Household Archaeology.' *American Behavioral Scientist* 25 (6): 617-639.

# Chapter 3

# Investigating Maya Ceramic Figurines: challenges to the use of non-invasive portable technologies in archived collections

Sandra L. López Varela

Universidad Nacional Autónoma de México; slvarela@comunidad.unam.mx

**Abstract**

*Jaina, a coastal site located 42 km north of Campeche, México, has produced a large number of ceramic figurines from burial deposits since the early 19th century. Unfortunately, the beauty of the 'Jaina figurines' has encouraged their illicit trafficking in the antiquities market. Modern excavations unearthed a large number of ceramic figurines from burial deposits. Few excavation reports and studies of the recovered materials have been published, leaving us with unanswered questions for their interpretation. In 2015, through a collaborative effort with Mexico's National Institute of Anthropology and History (Instituto Nacional de Antropología e Historia-INAH) Center in Campeche, a team of investigators analyzed a collection of 128 figurines with non-invasive portable technology, mainly, fiber optic reflectance spectroscopy (FORS) in the ultraviolet/visible and near infrared (UV/VNIR) and X-ray fluorescence (XRF) spectroscopy to characterize the chemical composition of the clay and pigmented surfaces. However, the potential of these techniques in the characterization and authentication of Maya ceramic figurines is limited in the absence of contextual information, as hereby discussed. When Maya ceramic figurines are witnesses of transnational antiquities crimes, archaeologists should not settle for chemical fingerprints and iconographic studies as an alternative to looting practices. Otherwise, use of scientific analysis risks the fabrication of erroneous stories and claims about the Maya past and Mexico's heritage.*

**Key words**
*Jaina, Ceramic Figurines, Children, Musical Instruments, Maya Archaeology*

## Introduction

The 19th century was a period of a very active intellectual engagement in the State of Campeche, encouraged by several European voyagers to the Americas (Charnay 1888; de Waldeck 1996). This setting, inspired by the collecting spirit of the Enlightenment, motivated two members of the Franciscan order to install a *Wunderkammern* (Cabinet of Curiosities) in the city of Campeche (Sellen 2010). By 1841, the 'Camacho brothers', as they were known at the time, created a museum exhibiting a collection of artifacts that included clay and stone idols, and musical instruments (Bancroft 1875, 265). The 'Camacho' collection included an exhibit of several figurines found in a tomb, containing a human skeleton, near the city of Campeche (Morelet 1857, 167-168).

The 'Camacho' collection seems to have been the source of many ceramic figurines now housed in museums around the world. This collection dispersed when it was moved to Mexico's National Museum under the orders of Emperor Maximilian I (Carvajal Correa 2014; Sellen 2010). Recently, Lowe and Sellen (2010, 149) do not rule out the possibility that part of the collection was acquired by Florentino Gimeno Echevarría, who owned a retail store in the city of Campeche, and was believed to have owned more than twelve thousand archaeological artifacts that he tried to sell to several museums in the United States and Europe. With their discovery of two catalogues at Mexico's National Museum of Anthropology (Museo Nacional de Antropología-MNA), carefully elaborated by Gimeno in 1869 and 1872, Lowe and Sellen (2010, 160, Figure 5) describe detailed information on the figurines, many of which, had been found at Jaina. The 'Gimeno Collection' somehow ended in Cuba after his passing, where it was acquired eventually by Adolf Bastian, founder of the Ethnological Museum in Berlin (Lowe and Sellen 2010, 149). Since Adolf Bastian exchanged the Campeche materials with other museums in the 19th century, they are the likely source of ceramic figurines on display in many museums around the world (Goldstein 1979, 19).

Nineteenth century accounts about Jaina sadly reveal the disturbance of its archaeological context by its visitors and inhabitants. Desiré Charnay (1888, 166) describes Jaina as a place dedicated to the interment of many 'bodies' brought from far away accompanied by vessels, idols, small statues, that have been broken, and then sold and disseminated everywhere. Charnay (1888, 168-169) explains how easy it was to identify the placement of graves because these were marked by a protruding big shell; and how those living at Jaina at the time used the urns recovered from these graves to store water. While Charnay (1888, 182) visited Jaina, he reports paying women and children for every object they collected.

The collecting practices of the nineteenth century resulted in the irreplaceable loss of archaeological information at Jaina. Therefore, the figurines exhibited at many museums around the world lack provenience. Unfortunately, modern excavations at Jaina (Benavides C. 2012; Carmen Cook de Leonard 1964; Fernández 1946; López Alonso and Serrano S. 1984; Moedano Koer 1946; Piña Chán 2001) have resulted in few published reports with limited descriptions of the context in which these figurines were found and of their associated materials. The figurines from these excavations thus pose analytical problems for their study and interpretation, despite the support of art historians and epigraphists (Martin and Grube 2000; Miller 1975; Miller and Martin 2004).

Given the unique and delicate characteristics of these figurines, answering questions related to their loci of production, chemical characterization, and authenticity was only possible with instrumental techniques, such as INAA (Instrumental Neutron Activation Analysis), that required their destruction. Non-invasive and non-destructive technologies are a good alternative to INAA to study the chemical composition of archived materials. In 2012, the INAH Center in Campeche decided to study their collection of Jaina figurines, using non-invasive and non-destructive technologies. Therefore, Dr. López Varela from UNAM, and Dr. Ioanna Kakoulli and Dr. Christian Fischer from UCLA, incorporated INAH's collection to the project entitled 'Chemistry, Variability, and Provenience of Jaina Figurines: a Multiscale-Multianalytical Approach', funded by UC Mexus-CONACyT in between 2012 and 2016. In this project, principal investigators applied non-invasive portable spectroscopic technologies to characterize a collection of 88 figurines from the Fowler Museum at the University of California Los Angeles and a collection of 128 ceramic figurines housed at the Centro INAH Campeche (BCC) and two museums, the Museo Arqueológico Hecelchakan (HKAN) and the Museo Fuerte San Martín (SM). The following discussion describes the challenges in investigating the variability in the chemistry and technology of the INAH collection of ceramic figurines.

**The archaeology of Jaina and its challenges for the interpretation of the ceramic figurines**

Situated in the wetlands of the Campeche coast (Figure 1), Jaina has been exposed to rising sea levels that have reduced its size considerably since the 19th century. Many of its buildings and burial sites are now underwater. Since rising sea levels have shaped the size of the island, Piña Chán (2001) suggested that Jaina was simply an extension of the mainland, shaped into an 'island' by seawaters. Earlier, de Waldeck (1996) had suggested the site

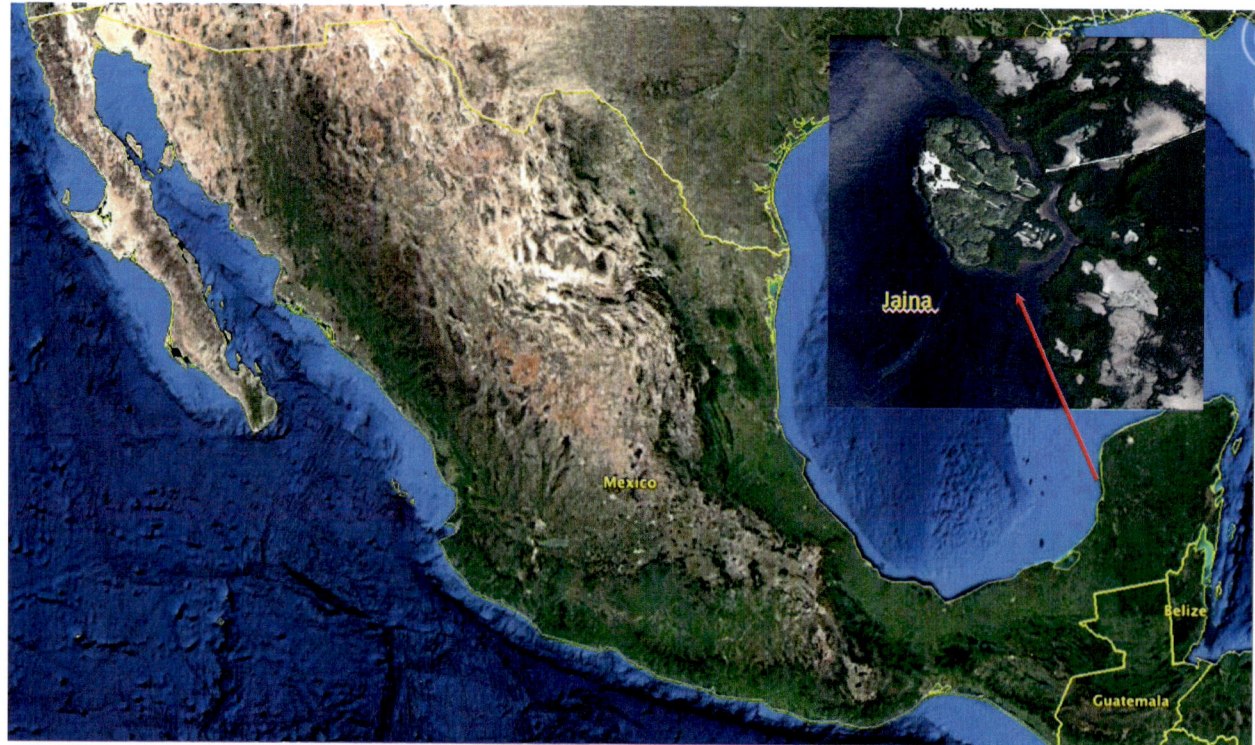

Figure 1. Map showing location of Jaina, off the coast of Campeche, Mexico, composed by López Varela, based on Google Earth

was a peninsula, whereas Charnay (1888) described Jaina as an island. In the absence of published geological and geomorphological studies, it is not possible to state unequivocally whether Jaina is an island or simply an extension of a portion of the Yucatán peninsula (Aveleyra de Anda and Ekholm 1966). Nevertheless, Jaina seems to be part of a network of islands along the Gulf Coast (Benavides C. 2002, 71), where multiple burials and figurines have been found (Charnay 1888; Inurreta Díaz 2004; Inurreta Díaz and Pat Cruz 2005; Shook 1955).

Within the site's 42 hectares, archaeologists have concentrated excavations in its two main architectural complexes, Zacpool and Zayozal, and their surrounding mortuary deposits. In the 1940s, archaeological excavations at Jaina (1940-1941 and 1941-1942) by Miguel Ángel Fernández (1946) and Hugo Moedano Koer (1946) produced 150 burials that were interred, either in urns or directly in the ground, that were never studied properly (Ochoa C. and Salas C. 1984a, 436). In addition, Moedano Koer (1946) reports the findings of platforms and rectangular house foundations. On two occasions, excavations of burial deposits at Jaina were conducted to enrich the collections of Mexico's National Museum of Anthropology and History (Ochoa C. and Salas C. 1984a, 436). Motivated by the desire to enlarge the collections of Jaina figurines for the premier opening of the museum at its current location in Mexico City (Piña Chán 1968), excavations were carried out in 1964, and yielded 400 burials.

Even though earlier excavations exposed more than a thousand burials and at least 600 figurines, limited contextual information was provided when they were submitted to INAH's Physical Anthropology Department (Ochoa C. and Salas C. 1984a, 436-437; Pijoan A. and Salas C. 1984, 471). This oversight left Jaina without a reliable stratigraphy and contextual information for interpretation of the associated figurines. Today, the Department of Physical Anthropology at the Museum contains 33 skulls, 16 jawbones, and various long bones from the Jaina excavations between 1940 and 1964 (Pijoan A. and Salas C. 1984, 471). With such little archaeological information (Aveleyra de Anda and Ekholm 1966), it is hard to determine if Jaina functioned as a necropolis (Charnay 1888; Piña Chán 2001), a religious center (Piña Chán 2001), or a trading station for coastal canoe traffic (Benavides C. 2005, 23).

*The scientific stage in the archaeology of Jaina*

The loss of archaeological materials and human remains from Jaina is simply tragic (Ochoa C. and Salas C. 1984a, 471; Pijoan A. and Salas C. 1984). Most archaeological data originates from excavations in the 1970s (López Alonso and Serrano S. 1984). These excavations recovered 106 burials and 43 figurines (Hernández Espinoza and Márquez Morfín 2007, 33; Márquez Morfín and Hernández Espinoza 2013, 60). These human remains have been investigated recently with new scientific tools (Batta, *et al.* 2013; Cucina 2015; Hernández Espinoza and Márquez Morfín 2007; Márquez Morfín and Hernández Espinoza 2013; Márquez Morfín and Hernández 2007; Serrano Sánchez and López Alonso 2007; Tiesler 2015).

Demographic studies of the human remains, for example, reveal a high infant mortality rate: 29.2% of the population studied reached one year of age, and 61.4% of the subadult population were about 15 years of age (Márquez Morfín and Hernández Espinoza 2013, Table 3). The mean age of interred adults ranges between 35 and 39 years and most were interred in a flexed position (López Alonso and Serrano S. 1984, 445). Biodistance analysis of these burials associated a small subgroup with the Mayapán and Chichén Itzá dental series defined by Cucina (2015, 80). The presence of fine and gray orange vessels, along with slate wares, in burials excavated during the 1973-1974 field seasons (Cucina 2015, 80), further associate those interred at Jaina with Terminal Classic and Postclassic populations of the Yucatán Peninsula.

*Previous studies of ceramic figurines*

No published radiocarbon dates are available from Jaina to establish an absolute chronology. Therefore, dating of the figurines is based on a relative ceramic sequence that places them in a chronological context based upon their ceramic technology and style (Butler 1935; C. Cook de Leonard 1971; C. R. Corson 1972; Piña Chán 1996; Ruz Lhuillier 1945). Piña Chán (2001), for example, classified the figurines into five types, placing Types 1-IV in the Early Classic. These figurines included hand and mold made human and zoomorphic figurines. Molded figurines, made with a fine orange or a fine cream paste, were assigned to the Late Classic Type V. Later studies assigned hand-modeled figurines to the Early and Late Classic (Tzakol-Tepeu ceramic phases) and mold-made figurines in the Late and Terminal Classic (Tepeu to the late pre-Mexican Puuc ceramic phases) [C. Corson 1976; Kellers 1973]. Recent ceramic research in the Maya region, however, no longer supports this chronological sequence of the figurines. Throughout the Maya region, excavations scarcely report the finding of Preclassic and Early Classic figurines, and if they do, these are very different from the Late Classic examples. Except for effigy censers produced later in the Postclassic period, the production of figurines is no longer significant after the end of the Late Classic.

In the absence of stratigraphic data to organize early ceramic sequences, Corson (1968, 5) examined nearly 500 figurines from Jaina. Most lacked provenience, but he ran a seriation program to create a typology based on several attributes, such as posture, gender, costume, and the clay matrix used in the making of these figurines. His results assigned the figurines to four chronological phases related to their geographical distribution (Jaina I-II, Jonuta, and Campeche). These specimens remain in the storerooms of the MNA, while small collections have been dispersed to regional INAH museums in Villahermosa, Campeche, Hecelchakan, and Mérida.

Using the foundation of Corson's study, Kellers (1973) assembled 1385 photographs of the ceramic figurines distributed in museums and private collections in the United States, Europe and Mexico to create a computerized classification and to identify the personages depicted by the figurines. Examination of Maya ceramic figurines in private collections and museums around the world has guided the reconstruction of Maya society and political networks (Grube, *et al.* 2001; Miller 1975). Whereas these studies have made invaluable contributions to the scholarship of Jaina style figurines, as noted by McVicker (2012, 218), they have reconstructed Maya social and political organization based on an uncritical acceptance of European courtly models (Inomata and Houston 2001; Martin and Grube 2000; Miller and Martin 2004), a system imposed in Mesoamerica with the Spanish Conquest.

In comparison to stylistic and iconographic studies, very few technological and compositional analyses of Maya clay figurines have been published. Invaluable to the Jaina literature is Goldstein's study (1979) of 400 figurines excavated at Jaina during the 1940s, along with specimens collected by Norman in the 19th century that ended up in the collections at the Smithsonian Institution in Washington, D.C. and the Brooklyn Museum of Art in New York City. Her study also included ceramic figurines recovered by Saville, now housed at the American Museum of Natural History; those gathered by Maler and stored at the Peabody Museum in Cambridge, Massachusetts; and those collected by Charnay, now stored at the Musée de l'Homme in Paris (Goldstein 1979, 19). In addition, Goldstein (1979, 8; 42) collected clay samples from Campeche archaeological sites, caves, river beds, even from potters, for comparative studies. A total of 1384 figurines were studied and classified based on their chemical characterization, style, and iconography. Figurines were cored for INAA (Instrumental Neutron Activation Analysis) at Brookhaven National Laboratories, under the direction of G. Harbottle and E. V. Sayre (Goldstein 1979, 48). These analyses revealed that at least eight distinct clays were used for the making of Coastal Campeche figurines (Goldstein 1979, 8). Chemical composition of the clay samples was compared using a statistical program, determining that several figurines were similar in chemical composition to those found in Comalcalco, Tortugero, Calatrava and Jonuta (Goldstein 1979, 52). Besides Goldstein's seminal study of the archaeology of Maya figurines, other scholars have continued publishing analyses of Maya ceramic figurines (García-Heras, *et al.* 2006; Halperin 2007; Sotelo Santos, *et al.* 2015). In addition, analytical studies of Maya Blue have contributed to our understanding of the production of the ceramic figurines (Arnold 2005; Arnold and Bohor 1975; Arnold, *et al.* 2007). While results from these analytical studies are pivotal to our knowledge on the chemical composition of Maya figurines, this crucial information answers part of the questions ceramicists are interested in to reconstruct the choices that potters made to produce these figurines.

## Studying the INAH Collection

In 2015, INAH provided us access to a collection of 128 ceramic figurines to determine their authenticity, by studying their production, distribution and use. Little is known about the provenience of most figurines because half of the collection came from a forfeiture that took place in 1994. The collection also includes 34 ceramic figurines recovered during the various field seasons of excavations undertaken at Jaina.

Although the 128 ceramic figurines were considered in this study, fiber optic reflectance spectroscopy (FORS) in the ultraviolet/visible and near infrared (UV/VNIR) and X-ray fluorescence (XRF) spectroscopy were applied to 61 ceramic figurines to characterize the clay body and painted surfaces without physical sampling (Figure 2). Use of a FieldSpec3® from Analytical Spectral Devices Inc. (ASD) and its flexible spot analyzer, with a high spectral resolution (3 nm @ 700 nm and 10 nm @ 1400/ 2100 nm) and a wide spectral range from 350 to 2500 nm, facilitated the systematic study of specific surface areas. The high spectral and spatial resolution of the spectrometer provided information and analytical fingerprints of the pigments used to decorate the clay figurines (especially the natural earth pigments and the synthetic pigment Maya Blue). A Thermo Scientific Niton® XL3t GOLDD+ handheld XRF equipped with a silver anode and a silicon drift detector was used to determine the elemental characterization of the clay figurines by taking readings from well-preserved areas and the weathered/altered regions of the ceramic matrix and painted decoration. Readings were taken with an 8 mm diameter spot size in both 'Soil' and 'Mining' modes, with an acquisition time of 90 and 120 seconds respectively. The technique gave qualitative and semi-quantitative information regarding the relative concentrations of major, minor, and trace elements. Minor and trace element concentrations were used to help in the classification of distinctive groups.

## Chapter 3   Investigating Maya Ceramic Figurines

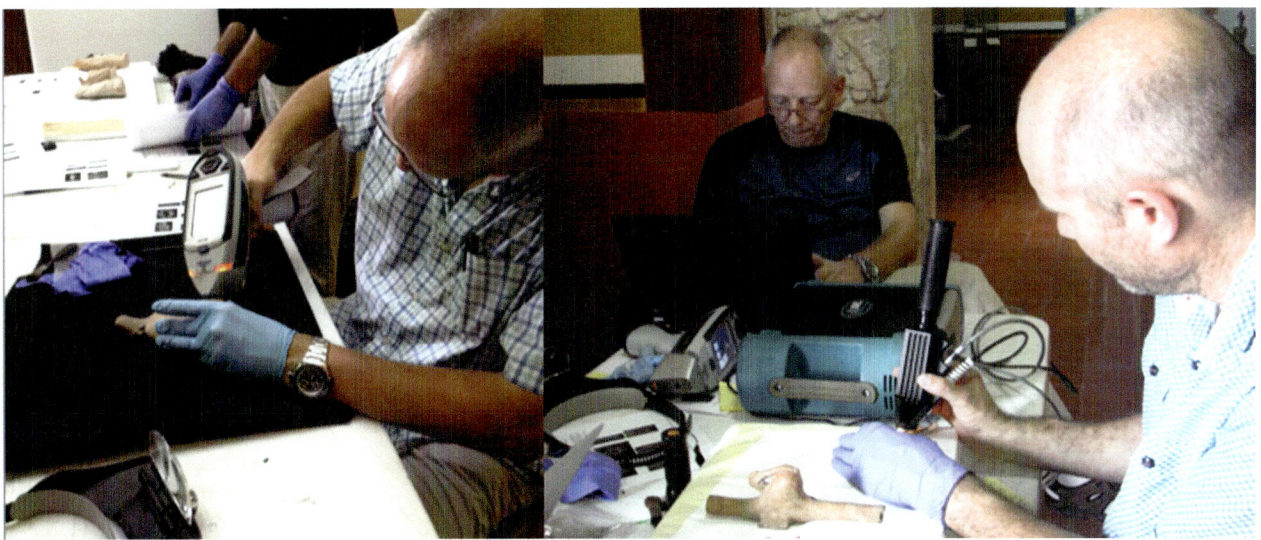

Figure 2. On-site analysis of the ceramic figurines at the Centro INAH Campeche: (A) use of a Thermo Scientific Niton® XL3t GOLDD+ handheld XRF spectrometer; (B) Use of a FieldSpec3® spectrometer from Analytical Spectral Devices Inc. (ASD) [©UCLA-UNAM_Jaina Project 2016]

Although the collected data will be published in more detail elsewhere, the study identified three main compositional groups based on the concentrations of major, minor and trace elements in the ceramic body. Analysis of the compositional data obtained for the body indicated important variations in trace elements such as Zr, Rb, Cr and Ti, revealing the different nature and/or source of the clay materials and temper. A group of figurines stylistically attributed to Teotihuacan/Veracruz were isolated based on their very low chromium levels. By way of contrast, the chromium concentrations of other groups were much higher and varied from 100 to almost 2000 parts per million. When compared to the Fowler Museum collection, the INAH figurines share similar grouping characteristics (Figures 3 and 4). Are these matching characteristics evidence to support their authenticity? Probably.

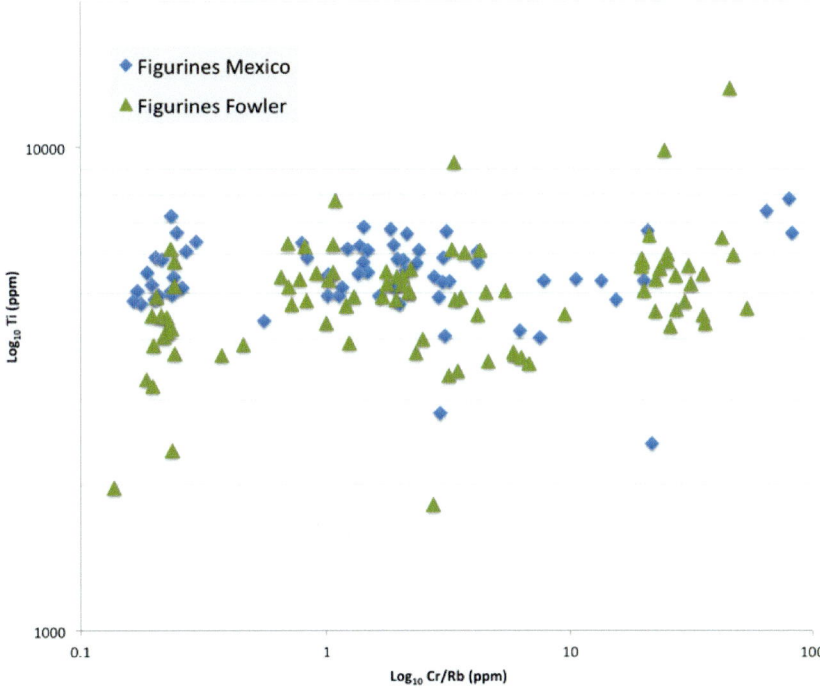

Figure 3. Bivariate plot of $\mathrm{Log}_{10}$ Ti (ppm) versus Cr/Rb (ppm) showing the separation of groups based on the abundances of trace elements Ti, Cr and Rb [©UCLA-UNAM_Jaina Project 2016]

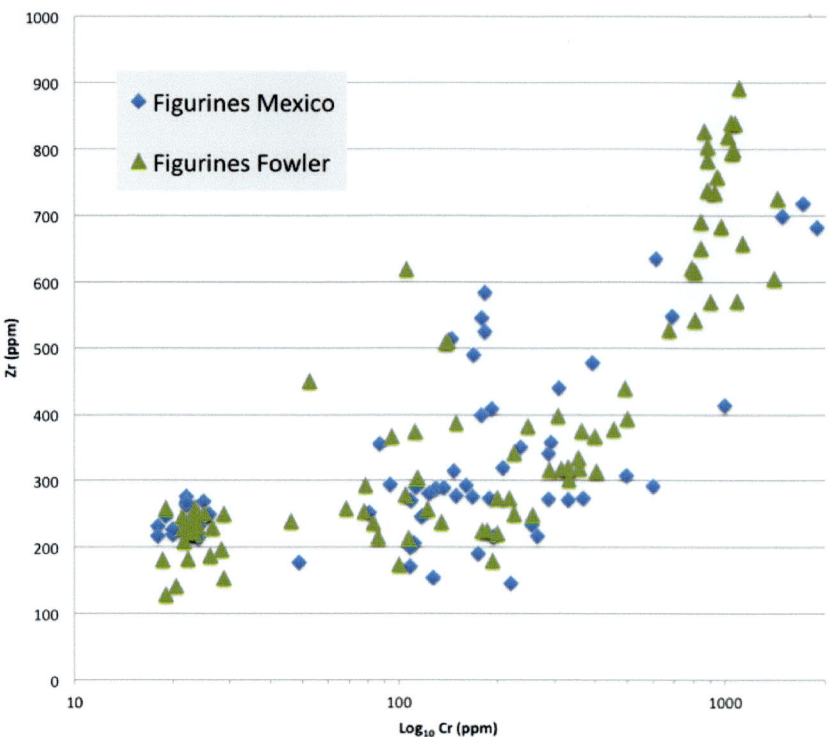

Figure 4. Bivariate plot of $\log_{10}$ Zr (ppm) versus $\log_{10}$ Cr (ppm) showing the separation of groups based on the abundances of trace elements Zr and Cr [©UCLA-UNAM_Jaina Project 2016]

FORS indicated that the yellowish to reddish colors of the body were primarily due to the presence of goethite and hematite. There is a possibility that the burials were sprinkled with hematite as part of a funerary ritual, given the distinctive red coloration on some bones (Batta, *et al.* 2013, 718). Analytical fingerprints of the pigments used to decorate the clay figurines have shown the use of Maya Blue and hematite-rich red ochre. For the white coatings, a clay-based material was often encountered. Gypsum (white) was also identified on selected figurines. Many of the figurines also show distinctive fire blackening. Black staining, erosion and encrustations on the surface were attributed to weathering. The nature of the weathered surfaces was further investigated based on the levels of chlorine and sulfur, which demonstrated to be good proxies for the associated weathering products. Some of the figurines also showed restorations mainly by means of refitting broken parts and an added fill of clay evidenced through reflectance and fluorescence imaging.

## *What have we learned from the application of these techniques?*

While the results from these studies are central to the technology and composition of Maya figurines, the analytical techniques used have limited potential for interpretation given the limitation of the contextual data of excavated materials from Jaina. In the absence of depositional and geological studies, the diagenic processes influencing the chemical composition of the major and minor element in the ceramics require in depth studies that can validate the trace element data (mainly of rare earth element profiles) and the ratios of isotopic element. Since the geochemical sources of the mineral raw materials and their exact production location of the ceramic figurines remain largely unclear, we cannot refer to these figurines as Jaina figurines', 'Jaina-style figurines', 'Jainas', or from Jaina (McVicker 2012; Miller 1975; Sambale 2001; Sotelo Santos, *et al.* 2015).

Indeed, the number of figurines recovered from Jaina has inspired the idea that the site was their production location and the origin of their finely modeled style. Excavations, to our knowledge, have not found any production sites. Even if these ceramic figurines could have been made at Jaina, clay had to be brought in from the mainland, as no naturally occurring clay sources exist on the island (Benavides Castillo 2007, 27). Acquiring clay for the making of pottery thus may have been a difficult endeavor. Without better data, it is not possible to assess whether the 34 figurines excavated at Jaina were made at the site. Why? Excavations have produced direct evidence of their production at other Maya sites (Gallegos 2009; Halperin 2007; Sanders 1963; Triadan 2007). Jaina is no longer the only site that has produced a large collection of ceramic figurines. One of the largest and intensively studied collection of figurines (N:2800) originates at Motul de San José (Halperin 2007, ix). Could these figurines have been brought to Jaina from distant sites as burial accouterments? In the absence of archaeological information, currently, this question cannot be answered.

It is now known that Maya potters were making ceramic figurines in large-scale numbers during the Late Classic for different purposes and uses. The published information associates the distribution of ceramic figurines only with interment practices. The discovery of figurines in middens and household contexts at other Maya sites (Gallegos 2009; Halperin 2014; Joyce 1992; Lesure 1997; Triadan 2007) diverge from the distribution of figurines at Jaina.

**Interpreting Maya Ceramic Figurines in the INAH collection**

The investigation of the 128 ceramic figurines in the INAH collection also identified key attributes to approximate the composition of Maya society and the animals associated with it. The collection includes figurative representations of individuals, mainly females (N:70), but also males (N:40), along with zoomorphic figurines (N:18). These figurines are no different from others found in the Maya region (Gallegos 2009; Halperin 2014; Joyce 1992; Lesure 1997; Triadan 2007). To interpret the ceramic figurines in the INAH collection, I am basing my assumptions on the available excavation reports and recent studies.

*Distribution and characteristics of male figurines*

Based on the available reports, the ceramic figurines have a distinctive distribution burial pattern at Jaina. Male burials were placed looking to the north, and interred with a male or a female figurine (Serrano Sánchez and López Alonso 2007, 82). One male burial was buried with a *metate* and a *mano* (Ochoa C. and Salas C. 1984b, 456), which are normally associated with women and the household, but are also used for preparing raw materials to make pottery. By comparison, female burials were interred looking to the south and had a male figurine placed between the waist and the shoulder (López Alonso and Serrano S. 1984, 446), with the exception of one burial that included a female figurine (Ochoa C. and Salas C. 1984b, 456). Even if these figurines are part of the accouterments of male and female burials at Jaina, their presence reveals a control of burial practices. The imagery portrayed in these male figurines identified them as rulers, high-rank individuals or *sahalob*, warriors, ball-players, individuals with achondroplasia, or as performing daily life activities.

The INAH collection includes several male figurines whose attire and pose invoke powerful images of Maya rulers displayed in monuments and stelae. These figurines wear an elaborate and heavy headdress or *hunal*, along with thick beaded necklaces or *uh*, and ear spools (Figure 5A-C). Several standing male figurines carry a fan shaped headdress, with a zoomorphic mask at the center, worn by Maya rulers at various sites in the Maya region. Usually, the fan-shaped headdress depicts the War Serpent imagery associated with governing titles, such as *k'inich* or *k'uhul ajaw* (Halperin 2014, Figure 3.2). Characteristic of most fan shaped headdresses is the application of a bird to the center of the feathered sprays that could be related to *Itzamnaaj*, an elderly creator deity (Halperin 2014). In the collection, several of these 'rulers' were portrayed either in a standing position, seated on a palanquin or on a ruling seat (Figure 6A-C).

In the collection, several male figurines wear a loincloth or *ex* (Figure 7A-D), painted in blue and red, characteristic of high-ranking individuals. Differences in the headdresses worn by these individuals, composed by several pieces of cloth wrapped differently around the head, express different ranks, according to Schele (1997, 59). The *saha*, a minor rank governor or administrator from Yaxchilan and Bonampak (Schele 1997, 71), wore a distinctive necklace with a spondylus shell. Complex designs mark the face of several individuals, possibly, having the rank of a *sahalob*, a member of Maya society who participated in war events.

Even if the War serpent headdress evokes war as a significant theme component of these male figurines, a low number of warriors are present in the collection (Figure 8A-C). Warriors from Yaxchilan and Bonampak wore a complex double strand feather headdress very similar to the one worn by a male figurine (Schele 1997, 100; Figure 8B) in the collection. Itzá warriors at Chichén Itzá (Schele 1997, 100) used a similar headband.

Other figurines in the collection evoke emblems of war. A male figurine, possibly a performer reenacting a warfare battle (Triadan 2007, 287) is dressed with the feather warrior suit (Figure 8C). Being a common theme in Maya and Teotihuacan warfare symbolism (Grube and Schele 1994), a musical instrument in the collection represents an owl (Figure 9A). The owl is also represented in a headdress worn by a ballplayer figurine (Figure 9B). The double strand necklace with a hanging *ahau* pendant identifies him as a high rank individual. Another ball player wears a thick yoke or *bate* around his waist and a complex headdress (Figure 9C).

## Innovative Approaches and Explorations in Ceramic Studies

Figure 5. Figurines depicting elements of power and war: (A) A ruler wearing a fan-shaped headdress depicting two zoomorphic figures (SM 10-342651); (B) A ruler holds a war related object and a fan shaped War Serpent headdress (SM 10-339781); (C) A masked ruler holding an ax on his left hand, wears a fan-shaped War Serpent headdress and a mantle (BCC-10-343434) similar to those represented at Stelae 13 of Tikal (Schele 1997:106).
(Photographs, courtesy of Centro INAH Campeche)

Figure 6. Representation of seated Maya rulers. (A) A male portrayed on his ruling seat, with a very elaborate headdress (HKAN 10-343413); (B) A ruler portrayed on a platform, inscribed with hieroglyphs, wearing a tunic and a zoomorphic fan-shaped headdress (HKAN 10-343413); (C) A ruler wearing a bird shaped headdress on his ruling seat (SM 10-342652).
(Photographs, courtesy of Centro INAH Campeche)

## Chapter 3  Investigating Maya Ceramic Figurines

Figure 7. (A) Male figurine wearing a cylinder pixom (HKAN 10-343354); (B) Male figurine wearing a complex cloth headdress and a spondylus shell identifying him maybe as a *saha* (HKAN 10-343415); (C) Male figurine wearing a rough application covering the chin and the cheek (SM 10-223510); (D) Male figurine wearing big ear spools and a complex design on his face, as well as a necklace formed by oliva snails (SM 10-342819). (Photographs, courtesy of Centro INAH Campeche)

Figure 8. (A) Male wearing a shield and a shell necklace (SM 10-397874); (B) A male warrior with a complex headdress, commonly, found among warriors at Chichen Itzá (HKAN 10-342655); (C) Male wearing a fan and a warrior suit (SM 10-339782). (Photographs, courtesy of Centro INAH Campeche)

Figure 9. (A) A musical instrument with one resonator chamber portrays an owl (SM 10-339778); (B) A male ruler wearing an owl headdress and a thick necklace with an ahau representation at the center (HKAN 10-343435); (C) Ball player wearing a protruding thick yoke around his waist and a wavy headdress still exhibiting traces of Maya blue (HKAN 10-343380). (Photographs, courtesy of Centro INAH Campeche)

Figure 10. (A) Elderly male with a female figurine (SM 10-342814); (B) A female figurine with a young adult male (SM 10-343125); (C) A female figurine holding a beaded strand (SM 10-522662); (D) A female figurine with a double necklace formed by thick beads (BBC 10-343340). (Photographs, courtesy of Centro INAH Campeche)

Besides the rich warfare symbolism expressed in the attires of male figurines, figurines were portrayed carrying folded pieces of paper or shaping a vessel. In the collection, figurines represent individuals with achondroplasia (Figure 8C), who performed as monkeys in ceremonies and festivals (Halperin 2014; Schele 1997). In the collection, figurines represent couples (Figure 10A-B). In these examples, the male is either standing in front of the female or seating on the shoulders of a young woman, who Schele (1997, 55) interpreted as the Moon Deity (Figure 10A).

## Children's burials and their musical instruments

The INAH collection includes at least 72 musical instruments, which I here dare to suggest might have originated from children burials. Burial practices suggest children were revered differently from adults, as their accouterments include musical instruments (Ochoa C. and Salas C. 1984b, 456). Excavations did not find musical instruments in male burials (Ochoa C. and Salas C. 1984b, 457). Only a few females were buried with a musical instrument (López Alonso and Serrano S. 1984, 445). The majority of these instruments portray women (N:49), which comes as no surprise because most children's interments were associated with a female figurine, although a few interments include a male or a zoomorphic figurine (Ochoa C. and Salas C. 1984b, 456).

These musical instruments depict women, wearing a blouse over a skirt and carrying in their hands a small bag, a fan, or a beaded strand (Figure 10C). All have long hair, with frontal sections of their hair cut in stepped stages, to form complex headdresses held by wrapping cloths around their head. Seated female figurines wear a much less elaborate blouse and skirt (Figure 10D). Most female figurines wear ear spools, multi-strand bracelets, double strand-beaded necklaces, and appear to have decorated their face with two protruding bands reaching their mouth. Scarcely portrayed in Maya imagery, several figurines show women taking care of children (Figure 11). However, such care was extended in children's burial by the placing of musical instruments depicting a female. Placing a musical instrument enhances the importance of music as part of children's internment practices (Ochoa C. and Salas C. 1984b, 456). Recently, Sotelo Santos *et al.* (2015) recreated the sounds produced by a musical instrument in a unique acoustic study of a female figurine found during the 1964 field season of excavations at Jaina.

There is a wide repertoire of musical instruments in the collection, mainly, ocarinas, flutes, whistles, and rattles (Figure 12A-C). A low number of instruments represent males (N:10) and animals (N:13). Ocarinas usually have the mouthpiece placed at the back of the figurine that forms a tripod with the front legs (Figures 12C). One counter example, however, places the mouthpiece to the side (Figure 12A). The broad-brimmed hat worn by this woman has been associated with cargos and market vendors (Halperin 2014). Most ocarinas have one resonator chamber and two stops.

Rattles have also been identified in collection (Figure 13A-D). These musical instruments represent women with their arms and hand palms placed in different positions. These women wear a blouse or *k'ub*, with intricate woven designs and a half-moon shaped headdress. Several rattle figurines depict symbols and Tlaloc imagery on their dresses, interpreted as Teotihuacan in style. Therefore, this type of figurines could date to the Early Classic, a time where their production was essential to Teotihuacan state politics in the Maya region. Chemically, this group of musical instruments is isolated from the remainder of the collection, suggesting that they were made from very different clays and tempers.

Figure 11. (A) A female figurine with a child placed on her lap (SM 10-398036); (B) A female figurine carries a child behind her back (SM 10-339983); (C) A female figurine with a red rounded bowl (SM 10-342637); (D) The same female figurine carries a child on her back (SM 10-342637). (Photographs, courtesy of Centro INAH Campeche)

Figure 12. (A) A musical instrument portraying a female figurine wearing a large hollow broad-brimmed hat over a complex hairdo exhibits three dots on her face (SM 10-290541); (B) A fragmented flute displaying a male with a bloated belly (SM 10-398032); (C) A mold made ocarina with one resonator chamber, recovered from the 1964 field season of excavations (SM 10-342828), represents a male wearing a mask representing a howler monkey. (Photographs, courtesy of Centro INAH Campeche)

Figure 13. (A) A female figurine with bent arms and outward hand palms served as a rattle (BBC 10-398097); (B) A similar rattle depicts a woman with one bent arm showing her outward hand palm, while the left arm rests on her left flank (SM 10-339983); (C) Another rattle depicts a woman with arms to her side and showing both outward hand palms (SM 10-49613); (D) A female articulated figurine exhibits a Tlaloc motive (BBC 10-398075 0/3). (Photographs, courtesy of Centro INAH Campeche)

These figurines are similar in attributes to those that have been recovered from Nopiloa, as these too, wear a blouse and skirt with applied designs representing the *atl* or Aztec water pictogram associated with the rain deity (Huckert 2009, 13). It might not be a coincidence then, that the elaborated designs depicted on their attire, express the structuring of the cosmos, divided into four regions (Huckert 2009). In central Mexico, ceremonies petitioning for rain include a dance performed by four women who raise and lower their arms, slowly moving their hands palms inward and outward (López Varela and Aguilar Escobar 2014). During the Xochipitzahuatl a traditional dance in Tejalpa, Morelos, women dance to the four winds near a cave, recreating these movements. Their dance is a tribute to the *cheneques* that live in this cave, taking care of its waters that provide them with everything they need for their livelihood.

**Final Remarks**

The authentication of Maya ceramic figurines and their interpretation in museum collections is a challenging endeavor, despite decades of studies combining instrumental and iconographic analyses. Indeed, results from these studies have matched Maya ceramic figurines and vessels to broad geographical areas, sites, and even painting schools. Without provenience, however, their place of manufacture and the extant of their distribution remain conjectural. Ceramicists are interested in this type of information to reconstruct ceramic production sequences. Without provenience, this type of information remains truncated, specially now, that we know that many of the so-called 'Jaina' figurines are musical instruments. The making of these musical instruments probably required a different selection of clays and tempers, as size, shape and material used, not only distinguishes each instrument, it influences the reproduction of sound.

When ceramic artifacts are witnesses of transnational antiquities crimes, archaeologists should not settle for chemical fingerprints and iconographic studies as an alternative to looting practices. Otherwise, using instrumental analyses risks the fabrication of erroneous stories and claims about the Maya past and Mexico's heritage.

**Acknowledgements**

Research was conducted at the Centro INAH Campeche, under a permit granted by INAH (Oficio 401B(4)19/2014/36/0717, April 24, 2014). This study was financed by a UC Mexus-CONACyT Collaborative Research Grant, awarded to the project 'Chemistry, Variability, and Provenience of Jaina Figurines: a Multiscale-Multianalytical Approach', conducted in between 2012-2016, by Dr. López Varela from UNAM and Dr. Ioanna Kakoulli and Dr. Christian Fischer from UCLA. I would like to express my gratitude to Dr. Christian de Brer, Head of the Conservation Department at the Fowler Museum-UCLA and Kim Richter at the Getty Research Institute for their collaboration in this project. In addition, I would like to thank Antrop. Marco Antonio Carvajal Correa of the Centro INAH Campeche, for supporting the analysis of the collection. I am very grateful to the Instituto Nacional de Antropología e Historia for providing us access to the graphic material included in this publication, as well as, the Universidad Nacional Autónoma de México, the Universidad Autónoma del Estado de Morelos, the University of California Los Angeles (UCLA) and UC Mexus-CONACyT for their support.

**References Cited**

Arnold, Dean E. 2005. 'Maya Blue and Palygorskite: A second possible pre-Columbian source.' *Ancient Mesoamerica* 16 (1): 51-62.
Arnold, Dean E., and Bruce F. Bohor. 1975. 'Attapulgite and Maya Blue, An Ancient Mine Comes to Light.' *Archaeology* 28 (1): 23-29.
Arnold, Dean E., Hector Neff, Michael D. Glascock, and Robert J. Speakman. 2007. 'Sourcing the Palygorskite Used in Maya Blue: A Pilot Study Comparing the Results of INAA and LA-ICP-MS.' *Latin American Antiquity* 18 (1): 44-58.
Aveleyra de Anda, Luis, and Gordon F. Ekholm. 1966. 'Clay Sculpture from Jaina.' *Natural History* 75 (4): 40-47.
Bancroft, Hubert Howe. 1875. *The Native Races of the Pacific States of North America.* Vol. IV. London: Longmans, Green, and CO.
Batta, Erasmo, Carlos Argáez, Josefina Mansilla, Carmen Pijoan, and Pedro Bosch. 2013. 'On yellow and red pigmented bones found in Mayan burials of Jaina.' *Journal of Archaeological Science* 40 (1): 712-722.
Benavides C., Antonio. 2002. 'Labores de campo en Jaina, Campeche, durante 2001.' *Mexicon* 4 (2): 67-72.
Benavides C., Antonio. 2005. 'Campeche Archaeology at the turn of the Century.' *Anthropological Notebooks* XI: 13-30.
Benavides C., Antonio. 2012. *Jaina: ciudad, puerto y mercado.* Vol. No. 1, Colección Justo Sierra. Campeche: Gobierno del Estado de Campeche.
Benavides Castillo, Antonio. 2007. 'Jaina en el contexto de las poblaciones del Clásico en el Occidente Peninsular.' In *La población prehispánica de Jaina, estudio osteogbiográfico de 106 esqueletos*, edited by Patricia O. Hernández and Lourdes Márquez, 13-31. México, DF: Instituto Nacional de Antropología e Historia.
Butler, Mary. 1935. 'A study of Maya Mouldmade Figurines.' American Anthropologist 37 (4): 636-672.
Carvajal Correa, Marco Antonio. 2014. 'Acopio, coleccionismo y museos en Campeche.' *Revista Maya*. doi:http://www.mna.inah.gob.mx/contexto/acopio-coleccionismo-y-museos-en-campeche-m-carvajal-correa.html.
Charnay, Désiré M. 1888. *Viaje a Yucatán a fines de 1886.* Translated by Francisco Cantón Rosado. Mérida: Imp. de la Revista de Mérida.
Cook de Leonard, C. 1971. 'Gordos y enanos de Jaina (Campeche, Mexico).' *Revista Española de Antropologia Americana* 6: 57-83.

Cook de Leonard, Carmen. 1964. 'Extraneous influences in Jaina figurines. [Summary].' *Actas y memorias* 1: 361.

Corson, Christopher Robert. 1972. 'Stylistic history and culture-historical implications of the Maya figurine complex of Jaina, Campeche.' PhD Diss. in Anthropology, University of California, Berkeley.

Corson, Christopher. 1976. *Maya Anthropomorphic Figurines from Jaina Island, Campeche*. Ballena Press studies in Mesoamerican Art, Archaeology, and Ethnohistory. Ramona, California: Ballena Press.

Cucina, Andrea. 2015. 'Population Dynamics during the Classic and Postclassic Period Maya in the Northern Maya Lowlands: the Analysis of Dental Morphological Traits.' In *Archaeology and Bioarchaeology of Population Movement among the Prehispanic Maya*, edited by Andrea Cucina, 71-84. New York: Springer.

de Waldeck, Federico. 1996. *Viaje pintoresco y arqueológico a la Provincia de Yucatán, 1834 y 1836*. México, DF: Consejo Nacional para la Cultura y las Artes. (Orig. pub. 1838.)

Fernández, Miguel Angel. 1946. 'Los adoratorios de la Isla de Jaina.' *Revista Mexicana de Estudios Antropológicos*, Sociedad Mexicana de Antropología 8 (1-3): 243-260.

Gallegos, Miriam Judith. 2009. 'Manufactura, iconografía y distribución de figurillas en Comalcalco, Tabasco.' In *XII Simposio de Investigaciones Arqueológicas en Guatemala 2008*, edited by J. P. Laporte, B. Arroyo and H. Mejía, 1051-1061. Guatemala: Museo Nacional de Arqueología y Etnología.

García-Heras, M., J. Reyes-Trujeque, R. Ruiz-Guzman, Miguel A. Avilés Escaño, A. Ruiz Conde, and P. J. Sánchez-Soto. 2006. 'Archaeometric study of Mayan ceramic figurines from Calakmul (Campeche, Mexico).' *Boletín de la Sociedad Española de Cerámica y Vidrio* 45 (4): 245-254.

Goldstein, Marilyn M. 1979. 'Maya Figurines from Campeche, Mexico: Classification on the Basis of Clay Chemistry, Style and Iconography.' Unpublished PhD Diss., Faculty of Philosophy, Columbia University.

Grube, Nikolai, Eva Eggebrecht, and Matthias Seidel. 2001. *Maya: divine kings of the rain forest*. Cologne: Könemann.

Halperin, Christina T. 2014. *Maya Figurines, Intersections between State and Household*. Austin: University of Texas Press.

Halperin, Christina Tsune. 2007. 'Materiality, Bodies, and Practice: The Political Economy of Late Classic Maya Figurines From Motul de San Jose, Peten, Guatemala.' PhD Diss. in Anthropology, University of California Riverside.

Hernández Espinoza, Patricia Olga, and Lourdes Márquez Morfín. 2007. 'El escenario demográfico de Jaina prehispánica durante el Clásico.' In *La población prehispánica de Jaina, estudio osteogbiográfico de 106 esqueletos*, edited by Patricia O. Hernández and Lourdes Márquez, 33-76. México, DF: Instituto Nacional de Antropología e Historia.

Huckert, Chantal. 2009. 'Nopiloa y la representación de la tierra fecunda.' *Anales del Instituto de Investigaciones Estéticas* XXXI (94): 5-26.

Inomata, Takeshi, and Stephen D. Houston. 2001. *Royal Courts of the Ancient Maya*. Vol. 1-2. Boulder: Westview Press.

Inurreta Díaz, Armando F. 2004. *Uaymil. Un puerto de transbordo en la costa norte de Campeche, Campeche*. México, DF: Instituto Nacional de Antropología e Historia.

Inurreta Díaz, Armando F., and Edgar D. Pat Cruz. 2005. 'Isla Piedras: asentamiento del Clásico Temprano en la costa norte de Campeche.' In *Los Investigdores de la Cultura Maya*, 255-266. Campeche: Universidad Autónoma de Campeche.

Joyce, Rosemary A. 1992. 'Images of Gender and Labor Organization in Classic Maya Society.' In *Exploring Gender Through Archaeology: Selected Papers from the 1991 Boone Conference*, edited by Cheryl Claassen, 63-70. Monographs in World Prehistory. Madison Wisconsin: Prehistory Press.

Kellers, James McW. 1973. 'A Tripartite Description of Jaina-style Figurines (three volumes).' PhD Diss., New York University, School of Education.

Lesure, Richard G. 1997. 'Figurines and Social Identities in Early Sedentary Societies of Coastal Chiapas, Mexico, 1550-800 b.c.' In *Women in Prehistory: North America and Mesoamerica*, edited by Cheryl Claassen and Rosemary A. Joyce, 227-248. Philadelphia: University of Pennsylvania Press.

López Alonso, Sergio, and Carlos Serrano S. 1984. 'Prácticas Funerarias Prehispánicas en la isla de Jaina, Campeche.' *XVII Mesa Redonda de la Sociedad Mexicana de Antropología*, 441-459. Volumen II, San Cristobal de las Casas, Chiapas. México: Sociedad Mexicana de Antropología.

López Varela, Sandra L., and Daniel Aguilar Escobar. 2014. 'Building Landscapes of Memory with Pots: Hermeneutic Expressions of Tlaloc in a Festivity of the Valley of Morelos, México.' In *Social Dyamics of Ceramic Analysis: new Techniques and Interpretations*, edited by Sandra L. Lopez Varela, 75-86. Oxford, England: Archaeopress.

Lowe, Lynneth S., and Adam T. Sellen. 2010. 'Una pasión por la antigüedad: la colección arqueológica de don Florentino Gimeno en Campeche durante el siglo XIX.' *Estudios de Cultura Maya* 36: 147-172.

Márquez Morfín, Lourdes, and Patricia Hernández Espinoza. 2013. 'Los mayas del Clásico Tardío y Terminal. Una propuesta acerca de la dinámica demográfica de algunos grupos mayas prehispánicos: Jaina, Palenque y Copán.' *Estudios de Cultura Maya* 42: 53-86.

Márquez Morfín, Lourdes, and Patricia O. Hernández. 2007. 'Estatus social y conteto funerario durante el Clásico en Jaina, Campeche.' In *El escenario demográfico de Jaina prehispánica durante el Clásico*, edited by Patricia Olga

Hernández Espinoza and Lourdes Márquez Morfín, 77-110. México, DF: Instituto Nacional de Antropología e Historia.

Martin, Simon, and Nikolai Grube. 2000. *Chronicle of the Maya Kings and Queens: Deciphering the Dynasties of the Ancient Maya*. London: Thames and Hudson.

McVicker, Donald. 2012. 'Figurines are us? The Social Organization of Jaina Island, Campeche, Mexico.' *Ancient Mesoamerica* 23 (2): 211-234.

Miller, Mary Ellen. 1975. *Jaina Figurines: A Study of Maya Iconography*. Princeton, NJ.: The Art Museum.

Miller, Mary Ellen, and Simon Martin. 2004. *Courtly Art of the Ancient Maya*. San Francisco and London. Fine Arts Museums of San Francisco and Thames and Hudson.

Moedano Koer, Hugo. 1946. 'Jaina: un cementerio Maya.' *Revista Mexicana de Estudios Antropológicos, Sociedad Mexicana de Antropología* 8 (1-3): 217-242.

Morelet, Arthur. 1857. *Voyage dans L'Amérique Centrale, L'ile de Cuba et le Yucatan*. Paris: Gide et J. Baudry, Librarires-Editeurs.

Ochoa C., Patricia, and Marcela Salas C. 1984a. 'Reseña sobre los diversos trabajos arqueológicos efectuados en la Isla de Jaina, Campeche.' XVII Mesa Redonda de la Sociedad Mexicana de Antropología, San Cristobal de las Casas, Chiapas, 431-439. México: Sociedad Mexicana de Antropología.

Ochoa C., Patricia, and Marcela Salas C. 1984b. 'Materiales culturales asociados a los enterramientos humanos de la isla de Jaina, Campeche (Temporadas 1973-1974).' XVII Mesa Redonda de la Sociedad Mexicana de Antropología, San Cristobal de las Casas, Chiapas, 453-459. México: Sociedad Mexicana de Antropología.

Pijoan A., Carmen, and Ma. Elena Salas C. 1984. 'La población prehispánica de Jaina, análisis osteológico.' XVII Mesa Redonda de la Sociedad Mexicana de Antropología, San Cristobal de las Casas, Chiapas, 471-480. México: Sociedad Mexicana de Antropología.

Piña Chán, Román. 1968. *Jaina, la casa en el agua*. México: Instituto Nacional de Antropología e Historia.

Piña Chán, Román. 1996. 'Las figurillas de Jaina.' *Arqueología Mexicana* 3 (18): 52-9.

Piña Chán, Román. 2001. *Breve estudio sobre la funeraria de Jaina*. Cuaderno No. 7. Campeche: Gobierno del Estado de Campeche, Museo Arqueologico Etnográfico e Histórico. (Orig. pub. 1948.)

Ruz Lhuillier, Alberto. 1945. 'Campeche en la arqueologia Maya.' *Acta Antropologica* 1: 2-3.

Sambale, Thomas. 2001. 'Die Jaina-Figurinen der Sammlung Jimeno des Ethnologischen Museums in Berlin.' MA Thesis, Universitaet Bonn.

Sanders, William T. 1963. 'Cultural Ecology of the Maya Lowlands.' *Estudios de Cultura Maya* 3: 203-241.

Schele, Linda. 1997. *Rostros ocultos de los Mayas*. Singapur: Impetus Comunicación, S.A. de C.V.

Sellen, Adam T. 2010. 'Los padres Camacho y su museo: dos puntos de luz en el Campeche del siglo XIX.' *Península V* (1): 53-73.

Serrano Sánchez, Carlos, and Sergio López Alonso. 2007. 'Estatus social y contexto funerario durante el Clásico en Jaina, Campeche.' In *La población prehispánica de Jaina, estudio osteogbiográfico de 106 esqueletos*, edited by Patricia O. Hernández and Lourdes Márquez, 77-110. México, DF: Instituto Nacional de Antropología e Historia.

Shook, Edwin M. 1955. *Yucatan and Chiapas*. Vol. 54: 289-295. Washington, D.C.: Carnegie Institution of Washington Year book.

Sotelo Santos, Laura Elena, Francisca Zalaquett Rock, Antonio Benavides Castillo, and Socorro del Pilar Jiménez Alvárez. 2015. 'Antiguas y nuevas noticias sobre una figurilla-silbato de Jaina. Contextos, Sonidos y Formas.' *Estudios de Cultura Maya* 46: 71-102.

Triadan, Daniela. 2007. 'Warriors, Nobles, Commoners and Beasts: Figurines from Elite Buildings at Aguateca.' *Latin American Antiquity* 18 (3): 269-293.

# Chapter 4

# Documenting Accommodation and Change in the Tarascan Ceramic Economy

## Amy J. Hirshman

Department of Sociology and Anthropology, West Virginia University, Morgantown, WV 26506;
amy.hirshman@mail.wvu.edu

### Abstract
*Recent research in Mesoamerica highlights our increasing understanding of the variability found in early state political economies. An aspect of that variability is the balance between the perseverance of pre-existing economic relationships and how political elites affected economic change over time. This study argues that not only was the overall economy of the Mesoamerican Late Postclassic Tarascan state (AD 1350-1525) highly varied, but even within a single class of objects, such as ceramic vessels, the organization of production, distribution, and consumption was a multifaceted, interactive mixture of commoners and elites. This study draws upon multiple lines of indirect indicators of ceramic production and market exchange, with a focus on a ceramic sequence stretching nearly 1500 years (ca. 50 BC to 1525 AD) in order to argue for the importance of persistent extra-household ceramic production and exchange activities in the Tarascan ceramic economy.*

### Key words
*Political economy, Early Markets, Tarascan State, Lake Pátzcuaro Basin*

### Introduction

Mesoamerican archaeology has shifted in the past several decades to incorporate greater complexity into our models of state political economies. One aspect of this shift is an altered focus from redistribution and tribute economies in twentieth century research to a broader understanding of the intricacies of economies within early complex states (e.g. Hirth 2013). Research on the various cultures comprising Mesoamerica over time (e.g., Berdan 1989, 2005; Hirth 1998; Minc 2009; Nichols *et al.* 2002; Smith and Berdan 2003), increasingly point to a dynamic interaction between tribute/state-controlled resources and robust markets, where markets are 'institutions predicated on the principles of market exchange of alienable commodities' (Garraty 2010, 6). Another aspect of this shift is the recognition of the significance of households and household craft production as a consistent feature within Mesoamerica (e.g. Feinman 1999; Hirth 2009; Carballo 2011). This multifaceted interaction between households, markets, and command economies is also central to how the political economies of states 'adjusted systems of mobilization to fit existing economic relations' (Earle and Smith 2012, 239). The balance of accommodation and change, therefore, is an outstanding question in the study of the emergence of states.

Ceramics produced within the Tarascan State (AD 1350-1525), centered in the Lake Pátzcuaro Basin of western Mexico (Figure 1) provides an opportunity to assess variability in the political economy of an early Mesoamerican state. As the second largest empire on the eve of the Spanish contact in Mesoamerica, the Tarascan state is known to have had political control of significant commodities, such as metal bells traded all over Mesoamerica (e.g. Pollard 1993). The Tarascans are further known for their distinctive, state-associated polychrome ceramics. Characteristically decorated with vibrant, swirling designs and liberal use of 'resist,' or a deliberate smudging of the surface involving a secondary refiring of the vessels, these fine wares are found in elite contexts such as elite burials and residential zones, as well as state ritual areas (e.g., Cabrera Castro 1996; Leal 1986; Pollard 1993, 2017).

However Tarascan elites did not control all aspects of the economy, as sixteenth century Spanish and native documents indicate that the political elites used both tribute and markets in their overall economic strategy (e.g., Gorenstein and Pollard 1983; Pollard 1993; *La Relación de Michoacán* 1980). Archaeological research on metallurgy and obsidian indicates variability in economic strategies (e.g., Pollard 1993) as well as persistent household production of various classes of ceramics after the state emerged (e.g. Hirshman 2008; Hirshman, Lovis and Pollard 2010; Hirshman and Ferguson 2012).

This review of Tarascan economic and ceramic data considers the importance of markets as well as the variation in ceramic-related economic strategies the state chose to pursue. I argue that not only was the Tarascan economic

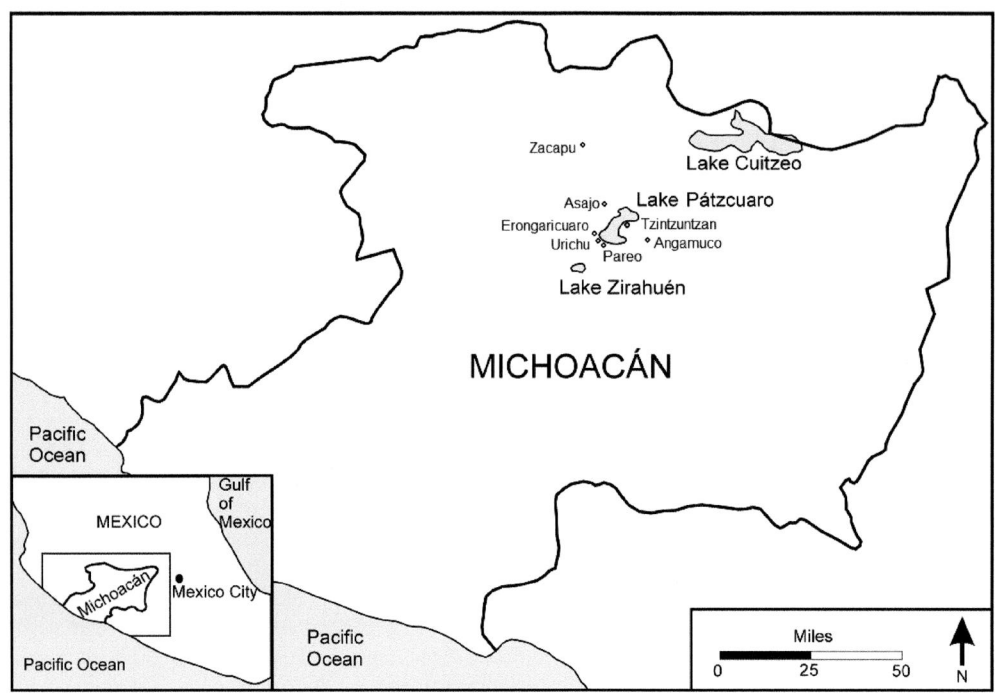

Figure 1. Map of the Lake Pátzcuaro Basin showing sites named in the text. (Used by permission of Hirshman)

strategy varied, but that significant aspects of the pre-state Basin economy were retained in the state period. I use multiple lines of indirect indicators of market exchange, with a focus on a ceramic sequence stretching nearly 1500 years (ca. 50 BC to 1525 AD) in order to argue for the persistent importance of household producers, markets and marketing activities in the Late Postclassic ceramic economy.

**The Tarascan State**

Prehispanic habitation within the Lake Pátzcuaro Basin, which eventually became the core of the Tarascan state (Figure 1), is archaeologically documented from the Late Preclassic (ca. 50 BC) to the Late Postclassic (AD 1525; Table 1; e.g., Pollard 2008). Approximately one-ninth the size of the Valley of Mexico, the Lake Pátzcuaro basin is a highland intra-drainage basin with a spring-fed freshwater lake ringed by volcanic cones. In this study 'Tarascan' refers to the ancient political entity rather than the ethnic identity of the commoners within the state or the descendant population today, who are known as the *P'urépecha*, which is also the name of their language (e.g., Pollard 2008).

Basin settlement and excavation data indicate two distinct episodes of elite activity dominated the cultural sequence within the Basin. Initially, ranked elites in small Basin polities ruled in the Early Classic through Early Postclassic periods (Loma Alta to Early Urichu phases; AD 350-1000/1100), and mortuary evidence from Urichu, an independent polity during this earlier period, include a group tomb for elite males containing status markers both imported to the basin and basin-made status markers, including local ceramics (Pollard and Cahue 1999).

| Period | Local Phases | Dates | Elite Activity |
|---|---|---|---|
| Late Postclassic | Taríacuri | A.D. 1350-1525 | Tarascan State |
| Middle Postclassic | Late Urichu | A.D. 1000/1100-1350 | Coalescing Elites |
| Early Postclassic | Early Urichu | A.D. 900-1000/1100 | Ranked Elites |
| Epiclassic | Lupe-LaJoya | A.D. 600/700-900 | Ranked Elites |
| Middle Classic | Jaracuaro | A.D. 500-600/700 | Ranked Elites |
| Early Classic | Loma Alta 3 | A.D. 350-500 | Ranked Elites |
| Late/Terminial Preclassic | Loma Alta 2 | 50 B.C. – A.D. 350 | Emerging Elites |

Table 1. Chronology for the Lake Pátzcuaro Basin (Hirshman, after Pollard 2008)

The second episode of elite activity began in the Middle Postclassic (Late Urichu; AD 1000/1100 to 1350) and involved elite competition and consolidation during a period of population growth and rising lake levels, with the eventual emergence of the Late Postclassic Tarascan state, with its capital at Tzintzuntzan (Pollard 2008). The mortuary pattern at Urichu, which became a tertiary Tarascan administrative center within the state (Pollard 1993), shifts from the earlier pattern to individual elite burials placed within the floors and walls of an elite residential/administrative area, with an emphasis on locally produced goods that emphasize the new Tarascan state identity, including ceramics (Pollard 2008; Pollard and Cahue 1999). The Tarascan state expanded during the Late Postclassic period to encompass most of what is today the modern Mexican state of Michoacán, becoming the Tarascan Empire, the second largest empire in Mesoamerica when the Spanish arrived in the early 1500s.

Broad population estimates for the Pátzcuaro Basin indicate growth from approximately 5000-8000 inhabitants in the Early Classic, to approximately 80,000 at Contact (Gorenstein and Pollard 1983; Pollard 2008). Approximately 30,000 people resided in Tzintzuntzan, the Tarascan capital and largest community in the region in the Late Postclassic (Pollard 1993). Pollard identified 92 Protohistoric (AD 1450-1520) basin communities within the ethnohistoric documentary record, 66 of which could be securely located by name with 26 more assigned probable locales (Gorenstein and Pollard 1983; Pollard 1993). Of particular note for this review are: Tzintzuntzan, the Tarascan capital located on the eastern lakeshore; Erongarícuaro, originally an independent center that became a secondary administrative center for the state, located on the western lakeshore; and Urichu, also independent prior to state formation, which became a tertiary Tarascan administrative center subject to Erongarícuaro located on the southwestern lakeshore (Figure 1). These sites were different in function and size, as Tzintzuntzan encompassed 674 hectares, Erongarícuaro covered 228 hectares, and Urichu was 90 hectares (Pollard 1993, 2003, 2005; Pollard and Cahue 1999).

**Ceramics in the Tarascan Market System**

The economy of the Basin prior to state formation most likely emphasized local market exchange, although some non-basin, exotic materials are noted (Gorenstein and Pollard 1983; Pollard and Cahue 1999). Most communities, with the exception of those on the islands, had natural access to a range of agrarian and lacustrine resources between the shore and higher forested slopes, a range that could be exploited by both communities and households (e.g., Toledo 1991). Although rich in resources, not all necessities were available; notably missing from the Basin were salt, obsidian, lime, and cotton (Darras 2009; Gorenstein and Pollard 1983; Pollard 1993; Williams 1999). A market system potentially enabled basin inhabitants to acquire necessities as well as off-set possible food-stuff shortfalls, especially as the population grew and rising lake levels covered agricultural lands within the basin (Gorenstein and Pollard 1983; Pollard 1982, 1993).

The sixteenth century documents provide less information regarding the Late Postclassic Tarascan market system than the tribute system. *La Relación de Michoacán* (1980) includes an illustration of a market scene and further indicates three Basin markets operating at the time of Contact, which could be closed in extreme circumstances such as the death of the king: two within the Basin at the capital Tzintzuntzan in the east and at Pareo in the south, and one just to the northwest at the Basin boundary at Asajo. However, the markets do not parallel the religious and political networks of the state (Gorenstein and Pollard 1983; Pollard 1993), suggesting that they at least in part reflect earlier economic configurations. Pollard (2017) details how P'urépecha dictionaries from the sixteenth century (*Diccionario Grande de la Lengua de Michoacán* 1991; Gilberti 1989) contain a range of terms relating to markets, marketing, participating in markets, and goods and services available in the market.

The 1000-year excavated ceramic assemblage at Urichu demonstrates continuity in color and form over time (e.g., Hirshman, Lovis, and Pollard 2010; Pollard 2001, 2008). In particular, little change is noted in the form or decoration of utilitarian wares in the Middle to Late Postclassic (Late Urichu to Tariacuri phases), including the persistence of low numbers of *comals* (griddles) and only punctate *molcajetes* (chili graters); thus these two periods are difficult to distinguish from surface collections alone within the Basin (e.g., Pollard 2001, 2008). A similar problem exists at culturally-related sites to the north, such as sites in the Zacapu Basin (e.g., Arnauld *et al.* 1993; Carot 2001; Migeon 1998).

*Assemblage Heterogeneity and Production Organization over time*

A study of 37,301 sherds from ceramic assemblage spanning over 1000 years from the site of Urichu focused primarily on general form, surface decoration and rim morphology to understand the changing nature of ceramic production organization in the basin (Hirshman 2008; Hirshman, Lovis and Pollard 2010). Decorative variables included slip,

| Phase | N | Shapiro-Wilk | Phase | Ess Range | |
|---|---|---|---|---|---|
| | Clusters | W Test | Mean Ess | Low | High |
| Tariacuri Area 5 | 61 | p=0.0001 | 0.111800 | 0.000 | 0.193 |
| Tariacuri Area 2 | 25 | p=0.0001 | 0.072935 | 0.000 | 0.547 |
| Tariacuri Area 1 | 31 | p=0.0005 | 0.048115 | 0.000 | 0.309 |
| Late Urichu | 16 | p=0.3400 | 0.050729 | 0.000 | 0.193 |
| Early Urichu | 59 | p<0.0001 | 0.103050 | 0.000 | 0.167 |
| Lupe | 52 | p=0.0015 | 0.081194 | 0.000 | 0.119 |
| Jarácuaro | 31 | p=0.0023 | 0.118600 | 0.000 | 0.185 |
| Loma Alta 3 | 10 | p=0.0856 | 0.070131 | 0.000 | 0.317 |

**ESS test for equal variance**  **Non-parametric anova**
Brown-Forsythe Test:   p<0.0001    Wilcoxon/Kruskal-Wallis Test:   p=0.0204

Table 2. Rim Sherd Within cluster Error Sum of Squares (ESS) One-Way ANOVA
(from Hirshman, Lovis and Pollard 2010, 272, Table 3)

paint, resist (intentional smudging from a second firing), physical manipulation of the surface including incision or application of decoration, and the extent of surface polish, if at all. Morphological attributes included closed or open vessels, and for rim sherds, shape of rim and lip. The sample was divided by time period and portion of vessel (rim/body/support) and polysynthetic clusters within each portion were identified through cluster analysis, and the Within cluster Error Sum of Squares analyzed within phases and across time to assess relative variability within the data set (e.g., Hirshman, Lovis and Pollard 2010 for complete details). The rim sherds (Table 2; rim sherd N=3089) provided the most sensitive portion of the data set. Variation between clusters of rim sherds within phases was assessed with the Shapiro-Wilk W Tes as statistically significant in all, but the Late Urichu period, and as statistically significant by the Brown-Forsythe test between phases. A One-Way Wilcoxon/Kruskal-Wallis non-parametric ANOVA of the Within Cluster Sum of Squares through time also indicated statistically significant difference over time. While the ceramic assemblage was never particularly uniform at any moment in time, a statistically significant decrease in ceramic variability occurred through the Late Classic to the Early Postclassic Periods (Loma Alta 3 to Lupe; ca. AD 600-1100), corresponding with the emergence of social ranking in the first episode of elite activity in the basin (Hirshman 2008; Hirshman, Lovis and Pollard 2010). Variation actually increases through time at this point, though it is not statistically significant. The greatest variation is indicated in the Late Postclassic commoner area, Taríacuri Area 2, while Taríacuri Areas 1 and 5 are elite zones at Urichu. The earlier shift towards assemblage similarity indicates ceramics were responsive to socio-political changes associated with the emergence of early elites in the basin and some production reorganization occurred. However, the lack of significant change with the emergence of the Tarascan political elites and the state indicates that the ceramic products did not fully incorporate into the changing socio-political circumstances of the basin. Coupled with the variability of the ceramic assemblage throughout the sequence, this analysis strongly indicates that decentralized, household organization of ceramic production persisted over time within the basin, even into the state period (Hirshman 2008; Hirshman, Lovis and Pollard 2010).

*Tarascan Ceramic Pastes over Time*

The ceramic typology for the basin is rooted first in the category of 'paste' as defined by Pollard on the basis of a range of visual and physical properties, and a total of 13 distinct paste categories have been identified in the basin from Tzintzuntzan, Erongarícuaro and Urichu (Table 3; Pollard 1993, Appendix 2; 2001, 2007). These pastes have different, but overlapping, patterns of distribution between the three sites, as well as between elite and commoner areas at each site (Haskell 2008; Hirshman and Haskell 2016; Hirshman, Lovis and Pollard 2010; Pollard 1993, Appendix 2, 2001; Pollard & Haskell 2006; Stawski 2008).

These visual paste categories identified by Pollard are not equivalent to chemically defined compositional groups. However, compositional data generated by neutron activation analysis (NAA) provides partial corroboration of the visual paste categories and confirms that the visual categories represent generally long-lived paste recipes within the basin (Hirshman and Ferguson 2012). The NAA analysis of select pastes identified at Tzintzuntzan (N=56), Erongarícuaro (N=45) and Urichu (N=70) identified six broad compositional groups. Three of these groups loosely affiliate with one another (MPG, PG3, and PG5) and also roughly correspond to the visual pastes Yaguarato Cream,

Table 3. Alphabetical Listing of Paste Categories Identified by Pollard (Hirshman, after Pollard 1993, 2001, Pollard and Haskell 2006)

| Paste Name | Location Identified |
| --- | --- |
| Black polished | Urichu |
| Ichupio Coarse | Tzintzuntzan, Erongarícuaro, Urichu |
| Patambicho Red | Tzintzuntzan, Urichu |
| Querenda White | Tzintzuntzan, Erongarícuaro, Urichu |
| Sanabria Red | Tzintzuntzan |
| Sipiho Grey | Tzintzuntzan, Erongarícuaro, Urichu |
| Tarerio Cream | Tzintzuntzan, Erongarícuaro, Urichu |
| Tariácuri Brown | Tzintzuntzan, Erongarícuaro, Urichu |
| Tariácuri Coarse | Tzintzuntzan, Erongarícuaro, Urichu |
| Tecolote Orange | Tzintzuntzan, Erongarícuaro, Urichu |
| Urichu Fine | Tzintzuntzan, Erongarícuaro, Urichu |
| Yaguarato Coarse | Tzintzuntzan, Erongarícuaro, Urichu |
| Yaguarato Cream | Tzintzuntzan, Erongarícuaro, Urichu |

Tariacuri Brown, and Sipiho Grey. These three compositional groups separate significantly from the other three compositional groups, which are also similar to one another (PG1, PG2, and PG4), and which correspond to the visual paste Querenda White and possibly Tecolote Orange. The two larger compositional groups, MPG and PG1, persist through time, both before and after state emergence (Hirshman & Ferguson 2012). The overall number of unassigned sherds is not particularly high for this type of study, and all but one sherd (of Thin Orange, from Erongarícuaro) appear to originate within the Basin (Hirshman and Ferguson 2012).

This division between the two sets of chemically similar groups also corresponds to a general north-south spatial division within the basin. None of the raw clays or 'ashy' samples (N=36) analyzed in the NAA study created matches to the two larger compositional groups, the only groups with sufficient numbers for comparison. Upon modeling mathematical 'clay+ash' combinations, several clays could be matched to either or both of the two larger compositional groups (Hirshman and Ferguson 2012). The clays that created 'clay+ash' matches indicate a broad and somewhat northern Basin production zone for PG1, PG2, and PG4 and a largely southern basin production zone for MPG, PG3, and PG5, with possible MPG production near Erongaricuao, though that is a tentative conclusion (Hirshman and Ferguson 2012). None of the significant matches were made with clay samples from Tzintzuntzan; this does not mean production did not occur there, only that the chemical analysis cannot be interpreted to suggest production at the Tarascan capital at this juncture, and probably not for the general fine wares in the NAA study.

Table 4 illustrates the appearance of pottery groups by site and time period. The MPG, PG1, and PG3, representing both of the main chemical trends in the basin, occur throughout the sequence at the sites of Erongarícuaro and Urichu. All six compositional groups appear in the Middle-Late Postclassic at Urichu, and three, MPG, PG1 and PG3, were present at Erongarícuaro. Only the MPG and PG1 occur at Tzintzuntzan, an unexpectedly low result, though the highest number of unassigned sherds from the Middle-Late Postclassic, 23%, come from Tzintzuntzan, which suggests greater ceramic variability than is captured by this study (Hirshman and Ferguson 2016).

Cohen (2016) also conducted a NAA study of 300 survey and excavation ceramic samples from elite and commoner areas at the site of Angamuco, in the southeast of the basin. The resulting 2015 report by Pierce and Glascock of the Archaeometry Laboratory, Research Reactor Center at the University of Missouri, Columbia, is Appendix B in Cohen's dissertation. Two of the compositional groups, 'Group A' and 'Group C' match the MPG and PG1, respectively, while Cohen interprets the other two compositional groups in her study as having derived from Angamuco or nearby (2016, 175-180). The compositional groups cross-cut decorative treatments and all four compositional groups are represented in elite and commoner contexts at the site, with either Group A or Group C being the most common compositional group in six of the seven areas of the site represented in Cohen's study (Cohen 2016, 177). As those two pastes originate elsewhere in the basin, their presence in much of Angamuco suggests they were acquired by market exchange.

Visual paste categories and chemical compositional groups indicate varied and long-lived paste recipes in the basin, and ceramics with these pastes were accessible to people at multiple sites through time. Although the compositional

| Compositional Group | Tzintzuntzan | | Erongarícuaro | | Urichu | | Total |
|---|---|---|---|---|---|---|---|
| | N | % sherds | N | % sherds | N | % sherds | |
| Main Pottery Group (N=88) | | | | | | | |
| *Middle-Late Postclassic* | 23 | 41% | 10 | 67% | 14 | 36% | 47 |
| *Early Classic-Early Postclassic* | ---- | | 27 | | 14 | | 41 |
| Pottery Group 1 (N=38) | | | | | | | |
| *Middle-Late Postclassic* | 20 | 35% | 1 | 7% | 4 | 10% | 25 |
| *Early Classic-Early Postclassic* | ---- | | 0 | | 13 | | 13 |
| Pottery Group 2 (N=5) | | | | | | | |
| *Middle-Late Postclassic* | 0 | 0% | 0 | 0% | 5 | 13% | 5 |
| *Early Classic-Early Postclassic* | ---- | | 0 | | 0 | | 0 |
| Pottery Group 3 (N=6) | | | | | | | |
| *Middle-Late Postclassic* | 0 | 0% | 1 | 7% | 2 | 5% | 3 |
| *Early Classic-Early Postclassic* | ---- | | 1 | | 2 | | 3 |
| Pottery Group 4 (N=4) | | | | | | | |
| *Middle-Late Postclassic* | 0 | 0% | 0 | 0% | 4 | 10% | 4 |
| *Early Classic-Early Postclassic* | ---- | | 0 | | 0 | | 0 |
| Pottery Group 5 (N=4) | | | | | | | |
| *Middle-Late Postclassic* | 0 | 0% | 0 | 0% | 4 | 10% | 4 |
| *Early Classic-Early Postclassic* | ---- | | 0 | | 0 | | 0 |
| Unassigned (N=25) | | | | | | | |
| *Middle-Late Postclassic* | 13 | 23% | 3 | 20% | 6 | 15% | 22 |
| *Early Classic-Early Postclassic* | ---- | | 1 | | 2 | | 3 |
| Total | 56 | 99%* of 56 | 44 | 101%* of 15 | 70 | 99%* of 39 | 170 |

\* figures may not total 100% due to rounding

Table 4. Compositional group by time and by site (from Hirshman and Ferguson 2012, 3202, Table 5)

data is site-level rather than household-level, as preferred by Hirth's 'Distributional Approach' (1998), compositional variation appears to increase over time, though not uniformly. While the variability at Tzintzuntzan, particularly in regards to its unassigned samples, may have been due to state-run institutions like tribute, and not simply local market exchange, the increase in paste variation at Erongarícuaro and Urichu is better explained by a marketing system.

*Decorated Ceramic fine Ware Patterns within the State*

Not only are there a significant number of pastes within the Basin, but research involving the ceramic assemblages of Tzintzuntzan and Urichu also indicates that the paste categories identified by Pollard crosscut otherwise morphologically and stylistically redundant categories within the basin (Hirshman, Lovis and Pollard 2010; Pollard 1993, 2001). Furthermore, decorated sherds comprise a significant component of the assemblages from commoner, lower elite, and upper elite contexts alike at Tzintzuntzan, Erongarícuaro, and Urichu (e.g., Haskell 2008; Hirshman, Lovis and Pollard 2010; Pollard 1993, 2001; Stawski 2008).

Using contextual evidence from excavations of upper and lower elite and commoner residences from Tzintzuntzan, Urichu, and Las Milpillas near Zacapu to the north, Stawski (2008) isolated the ceramic household assemblages associated with each social class known from the ethnohistorical documents. For commoner residences vessel forms include convex and incurved rim bowls, and everted and incurved rim jars, which are unslipped, unpainted, undecorated or monochrome, and made of one of the three common coarse wares. Small quantities of decorated pottery may be found in their houses. Lower elite residences, or lords in lower ranked centers like Urichu, include the ceramics found at commoner houses, but also include some spouted vessels, slipped and painted bowls and jars generally without resist decoration, and a wider variety of vessel supports. In the upper elite residences ceramics include, in addition to the above pottery, miniature jars and bowls, larger numbers of spouted vessels, spout handle-jars, braziers, and plates. Decoration includes resist and appliqué pellets, polychrome paint on slips and a wide variety of supports. Notably, these assemblages generally include a great variety of fine ware pastes.

At Erongarícuaro the distribution pattern of pastes and of decorated sherds overlapped between the elite and commoner areas, varying in frequency rather than each having a distinctly different pattern (Haskell 2008; Pollard and Haskell 2006). In comparing the survey and excavation-derived ceramic assemblages from the elite residential zone to the commoner zone in the Middle to Late Postclassic, elites consistently utilized a smaller range of pastes than did the commoners, but the pastes they used were the same as those used by the commoners (Haskell 2008; Hirshman and Haskell 2015; Pollard and Haskell 2006).

A similar pattern was identified for Urichu, which would have had only lower elites in residence as a tertiary center in the basin. As at Erongarícuaro, these elites had a smaller, but overlapping, range of pastes in comparison with the commoners. Commoners also had a higher percentage of decorated sherds within their portion of the assemblage, as well as sherds exhibiting resist, than did the assemblage from the elite area at Urichu (Hirshman and Haskell 2016; Hirshman, Lovis and Pollard 2010; Pollard 2001).

While unsurprising for commoners to have more utilitarian, undecorated pottery than elites, if commoners and elites were both accessing most of their ceramics through the market, then their assemblages should overlap in terms of paste category diversity. At both sites this is true for the non-burial, survey and excavation assemblages. Furthermore, both sites meet the market expectation (Hirth 1998) that both elite and commoner assemblages include an overlapping range of decorated sherds, especially if both groups are engaged in state-oriented feasting and other communal activities. The relatively even distribution of fine ware pastes and decorated sherds at these two sites, in contrast to the highly restricted distribution of a particular class of spouted fine ware vessels, for example, and as noted below, points toward a market mechanism for the distribution of the majority of ceramic fine wares in the basin.

*Marketing System and Transportation within the Basin*

Decentralized, household-based ceramic producers would need to be able to transport their wares to markets, and an assessment of the technology of transportation and distances within the Basin demonstrates the general efficiency of the basin transport system, as well as supports the practicality of household producers carrying their own products to the known markets in the basin (Hirshman and Stawski 2013). Transportation in the Basin relied upon people carrying burdens using tumpline hung frames and/or canoes. Drawn from ethnohistoric and ethnographic literature from the *P'urépecha* region, Highland Mexico and elsewhere, as well as GIS methodologies, a feasibility model of a 23 kg load of 38 to 100 vessels, depending upon vessel size, carried at an average walking velocity of 4.5 km/hour would imply that all but one of the known Late Postclassic communities in the Basin were located within an approximate 18 km, a four hour walking-distance with a heavy load, to a known market community during the Late Postclassic (Hirshman & Stawski 2013; Pollard 1993). Moreover, 72% of the Late Postclassic communities identified by Pollard (1993) were located within approximately two walking hours to a market (Hirshman and Stawski 2013). Canoes would enable even longer trips (Hirshman and Stawski 2013).

Nothing in the sixteenth century documents indicates a coercive extension of control over transportation routes on land or water or a shift of transportation control from commoners to the state (Hirshman and Stawski 2013). Only with the enormous transportation transformations of paved roads and the ability to carry larger loads more quickly with buses and trucks in the 20th century were household producers in the basin significantly affected, indicating substantial meddling by the prehispanic Tarascan State would have been necessary to transform the organization of ceramic production in their political core (for a fuller discussion, e.g., Hirshman and Stawski 2013). Rather, transportation was not a limiting factor for market exchange and well within the ability of both household producers and consumers in the basin.

**Ceramics and the Tarascan command Economy**

In contrast to the emerging understanding of the Tarascan marketing system, Spanish and native sixteenth century documents provide greater background information for Tarascan activities (e.g., Acuña 1987; Beltrán 1982; Gorenstein and Pollard 1983; *La Relación de Michoacán* 1980; Paredes 1984; Pollard 1993; Warren 1968, 1985). The state is particularly noted for its control of metallurgy, and both ethnohistoric sources and archaeological research indicate that the Tarascan state positioned itself to control at least some aspects of the mining regions and the mining-smelting process early in its history through both tribute demands and direct control (e.g., Gorenstein and Pollard 1983; Maldonado 2008; Pollard 1993, 2017; Warren 1968, 47, 50).

These documents further indicate the political elite controlled a wide range of utilitarian and luxury items brought to the capital at Tzintzuntzan and maintained in state storehouses, providing the basis of elite support and elite finance, as well as potential famine relief (Pollard 2003). For example, maize, known from ethnohistoric sources (Gorenstein and Pollard 1983; Paredes 1984; Pollard 1982), moved through both the command and market systems. Moreover, quantities of obsidian increased dramatically in the state period (Pollard 2017). While the state probably controlled obsidian from one source, Ucareo (Pollard 2017; Hernández and Healan 2008), as well as most lapidary consumption (e.g. Pollard 2017; Rebnegger 2013), obsidian used as prismatic blades from other sources moved through market systems (Darras 2009; Pollard 2017). In addition to tribute, the Tarascan elite sponsored long-distance trade (Pollard 1993), including long-distance ethnic *nahua* merchants from Central Mexico (Monzón, Roskamp and Warren 2009).

While ceramic assemblages from Urichu and Erongarícuaro generally demonstrated continuity over time, ceramics also reflected change as the state emerged. New ceramic forms and decorative motifs appear in the Urichu assemblage in the Middle to Late Postclassic, including spouted vessels, eccentric zoomorphic vessels, and miniature vessels (e.g., Pollard 2001, 2017; Pollard and Washburn 2017). Along with new forms, a new 'design grammar' is found on decorated fine wares. A symmetry analysis of whole vessels from the Middle Preclassic to the Late Postclassic (N=143, 60 from within the basin) demonstrates significant changes in ceramic decorative expression concurrent with the emergence of the state in the Late Postclassic. The changes are more significant than in any other period in the study, including the Classic to Early Postclassic, in which social ranking becomes apparent in the basin (Pollard and Washburn 2017).

Nearly all of these new forms from excavations at Urichu are found in elite-associated contexts (Pollard 2001). Elsewhere, these elite fine wares are generally associated with the ritual zones at the Tarascan capital of Tzintzuntzan and secondary Tarascan centers such at Erongarícuaro, as well as elite-associated residential zones (e.g., Cabrera Castro 1996; Castro Leal 1986; Macías 1990; Pollard 2017; Pulido 2006; Valdez and Liot 1994). The spouted vessels were used for elite cacao consumption (Pollard 2017) and are predominantly, though not exclusively, found in low numbers as sherds within elite residential zones at Tzintzuntzan, Erongarícuaro, and Urichu and in burials (e.g., Pollard 2001, 2017; Pollard and Haskell 2006; Stawski 2008).

This circumscribed numbers and distribution of these forms contrasts with the higher frequencies and broader distribution of other fine ware ceramics, as discussed above for Erongarícuaro and Urichu (e.g., Hirshman and Haskell 2016). Pollard hypothesizes the restricted forms moved by means of elite patronage and gift-giving networks rather than more intensive provisioning mechanisms (Pollard 1993; 2017).

Within the lake basin, Aguilar (2005:190-212) notes that in *La Relación de Michoacán,* the Tarascan (*P'urépecha*) term for tribute collectors from basin communities, *uhcámbecha,* refers to a 'boss' or labor manager and interprets this as indicating that tribute within the Basin was in service, not goods. Pollard (personal communication) suggests service tribute indicates decorated pottery was not a general tribute item from communities within the Pátzcuaro Basin. As *La Relación de Michoacán* 1980) names a court official who possibly oversaw pottery production, it is possible these very high status ceramics were made at Tzintzuntzan under the control of the political elite.

If indeed gift-giving, rather than redistribution, of ceramics was central to the state elite strategy of ceramic usage, then little in the way of significant storage would be needed by the Tzintzuntzan elites. The nature and extent of centralized, state-associated storage is cited as a significant variable for distinguishing between redistribution and market exchange (Stark and Garraty 2010). Using predominantly ethnohistorical, rather than archaeoglical, evidence, Pollard (2012) identified state-associated storehouses (treasuries; kingly wealth; and aforementioned storehouses for tribute). Though there is little archaeological evidence for state storehouses, the few households excavated in the basin and to the north provide indicators for elite household storage, including a cache of high status ceramics at Urichu (Pollard 2001), and commoners, including what appear to be conical storage structures (see Pollard 2012). Even less evidence exists for community-level storage; this absence of storehouses for local elites in the Tarascan state reinforces the important role for markets in provisioning all households (e.g., Pollard 2012).

Two other ceramic categories complicate the relationship between the state and householders. Ceramic pipes for Tabaco smoking also appear in the Late Postclassic and are strongly associated with the state ritual; they are found in public ritual areas within the three sites, but not in other elite associated contests, such as residences or burials (e.g., Pollard 2017). Pipes are found in higher numbers than other elite-associated ceramics, such as the spouted, miniature, or zoomorphic vessels, and Pollard argues they are predominantly made locally, and were possibly available in the market (Pollard 2017). Another strongly elite-associated ceramic product, cotton spindle whorls, are limited in number (compared to maguey spindle whorls), and occur occasionally in elite residences, though more frequently in male or female elite burials (Pollard 2017). Cotton spindle whorls required cotton, mainly imported to the basin through the tribute system, but the whorls appear to be locally made, based on visual inspection of the pastes (e.g., Pollard 2017). These categories suggest household production of ceramics for restricted ritual or elite use in addition to production of fine wares for both elite and commoner consumption as argued above.

**Discussion: Ceramic production and exchange**

The evidence reviewed here indicates the Tarascan state utilized a mixed economic strategy, involving tribute and market exchange. Tribute, well-known from the documentary sources, appears to have brought wealth and goods into the state from outside the basin, while within the basin, most tribute was in the form of service rather than goods (e.g., Aguilar 2005). The state expressly provisioned the highest elite and maintained control over some resources, such as metal and specific obsidian sources. Yet, the political elite seemed to manage the production of only select categories of ceramic products, notably high status fine wares such spouted vessels. Other status and ritual ceramics, such as pipes and cotton spindle whorls, appear to be the product of household producers and, at least with the pipes, potentially circulated in the market system. The majority of the decorated vessels were accessible to both elites and commoners, and in more even percentages than the restricted classes of ceramics. The long-term temporal and spatial diversity in the ceramic assemblage, both in terms of decoration and fabric composition, indicates persistent and decentralized production organization. Productive organization did not demonstrably change with the emergence of the state, despite the appearance of some new forms.

The expectations of marketing models posit smoother distributions of marketed artifact classes, in this case represented by the decorated paste categories at Erongarícuaro, a secondary Tarascan center, and Urichu, its subsidiary site. Both between the sites, and between the elite and commoner zones within each of the sites, the differences appear to reflect the wealth of the elites more than absolute differences in ceramic accessibility between the classes. In a context of significant household rather than community storage, long-term household ceramic production, growing populations, and decreasing agricultural resources due to lake level rise, market exchange for the bulk of the ceramic needed within the basin makes the most sense. In this way the state elites accommodated preexisting economic efficiencies while focusing on select status and tributary goods that marked the emergence of the state and elite status.

**Conclusions**

Household production was common in ancient Mesoamerica (e.g. Hirth 2009), and market oriented economies are a marker of Late Postclassic Mesoamerica more generally (e.g., Smith and Berdan 2003). The model presented here for the Late Postclassic Tarascan state is one of persistent decentralized household ceramic production for market exchange, including both utilitarian and most of the decorated fine wares. This production was rooted in long-term household production and never strongly consolidated or reorganized with the emergence of the state. While there was the introduction of new design motifs and vessel shapes with the emergence of the state, and the emergence of highly specialized ceramics associated with the state and state ritual such as pipes and spouted vessels, the production and distribution of few of those ceramics appear to be under direct state control.

More archaeological data is still necessary for a definitive statement on the interrelationship between markets and ceramics in the Tarascan state. Questions remain regarding pre-state economic relationships within the basin, as well as details regarding households, the configuration of the marketing system, and the extent and nature of marketing integration within the basin during the state. Yet the multiple lines of indirect evidence in this study consistently point in one direction: the state utilized existing productive and distributive relationships and reorganized only aspects of the ceramic economy in their political core, the Lake Pátzcuaro Basin. This more nuanced understanding of the Tarascan state and its relationship to complex social institutions such as markets and households, as reflected in this current study, enhances our understanding of cultural variation in the Mesoamerican Late Postclassic Period, and more fully develops our understanding of the patterns and exceptionality in the past.

**Acknowledgements**

Funding for the technical analyses in this manuscript came from a number of sources, including NSF grant BCS-0102325 to the Archaeometry Laboratory of the Research Reactor, University of Missouri (MURR), National Science

Foundation SBR 9507673 (ORD No. 63560), National Endowment for the Humanities RK-20087 to Dr. H. Pollard, PI. Funding for the Erongarícuaro excavations was provided by the Heinz Foundation and the Wenner-Gren Foundation for Anthropological Research to H. Pollard. Particular thanks to Dr. Helen Pollard for reviewing several versions of this manuscript and for on-going conversations regarding all things Tarascan. Various researchers lent their expertise to this project, including Drs. Michael Glascock, Jeffrey Ferguson and Jeff Speakman at MURR, and Dr. William A. Lovis , Michigan State University, and Dr. Christopher Stawski, San Francisco State University, and Dr. David L. Haskell, Ohio State University. Dr. Sarah Surface-Evans assisted with Figure 1.

**References Cited**

Acuña, René, ed. 1987. *Relaciones Geográficas del Siglo XVI: Michoacán.* Vol. 9. México, DF: Universidad Nacional Autónoma de México.

Aguilar González, José Ricardo. 2005. 'Tzintzuntzan Irechequa. Política y sociedad en el Estado tarasco.' Tesis de Licenciatura en Historia, Universidad Michoacana.

Arnauld, Charlotte, Patricia Carot, Marie-France Fauvet-Berthelot, and Dominique Michelet. 1993. 'La cerámica de las lomas en la secuencia cerámica regional.' *Arqueología de las lomas en la cuenca lacustre de Zacapu, Michoacán,* 149-155. Collection Études Mesoaméricaines II-13/Cuadernos de Estudios Michoacanos 5. México, DF: Centre d'Etudes Mexicaines et Centraméricaines.

Beltrán, Ulises. 1982. 'Tarascan State and Society in Prehispanic Times: An Ethnohistorical Inquiry.' PhD Diss., University of Chicago. Ann Arbor: University Microfilms.

Berdan, Frances F. 1989. 'Trade and Markets in Precapitalist States.' In *Economic Anthropology,* edited by Stuart M. Plattner, 78-107. Palo Alto, CA: Stanford University Press.

Carballo, David M. 2011. 'Advances in the Household Archaeology of Highland Mesoamerica.' Journal of Archaeological Research 19 (2):133-189.

Cabrera Castro, Rubén. 1996. 'Cerámica suntuaria de Tzintzuntzan, Michoacán.' *Tiempo y territorio en arqueología. El centro norte de México* (Colección *científica 323),* edited by Ana María Crespo y Carlos Viramontes, 37-58. México: Instituto Nacional de Antropología e Historia.

Carot, Patricia. 2001. *Le site de Loma Alta, Lac de Zacapu, Michoacan, Mexique,* BAR International Series 920. Oxford: British Archaeological Reports.

Castro-Leal, Marcia. 1986. *Tzintzuntzan capital de los tarascos.* Morelia, Mich.: Editorial del Gobierno de Michoacán.

Cohen, Anna. 2016. 'Creating and Empire: Local Political Change at Angamuco, Michoacán, Mexico.' PhD Diss., University of Washington.

Darras, Véronique. 2009. 'Peasant Artisans: Household Prismatic Blade Production in the Zacapu Region, Michoacan (Milpillas Phase 1200-1450 AD).' In *Housework: Craft Production and Domestic Economy in Ancient Mesoamerica,* edited by Ken G. Hirth, 90-114. Archaeological Papers of the American Anthropological Association 19. Washington, DC: American Anthropological Association.

*Diccionario Grande de la Lengua de Michoacán.* 1991. Introducción, paleográfia y notas por J. Benedict Warren. Morelia, Mexico: Fimax Publicistas.

Earle, Timothy and Michael E. Smith. 2012. 'Household Economies Under the Aztec and Inka empires: A Comparison.' In *The Comparative Archaeology of Complex Societies,* edited by M. E. Smith, 238-284.Cambridge: Cambridge University Press.

Feinman, Gary M. 1999. 'Rethinking Our Assumptions: Economic Specialization at the Household Scale in Ancient Ejutla, Oaxaca, Mexico.' In *Pottery and People: A Dynamic Interaction,* edited by James M. Skibo and Gary M. Feinman, 81-98. Salt Lake City: The University of Utah Press.

Garraty, Christopher P. 2010. 'Investigating Market Exchange in Ancient Societies: A Theoretical Review.' In *Archaeological Approaches to Market Exchange in Ancient Societies,* edited by Christopher P. Garraty and Barbara L. Stark, 3-32. Boulder, CO: University Press of Colorado.

Gilberti, R. P. Fr. Maturino. 1989. Diccionario de la lengua tarasca o de Michoacán. Introducción, paleográfia y notas por J. Benedict Warren. Morelia, Mexico: Fimax Publicistas. (Orig. pub. 1559.)

Gorenstein, Shirley, and Helen P. Pollard. 1983. *The Tarascan Civilization: A Late Prehispanic Cultural System.* Publications in Anthropology 28. Nashville: Department of Anthropology, Vanderbilt University.

Haskell, David L. 2008. 'Tarascan Kingship: the Production of Hierarchy in the Prehispanic Pátzcuaro Basin, Mexico.' Ph.D. Diss. University of Florida.

Hernández, Christine L. and Dan M. Healan. 2008. 'The Role of Late Pre-contact Colonial Enclaves in the Development of the Postclassic Ucareo Valley, Michoacan, Mexico.' *Ancient Mesoamerica* 19 (2): 265-282.

Hirshman, Amy J. 2008. 'Tarascan Ceramic Production and Implications for Ceramic distribution.' *Ancient Mesoamerica* 19 (2): 299-310.

Hirshman, Amy J. and Jeffrey R. Ferguson. 2012. 'Temper Mixture Models and Assessing Ceramic Complexity in the Emerging Tarascan State.' *Journal of Archaeological Science* 39 (10): 3195-3207.

Hirshman, Amy J and David Haskell. 2016. 'Evaluating Contrasting Models of Ceramic Production in the Tarascan State: Negotiations in Clay.' In *Cultural Dynamics and Production Activities in Ancient Western Mexico*, edited by Eduardo Williams and Blanca Maldonado, 201-214. Oxford, UK: British Archaeological Reports International Series.

Hirshman, Amy J., William A. Lovis, and Helen P. Pollard. 2010. 'Specialization of Ceramic Production: A Sherd Assemblage Based Analytic Perspective.' *Journal of Anthropological Archaeology* 29 (3): 265-277.

Hirshman, Amy J. and Christopher J. Stawski. 2013. 'Distribution, Transportation, and the Persistence of Household Ceramic Production in the Tarascan State.' *Ethnoarchaeology* 5 (1): 1-23.

Hirth, Kenneth G. 1998. 'The Distributional Approach: A New Way to Identify Marketplace Exchange in the Archaeological Record.' *Current Anthropology* 39 (4): 451-476.

Hirth, Kenneth G. 2009. 'Craft Production, Household Diversification and Domestic Economy in Prehispanic Mesoamerica'. In *Housework: Craft Production and Domestic Economy in Ancient Mesoamerica*, Archaeological Papers of the American Anthropological Association 19, edited by Kenneth G. Hirth, 13-31. Washington, DC: American Anthropological Association.

Hirth, Kenneth G. 2013. 'The Merchant's World: commercial Diversity and the Economics of Interregional Exchange in Highland Mesoamerica.' In *Merchants, Markets, and Exchange in the Pre-Columbian World*, edited by Kenneth G. Hirth and Joanne Pillsbury, 5-112. Washington, DC: Dumbarton Oaks Research Library and Collection.

*La Relación de Michoacán.* 1980. Versión paleográfica, separación de textos, ordenación colloquial, Reconocimiento prelinimar y notas de F. Miranda. Estudios Michoacanos. Morelia, Michoacán: Fimax Publicistas. (Orig. pub. 1541.)

Macías Goytia, Angelina. 1990. *Huandacareo: Lugar de juicios, tribunal*. Colección Científica, No. 222. México, DF: Instituto Nacional de Antropología e Historia.

Maldonado, Blanca E. 2008. 'A Tentative Model of the Organization of Copper Production in the Tarascan State.' *Ancient Mesoamerica* 19 (2): 283-297.

Minc, Leah D. 2009. 'Style and Substance: Evidence for Regionalism within the Aztec Market System.' *Latin American Antiquity* 20 (2): 343-374.

Monzón, Cristina, Hans Roskamp and Benedict Warren. 2009. 'La memoria de don Melchor Caltzin (1543): historia y legitimación en Tzintzuntzan, Michoacán.' *Estudios de Historia Novohispana* 40: 21-55.

Nichols, Deborah L., Elizabeth M. Brumfiel, Hector Neff, Mary Hodge, Thomas H. Charlton, and Michael D. Glascock. 2002. 'Neutrons, Markets, Cities, and Empires: a 1000-year Perspective on Ceramic Production and Distribution in the Postclassic Basin of Mexico.' *Journal of Anthropological Archaeology* 21 (1): 25-82.

Paredes Martínez, Carlos S. 1984. 'El tributo indígena en la región del lago de Patzcuaro.' In *Michoacan en el Siglo XVI*, edited by Carlos S. Paredes Martinez, Marcela Irais Pinon Flores, Armando M. Escovar Olmedo, and Maria Trinidad Pulido Solis, pp. 21-104. Morelia, Mexico: Fimax Publicistas.

Pollard, Helen Perlstein. 1982. 'Ecological Variation and Economic Exchange in the Tarascan State. *American Ethnologist* 9 (2): 250-268.

Pollard, Helen Perlstein. 1993. *Tariacuri's Legacy: The Prehispanic Tarascan State*. Norman: University of Oklahoma Press.

Pollard, Helen Perlstein. 2001. 'Informe Final, Tomo 3: La cerámica.' Report to the Consejo de Arqueología, Instituto Nacional de Antropología e Historia.

Pollard, Helen Perlstein. 2003. 'Central Places and Cities in the Core of the Tarascan State.' In *Urbanism in Mesoamerica*, edited by William T. Sanders, Alba Guadalupe Mastache, and Robert H. Cobean, 345-390. Bilingual edition: *El Urbanismo en Mesoamérica*, Lugares Centrales y Ciudades en el Núcleo del Estado Tarasco. México, DF and University Park, PA: Instituto Nacional de Antropología e Historia and Pennsylvania University Press.

Pollard, Helen Perlstein. 2008. 'A model of the Emergence of the Tarascan State.' *Ancient Mesoamerica* 19 (2): 17-230.

Pollard, Helen Perlstein. 2012. 'La economía política del almacenaje en el Estado tarasco prehispánico.' *Almacenamiento prehispánico, del Norte de México hasta el Altiplano central*, edited by Séverine Bortot, Dominique Michelet and Véronique Darras, 131-144. México: Laboratoire d'Archéologie des Amériques of the CNRS (Paris), Université Paris I Panthéon-Sorbonne, Universidad Autónoma de San Luis Potosí, and Centro Francés de Estudios Mexicanos y Centroamericanos.

Pollard, Helen Perlstein. 2017. 'Markets, Tribute, and Class in Tarascan Commodity Consumption: the Lake Pátzcuaro Basin.' *Americae 2*. URL: http://www.mae.u-paris10.fr/articles-articulos/markets-tribute-and-class-in-tarascan-commodity-consumption-the-lake-patzcuaro-basin/.

Pollard, Helen Perlstein, and Laura Cahue. 1999. 'Mortuary Patterns of Regional Elites in the Lake Pátzcuaro Basin of Western Mexico.' *Latin American Antiquity* 10 (3): 259-280.

Pollard, Helen and David Haskell. 2006. 'Proyecto Erongarícuaro. Informe técnico parcial. Temporada II.' México DF: Consejo de Arqueología, Instituto Nacional de Antropología e Historia.

Pollard, Helen Perlstein, and Dorothy K. Washburn. 2017. 'Burial Goods in the Lake Pátzcuaro Basin as Evidence of Social Change.' Paper presented at the annual Midwest Conference on Mesoamerican Archaeology and Ethnohistory, Wayne State University, Detroit, Michigan, March 11.

Pulido Méndez, Salvador. 2006. *Los Tarascos y Los Tarascos-Uacúsecha: Diferencias Sociales y Arqueológicas en un Grupo.* Colección Divulgación. México DF: Instituto Nacional de Antropología e Historia.

Rebnegger, Karin J. 2013. 'Obsidian consumption and Production in the Tarascan State.' PhD Diss., Michigan State University.

Smith, Michael E. and Francis F. Berdan. 2003. 'Postclassic Mesoamerica.' In *The Postclassic Mesoamerican World*, edited by Michael Smith and Francis Berdan, 1-13, Salt Lake City: University of Utah Press.

Stark, Barbara L. and Christopher P. Garraty. 2010. 'Detecting Marketplace Exchange in Archaeology: A Methodological Review.' In *Archaeological Approaches to Market Exchange in Ancient Societies*, edited by Christopher P. Garraty and Barbara L Stark, 33-58. Boulder: University Press of Colorado.

Stawski, Christopher James. 2008. 'Residential Zoning at Prehispanic Tzintzuntzan, Mexico Revisited: A Quantitative Analysis.' Master's thesis, Michigan State University.

Toledo, Victor M. 1991. 'Pátzcuaro's Lesson: Nature, Production, and Culture in an Indigenous Region of Mexico.' In *Biodiversity: Culture, Conservation, and Ecodevelopment*, edited by Margery L. Oldfield and Janis B. Alcorn, 147-171. Boulder: Westview Press.

Valdez, Francisco and Catherine Liot. 1994. 'La cuenca de Sayula: yacimientos de sal en la frontera oeste del estado tarasco.' In: *El Michoacán antiguo*, edited by Brigitte Boehm de Lameiras, 285-305. Zamora: El Colegio de Michoacán and El Gobierno del Estado de Michoacán.

Warren, J. Benedict. 1968. 'Minas de Cobre de Michoacan, 1533.' *Anales del Museo Michoacano, Series* 2 (6): 35-52.

Warren, J. Benedict. 1985. *The Conquest of Michoacán: The Spanish Domination of the Tarascan Kingdom in Western Mexico, 1521-1530.* Norman: University of Oklahoma Press.

Williams, Eduardo. 1999. 'The Ethnoarchaeology of Salt Production at Lake Cuitzeo, Michoacan, Mexico.' *Latin American Antiquity* 10 (4): 400-414.

# Chapter 5

# Forming Pots and Community: Pottery Production and Potter Interaction in an Ancestral Wendat Village

## Sarah Striker
Arizona State University; Sarah.Striker@asu.edu

## Linda Howie
HD Analytical Solutions/Western University; linda.howie@hdanalyticalsolutions.com

## Ronald Williamson
Archaeological Services Inc.; RWilliamson@asiheritage.ca

**Abstract**

*The Mantle site is a sixteenth century Ancestral Wendat settlement near Toronto, Ontario, Canada. The site, a large and well-planned village, emerged from a period of coalescence, which saw the integration of several smaller communities into a socially cohesive yet cosmopolitan settlement. The potters at Mantle likely came from diverse, perhaps even far-flung communities. Through their pottery, we can recognize a dynamic community of potters using a wide range of decorative styles and continuously refining technological practice. We compare two groups of pottery from the Mantle collection: 1) typical vessels that are characteristic in size, form, and decoration for Wendat sites of this period and comprise the bulk of Mantle pottery assemblage; and 2) 'learner vessels' that are conventionally interpreted as the products of beginner potters due to a combination of irregularities including small size, atypical form, poorly executed or atypical forming technique, and/or poorly executed or atypical decoration as compared to typical vessels. A petrographic study of these vessels show that a large proportion of both vessel types did not convincingly match raw material resources identified in the immediate vicinity of the site. We find that many vessels, especially those categorized as learner vessels, are evidence of both novices learning basic skills of the craft and ongoing learning and experimentation by more experienced potters. Experienced potters made expedient vessels to test local, possibly unfamiliar, raw materials while young potters learned fundamental techniques. We demonstrate how this pattern is the result of both the social and geological context in which Wendat potters were practicing their craft. This case study illustrates how pottery marks community integration, how resource availability prompts innovation, and elucidates the training of new potters as they create culturally-informed products.*

**Key words**
*Ceramic petrography, ceramic provenance, communities of practice, skill, archaeology of children, Wendat, Iroquoian*

## Introduction

Atypical ceramic vessels that are thought to be the work of children or inexperienced potters learning how to make pottery are common finds at Iroquoian village sites. At the Mantle site, these atypical vessels exhibit considerable variation across the criteria that form the basis of their identification. Some are small, crudely made pinch pots bearing direct evidence that they were made by children such as tiny fingerprints and/or finger nail impressions. Others are comparatively small but with well-executed forms and decorative elements as compared to typical vessels – those vessels identified as characteristic of Wendat sites of this period in form, size, and decoration. Many of these atypical vessels have undecorated, and often crudely smoothed surfaces or only simple, often unevenly rendered decoration. While use-wear evidence relating to cooking or heating was not recorded consistently as categorical data in the original analysis, subsequent detailed inspection by Striker determined that none of the juvenile vessels displayed evidence of having been used for cooking.

Despite the variability of the category, we have grouped these vessels together – as is common practice in Iroquoian ceramic studies – and adopt the term 'learner vessels' following Dorland (2016a, 2016b), although the terms 'juvenile' and 'novice' vessels are also common in the Iroquoian literature. We acknowledge, as other scholars do (e.g., Braun 2012; Dorland 2016a, 2016b, 2017; Martelle 2002; Smith 1998), that the distinction between learner and typical vessels is problematic as it is not based on a consistently applied set of criteria and ignores differences in intended function. Miniature vessels made for special uses and vessels made expediently by skilled potters for purposes that did not require higher quality such as raw material testing or for short term use all exhibit similar characteristics. Our objective is to extend understanding of the variation within this problematic category and how it relates to the learning process by examining and comparing the compositional characteristics of the ceramic bodies and what they reveal about clay selection and tempering practices, as a realm of know-how that must be learned. Using petrographic analysis by Howie, we compare clay and temper choices in pottery previously identified as learner-made with clay and temper choices for typical vessels. The approach developed here allows us to explore the nuances of how, where, and when learning about different aspects of pottery production took place, and to identify skills that may have been especially important for novice Mantle potters to develop as they become proficient in their craft.

*The Mantle Community*

Mantle is an early sixteenth century Wendat village located near Toronto, Ontario. The Wendat are 'Iroquoian,' which refers to both a cultural pattern and a linguistic family, the latter of which includes the Northern Iroquoians of the Great Lakes Region as well as Cherokee, spoken in the southern Appalachians, and Tuscarora, spoken near the mid-Atlantic coast. The essential elements of the Iroquoian cultural pattern were a primary reliance on horticulture for subsistence, villages containing bark-covered longhouses shared by (usually matrilineal) related extended families, clan membership extending beyond each village to other communities, which integrated villages within tribes and confederacies, and a set of shared governance structures and religious practices (Trigger 1976, 91-104). This pattern is not fully recognizable archaeologically until the turn of the fourteenth century (e.g., Engelbrecht 2003; Warrick 2000, 2008; Williamson 2012).

Mantle is one of the latest villages in a long sequence of continuous occupation in the Rouge-Duffins river drainage from Middle Woodland times (ca. BC 200-500 AD) through the mid-to-late sixteenth century. Settlement pattern and ceramic analyses have been used to trace the movement of a single community from the small dispersed villages of the mid-fourteenth century to the Draper, Spang and finally Mantle sites (see Birch 2010a, 2010b; Birch and Williamson 2013a). Prior to the mid-fifteenth century, Wendat communities in the north shore area were typically small and consisted of four to nine longhouses; some like the Alexandra site reflect reoccupation over long periods of time (Williamson 2014, 19). Each river drainage was occupied by a few of these small, matrilineal communities. By the mid-fifteenth century, these communities were aggregating. This aggregation was probably due to several factors although clear evidence for substantial interpersonal violence (Jenkins 2016); Williamson 2007) and the construction of large palisades along with defensive village locations suggest that the threat of violence was a major concern. Communities may, therefore, have come together in part for defense. In the Rouge-Duffins drainage, aggregation is documented at the Draper site, which expanded several times during its occupation (Finlayson 1985). With each expansion, a cluster of longhouses was added, each approximately the same size as one of the earlier communities found in the same area. The community may have then relocated to the Spang site although it has only been subject to limited excavations (Birch and Williamson 2013a, 61-62), so its position in this sequence is less certain. Recent work by Jennifer Birch suggests that Spang was potentially more spatially integrated than the Draper site (Birch 2016).

By the early sixteenth century, the community had moved again and established the Mantle village. Mantle is remarkable for its size (3 ha) and the complexity of the village plan. Unlike at the Draper site, where each village segment maintained some spatial separation, the Mantle site was well integrated. Houses were systematically organized, with the longhouses in the center of the site built radially around a central plaza. This evidence suggests that at the time of construction, social mechanisms were in place to support the cooperation of a larger group of people (Birch 2010a, 2010b, 2012; Birch and Williamson 2013a, 2013b).

Jennifer Birch has redefined this process of aggregation and community integration as 'coalescence' (Birch 2010a, 2010b, 2012). Coalescence is a regional process of settlement nucleation that brings once-separate communities together in single, socially cohesive village (Kowalewski 2006). This transformation from small dispersed settlements to a few large but socially integrated communities has been observed among Iroquoian communities throughout Ontario and New York (Birch and Williamson 2013a). Coalescence also brings changes to the nature of interaction among neighboring communities (Kowalewski 2006). Where local interaction among those few closest communities in the same river drainage was once most important, longer distance and more varied contacts are seen at large communities like Mantle. The most obvious change is that 'local' communities who had come to live together had each brought their own interaction networks. Coalescent communities also tend to attract long-distance relationships, possibly because of their large size and increasing sociopolitical complexity (Kowalewski 2006, 117).

There is evidence for these changes at Mantle, suggesting significant social shifts (Birch and Williamson 2013b). The Mantle ceramic assemblage has evidence of interaction with a greater number of distant groups rather than more intensive interaction with a select group of neighbors. For example, there is a greater diversity of pottery decorative types present in the Mantle assemblage than at earlier sites though they are represented by fewer vessels (Birch and Williamson 2013a, 138-140; Birch et al. 2016). The exact nature of this interaction is not yet clear. One key question is to what extent people from distant communities were coming to live at Mantle versus simply exchanging materials with Mantle residents. At least some of the pottery, especially those vessels with non-local decoration, appears to have been made elsewhere – especially from the St. Lawrence River Valley area and New York State (ASI 2012). While the clays and tempers used to make many of these non-local decorative types do not match samples collected from around the Mantle site, we have not yet identified their sources (Howie 2012).

**Community of Practice at Mantle**

Learning craft production cannot be divorced from the situation in which the activity is practiced (see Crown 2014). Lave and Wenger (1991) describe this process as 'situated learning' which develops through continuous, sustained interactions with others as part of a community of practice (a group of people who share a craft). Learning is conceptualized not as a transfer of knowledge from more skilled workers to novices, but as the gradually increasing participation of an individual in a community of practice. As individuals continue to work together, they play a greater role in the development of community knowledge.

Making pottery is a complex process requiring specialized knowledge at each stage of production. Members of communities of practice share information about situations that they encounter and the solutions they devise, alone or as part of a group. As this new information is shared, it becomes community knowledge. Novices are integrated into this process gradually, contributing more new knowledge as their own experience grows. Consequently, communities of practice develop certain ways of doing things – processing temper, forming, applying decorations – that their members share (Gosselain 2000). Often, their practice is one of many possible methods for completing the same step in the task. Archaeologists commonly identify members of a community of practice by identifying shared techniques in the finished pottery they produce (e.g., Herbich 1987; Neuzil 2005; Parkinson 2006; Stark 1998; Stark, et al. 2000).

We would expect that the knowledge shared by a community of practice would be shaped by the context in which its members practice their craft. Part of this context is social (e.g., intra-group dynamics, organization of production, relationships with other potting communities), but context can also be technological (e.g., specific challenges for potters working in a given environment, available raw materials, desired characteristics of finished objects). Here, we consider the importance of context for interpreting variability in a pottery assemblage that includes both learner and typical adult vessels. Our focus is the social and geological context as each significantly shaped pottery practice at Mantle.

Ethnohistorical analogy suggests that a community like Mantle was comprised of several clans that would have functioned as a social integrative force for the various extended matrilineal families within the village. Representatives of each clan could have been part of a village council. Clans may have been important units of production and likely had their own trade relationships. In this social setting, households and clans would have been essential contexts within which craft production took place (Birch and Williamson 2013a, 2013b).

Although there are extensive historical accounts of life in Iroquoian villages, pottery-making is rarely discussed. Descriptions by Boucher, Sagard, and Lafitau note that pottery was made by women and Sagard describes in some detail vessel forming using a paddle and anvil technique (cited in Martelle 2002, 6-9). It is not clear to what degree potters at the Mantle site were integrated as a single community of practice. Potters from the same household or clan may have worked together or the potters of the entire village may have worked collectively, particularly for laborious, time-consuming tasks like extracting and transporting raw materials (natural clays, tempering materials and water) to work areas, processing clays and tempers and preparing paste mixtures, and preparing for firing where a 'group effort' might have been more expedient.

Ethnohistoric sources indicate that subsistence pursuits such as hunting (e.g., Biggar 1922, 60-61, 82-85), fishing (e.g., Wrong 1922, 81) and planting and harvesting were carried out by men's and women's work parties respectively, and organized at the lineage level. Sometimes, the entire village would come together to accomplish a task such as house building (e.g., Wrong 1968, 81). Pottery production or specific stages of manufacture might have been similarly organized. If Mantle potters did work together during any or all stages of the manufacturing process, close social ties among members of the same household or clan may have influenced which potters worked together, as well as the specific approaches and procedures followed by individual potters. Newcomers, if present, may have brought new ideas or techniques with them.

## Clay and Temper Choice and the Geological Environment of Southern Ontario

The geological environment is also an important influence on how potters practice their craft. The composition and texture of clays and tempers used to make pottery contribute to the physical and mechanical performance characteristics of the vessels made from them. In regions where potters consistently use the same raw material sources or parent materials, this task may be quite straightforward. For novices, learning this skill might require simply becoming familiar with source locations, processing procedures and desired sensory or physical characteristics. In Ontario, the geology is extremely variable, so potters moving about the landscape might encounter many natural clay deposits and potential tempering agents during their everyday activities, each with significantly different observable characteristics.

The bedrock geology of Ontario can be divided into two broad types based on age: the Precambrian crystalline igneous, sedimentary and metamorphic rocks that form the Canadian Shield and are exposed in the north, and the younger Paleozoic and Mesozoic sedimentary rocks (primarily clastic carbonate rocks and shales) that subsequently developed in the large marine basin bordering the Shield in the south (Thurston 1991). The varying topography of southern Ontario, ranging from flat plains to rolling uplands and uplands intersected by ridges and escarpments, reflects a complex history of extensive pre-Quaternary erosion and Quaternary glaciation, which both infilled and eroded the preglacial land surface (Baldwin *et al.* 2000). During the last glacial period (ca. 110,00 to ca. 11,700 BP) periodic advances and retreats of ice sheets severely altered the geography of the region, scouring and sculpting the land and transporting, comminuting and depositing material. In the Toronto region, successive deposition of layers of sediments ultimately formed till deposits up to 200 m thick on top of the Paleozoic bedrock (Eyles and Eyles 2004).

Glacial sedimentary deposits are widespread and unevenly distributed across the landscape (Figure 1). Ice sheets essentially act as giant 'conveyor belts' picking up, carrying and depositing material as they advance and retreat (Boulton *et al.* 1985). As they advanced southward they brought transported material from the north – much of it igneous and metamorphic rock from the Canadian Shield. These unsorted rock debris and sediments were dragged along under the ice, mixed with younger carbonate and other sedimentary rock picked up along the way, and deposited in long drumlins or pushed along the front edge of the advancing sheet and deposited in ridges called moraines. Flowing water from ice melt created streams, rivers and lakes which deposited a variety of comparatively well-sorted sediments in the form of eskers (well-sorted and cross-bedded sand and gravels), kames (mounds of stratified till) and varved lake and pond sediments (repetitive contrasting layers of sandy, silty or clayey material). The result of this movement, comminution and mixing of material is sediments consisting of a 'mixed bag' rock and mineral assemblage, derived from both Shield and younger sedimentary rock formations, often with a significant carbonate rock derived component.

This palimpsest of compositionally and texturally varying glacial landforms, along with ongoing erosion, sedimentation and deposition since the Holocene, created distinctive soil complexes (Baldwin *et al.* 2000). The implication is that the clayey soils formed in different localities on the landscape – all natural clays potentially suitable for pottery production – often differ in their specific textural and compositional properties, reflecting parent material contributions and soil-formation-related characteristics specific to their genesis and history. These differentiable natural clays may be in close proximity on the landscape, however, and share the same general mineralogy. For example, a natural clay formed in a varved glacial lake bottom versus a recent streambed or a sandy moraine deposit will have different characteristics, but the mineralogy of the rock and mineral clasts they contain might be very similar (Figure 2).

Quantifying this variability for south-central Ontario alone is difficult. Clay, gravel and shale deposits are well mapped for the region surrounding Mantle due to a major aggregate and clay industry (e.g., Guillet 1967, 1977; Guillet and Joyce 1987; Hewitt and Cowan 1969). Additionally, the Oak Ridges Moraine, situated to the north of the Mantle site, overlies an important aquifer system and has been studied in considerable detail (Sharpe *et al.* 1999; Sharpe and Russel 2016). These studies, however, only map boundaries between major geological units, formations and landforms and describe general lithological and textural variation. Local variability can be considerable, which is noted, but this variation is not documented and described in the detail desired for artifact provenance studies. For example, published lithological assessments of the gravel and sand in different areas of the Oak Ridges Moraine

# Chapter 5 Forming Pots and Community

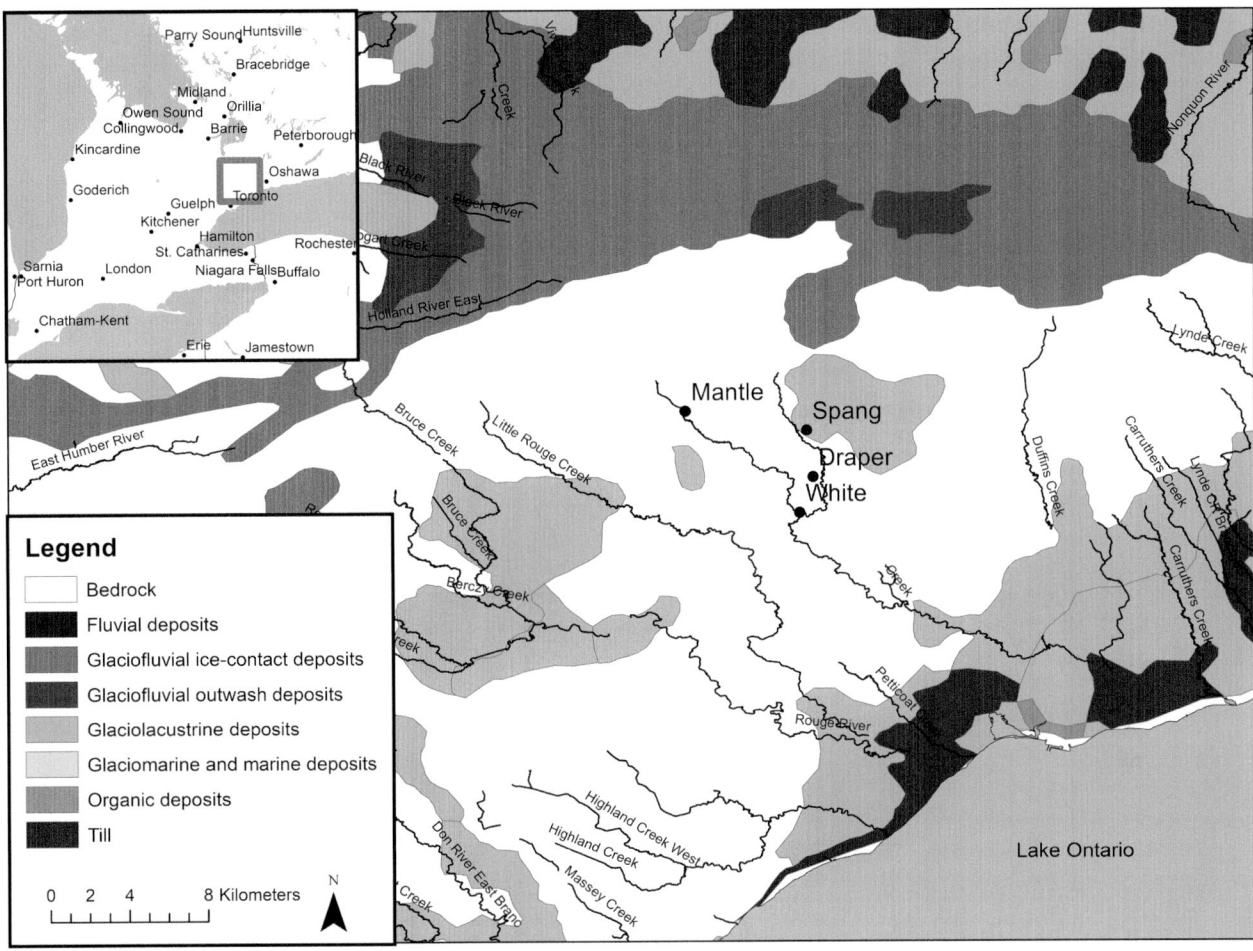

Figure 1. Surficial geology of south-central Ontario. Data from the Ontario Geological Survey (1997), Esri, TomTom and contains information licensed under the Open Government Licence – Canada

(Hewitt and Cowan 1969) report pebble assemblages consisting of varying quantities of limestone, dolomite, shale, siltstone, acid igneous, basic igneous and metamorphic rock, presented as relative frequencies (flood, common, rare, very rare, trace) and specific types of igneous metamorphic and carbonate rock are not distinguished. Geologists and soil scientists are interested in a different scale of variability so archaeological studies require additional geological sampling, ideally based on visual, tactile and other characteristics that might have mattered to potters. For example, we conducted a comparative study of the macro and microscopic characteristics of clays and sediments that form in two different environments in the immediate vicinity of the Mantle site, and observed significant textural and compositional differences, even between samples taken different areas of the same deposit and separated by less than one meter.

In a landscape like south-central Ontario we would expect that potters would encounter many clays in their daily activities – especially while travelling to and working in the maize fields. Birch and Williamson estimate that by the end of the occupation of the Mantle site, the distance from the edge of the maize fields to the village would have been approximately 1.6 km in any direction (Birch and Williamson 2013a, 99-100). By that estimate, women working the fields would be regularly walking, exploring, and digging in around 8 km² of land. Moving every 25 years or so to a new village situated only a few kilometers away, as this community did in their move from Draper to Spang and then Mantle, might also mean potters would have encountered many geographically separated clay sources exhibiting a wide range of textural and compositional properties within their lifetime.

Ethnoarchaeological studies demonstrate that potters do not select clays and tempers at random (Costin 2000, 380) and although potters tend to use nearby resources – most communities of potters travel no farther than 5km for primary ceramic raw materials (Arnold 1985; 2015, 16) – there is far more to raw material selection than proximity to where you live. Natural variability in clay sources leading to inconsistent behaviors, decisions about desired performance characteristics of finished vessels, cultural preferences, energy required to procure resources, restrictions on access, the organization and technology of procurement, processing requirements and fabrication strategies *all* influence raw material selection criteria, and consequently, the relationship between raw materials and the end characteristics of finished ceramic bodies (Costin 2000, 380-381). Among modern potters, experimenting with the performance characteristics of different clay types, paste recipes and how theses can be manipulated/altered to achieve desired ends is an important part of learning how to become a competent potter (Muller and Zamek 2011; Pitelka 2001; Zakin 1990). We would expect that in an environment in which a potter might encounter many different clay resources in their lifetime, that this would constitute essential knowledge to learn, and therefore would have been an important facet of community knowledge.

**Ceramic Petrography of Vessels from the Mantle Site**

With this social and geological context in mind, we compare the clay selection and tempering practices associated with learner and typical pottery found at the Mantle site. A total of 1992 identifiable typical vessels were found at Mantle and another 193 were identified as learner vessels based on their comparatively small size, the quality of execution of forming and finishing, forming technique, and the nature and quality of execution of decorative embellishments (surface and morphological). Sherd counts were obtained from different anatomical areas of a vessel, surface treatments recorded, decorative treatments and morphological embellishments (e.g., castellations) were recorded for sherds with intact rims, and analyzable sherds were assigned type designations using ASI's standard procedures following MacNeish (1952).

Petrographic analysis of 62 rim and partial vessel fragments from the Mantle site was undertaken by Howie. Nineteen of these fragments were from learner vessels. The objectives of this study were to: 1) investigate compositional variability within the ceramic assemblage, 2) to document technological and provenance characteristics of vessels and, 3) to identify vessels produced locally, based on compatibility with geological samples taken from the immediate vicinity of the site. Vessel fragments selected for analysis were chosen at random from the total assemblage with the aim of sampling across the range of variation in skill level and provenience (association with architectural and cultural features). Sampling of the typical vessel assemblage was random and stratified by decorative type and provenience. Natural clay samples were collected from the vicinity of the site by Andrea Carnevale (ASI) and Williamson. These samples derive from exposed clay deposits located along on the east and west banks of the creek adjacent to the site. Samples were taken from different localities within the larger exposed deposit to capture the range of variation observed in textural and compositional characteristics. These natural clay samples provide a comparative baseline of locally available clays for the ceramic samples. They provide evidence of both the nature of naturally occurring mineral and rock assemblages and characteristics of clays formed along a water course adjacent to the site.

Thin section petrography is well-established as a powerful and effective means of analyzing compositional variation among pottery vessels on the microscopic level, and of differentiating and characterizing them according to the geological characteristics of the raw materials used in their production (e.g. Bishop *et al.* 1982; Freestone 1991; Peacock 1970; Shepard 1956; Shotton and Hendry 1979; Whitbread 1995). These data, once integrated with comparative geological information enables the analyst to predict, or in some cases to identify, parent raw materials or geographic source areas. The methods employed in this study follow the descriptive system developed by Whitbread (1989; 1995, 365-396) specifically for the examination and characterization of 'ceramic fabrics'.

As used by Whitbread (1995, 368), the term ceramic fabric refers to the arrangement, size, shape, frequency and composition of components of a ceramic material, and encompasses a broad range of compositional attributes relating to its geological, mineralogical, textural and microstructural characteristics. These attributes not only describe the types and frequency of the rock and mineral fragments present, but also the nature of the clay matrix, the character, spatial distribution and frequency of voids, mineral and organic inclusions, and features relating to soil genesis and formation processes, as well as the interrelationships of these different components. The strength of the descriptive system approach is that it permits examination and comparison of multiple aspects of technology, including the treatment of raw materials, paste recipes, forming techniques and firing methods (Freestone 1991; Whitbread 1989, 1995, 1996; Tomkins *et al.* 2004). This information not only informs about production methods, but also variation in technical practices, enabling an additional basis for differentiating pottery vessels according to technological criteria (i.e., fabrication processes), even when they are mineralogically similar. These broader descriptive criteria acknowledge the inherent complexity and composite nature of ceramic bodies, that they are 'human-made' materials and, consequently, that fabric properties not only reflect geological characteristics of the raw materials used to create them, but also human habit/choice in manufacturing procedures. Viewed from this perspective, ceramic fabrics not only document how people made their pottery, but are material expressions of group identity and interaction, including transference of knowledge.

Thin sections of geological and pottery samples were prepared using standard procedures. A sample approximately 1cm thick was cut from the rim to neck area, perpendicular to the vessel lip. All samples were impregnated with epoxy resin under vacuum conditions. Impregnated sample blocks were ground and polished on a lap wheel and mounted to glass slides with a UV curing optical adhesive. The slide-mounted samples were trimmed to a 1-2 mm thickness, lapped and polished to a uniform 30 micron end thickness and covered with a glass coverslip.

The geological samples were evaluated using an adapted form of Whitbread's descriptive system for ceramics. The objective of this approach, which is not standard practice in ceramic petrography, was to define essential textural, compositional and mineralogical characteristics, thereby facilitating a direct and meaningful comparison with the archaeological samples using a single set of criteria. This treatment also aided the identification of added temper in the ceramic fabrics and evidence of raw material processing. As the geological samples all derive from exposed deposits bordering a creek, they provide evidence of the characteristics of natural clays that form in this specific environmental context and provide a basis for identification of locally produced pottery on geological grounds. We acknowledge that our 'local geological baseline', as presently defined, is far from complete and offers a restricted view of the diversity of natural clays. It has proved useful, however, as a general guide, enabling a more nuanced understanding of the pottery samples than would be possible otherwise.

The compositional characteristics of the six samples of natural clay (MC2-MC7) collected from the immediate vicinity of the Mantle site are summarized in Tables 1 and 2, and exemplary photomicrographs are presented in Figure 3. There are significant differences among the samples from different localities within the deposits in terms of their textural characteristics, the physical characteristics and mineralogy of the rock and mineral inclusions they contain, as well as other compositional features such as the nature and prevalence of textural and amorphous concentration features. Three texturally and compositionally different clay sources can be differentiated, including a *silty clay*, two *fine sandy clays* and three *coarse sandy clays*. Characteristics that the clay samples share are:

1. The presence of calcitic inclusions, including lumps of micrite, limestone fragments and discrete grains and rhombic crystals of calcite.
2. A highly calcareous clay matrix as indicated by either optical properties of the clay domains or the abundance of silt-sized grains of crystalline calcite.
3. The general paucity of fragments of igneous rock, especially examples comprising quartz, feldspar and ferromagnesian minerals. In all the clay samples except MC3 and MC7, igneous rock fragments are rare to very rare and only in the case of MC3 do the fragments have a ferromagnesian mineral component (biotite and amphibole). It is also significant that in all the clay samples the igneous rock fragments exhibit an intermediate roundness (subangular to subrounded) and are never particularly angular (very angular to subangular).
4. The presence of fine (very-fine-sand to silt-sized), subrounded to rounded ferromagnesian mineral fragments (amphibole, pyroxene, olivine) and fine needle-like biotite laths.

These characteristics served as a comparative baseline for identification of pottery samples geologically compatible with the natural clay samples. They also aided the identification of tempering materials, intentionally added as a paste ingredient.

*Assemblage-Wide Patterns*

The petrographic analysis of the 62 pottery vessels revealed 11 compositionally distinct 'types' of ceramic bodies, which were broadly split into two groups based on the presence/absence of calcite inclusions and fragments of carbonate rock (Tables 1 and 2). Ceramic fabrics containing these inclusions (Group A) were identified as geologically compatible with natural clays that occur in the immediate vicinity of Mantle. Group B fabrics, do not contain these inclusions and are therefore geologically incompatible with the clay samples. Five compositionally and/or texturally distinct fabrics were distinguished among the pottery samples containing calcite and carbonate rock fragments (Group A) and two of these were found to contain temper intentionally added by the potter. In one case this is crushed igneous rock while in the other it is crushed limestone. Certain fabric types are strikingly similar to specific natural clay samples and may derive from the local deposits that were sampled (Table 1). In other cases, mineralogical similarity to the natural clays generally connects these pottery samples to the geology of local clay

| Fabric Type / Samples | Distinguishing Characteristics |
|---|---|
| | **Group A Fabrics:** mineralogically compatible with the natural clay samples from Mantle, containing calcitic inclusions (lumps of micrite, rhombic crystalline calcite spar (calcite crystals) and fragments of limestone) in addition to quartz, feldspar and small quantity of the ferromagnesian minerals biotite, amphibole and pyroxene. The fabric types, each unique in their own right, derive from compositionally different clay sources. |
| A-2<br><br>54 | **Occurrence:** 1 learner vessel<br>**Paste recipe:** a well sorted micritic clay (rich in micrite) containing rounded, fine- to medium-sand-sized inclusions of monocrystalline quartz, feldspar, micrite and a small quantity of biotite, amphibole, pyroxene and olivine, tempered with crushed limestone. Limestone temper is a bioclastic limestone comprising crystalline shell structures and crystalline calcite spar in a micritic cement.<br>**Distinguished by:** 1) the presence of the limestone temper, 2) the complete absence of igneous rock fragments a<br>**Geological Associations:** textural and compositional characteristic of the clay component are comparable to clay sample MC2. The limestone temper It is comparable to limestone clasts observed in the local coarse sandy clays (MC3, MC6 and MC7) |
| A-3<br><br>58, 59 | **Occurrence:** 2 learner vessels<br>**Paste recipe:** an untempered, non-uniform mixture of texturally different clay, possibly a lensed clay. One component is a well sorted, fine-textured, sandy, calcareous (calcium carbonate rich) clay containing abundant, very-fine-sand-sized, angular inclusions of monocrystalline quartz and feldspar, and a small quantity of biotite, amphibole, pyroxene olivine and calcite (micrite and discrete grains); the other is a poorly sorted calcareous clay containing comparatively few inclusions, predominantly subangular to rounded inclusions of monocrystalline quartz, feldspar, micrite, and limestone, the size of which ranges from very coarse to very fine sand, and a small quantity of ferromagnesian minerals (same as above) and mudstone clasts. Channel voids border the areas of sandy clay, which occurs as bands and swirls within the clay component containing fewer inclusions.<br>**Distinguished by:** a clay consisting of two, texturally different, yet mineralogically similar components, 2) the paucity of igneous rock fragments and the complete absence of large angular fragments of any rock or mineral<br>**Geological Associations:** compositional, mineralogical and textural characteristic of the fine-textured, sandy component are comparable to the samples of local fine sandy clay (MC4 and MC5). The mineralogical and compositional characteristics of the poorly sorted component are comparable to the samples of coarse sandy clay (especially MC3), except it contain significantly fewer rock and mineral inclusions and granule to very coarse-sand sized inclusions, although present, are comparatively infrequent. |
| A-4<br><br>57 | **Occurrence:** 1 learner vessel<br>**Paste Recipe:** an untempered, poorly sorted, sandy clay containing abundant silt-sized grains of crystalline calcite, coarse to medium sand sized inclusions monocrystalline quartz, feldspar, micritic limestone and crystalline calcite, a small quantity of ferromagnesian minerals (amphibole, pyroxene, olivine and biotite) and igneous rock fragments.<br>**Distinguished by :**1) a clay matrix dominated by silt-sized grains of crystalline calcite, 2) the complete absence of large angular fragments of any rock or mineral, 3) a paucity of igneous rock fragments, and 4) the rarity of biotite inclusions.<br>**Geological Associations:** comparable to the coarse sandy clay sample MC3, as the clay matrix is dominated by silt-sized grains of crystalline calcite. The size distribution of inclusions is different: granule sized inclusions are absent and very coarse sand sized inclusions are comparatively infrequent. This textural difference might be interpreted as resulting from clay processing (e.g. sieving or screening) to remove unwanted and inappropriately large inclusions. |
| A-5<br><br>60 | **Occurrence:** 1 learner vessel<br>**Paste recipe:** an untempered, highly micritic, fine-textured clay containing abundant rounded lumps of micrite, as well as monocrystalline quartz, feldspar and crystalline calcite inclusions, a small quantity of ferromagnesian mineral inclusions (biotite, amphibole, pyroxene and olivine) and igneous rock fragments.<br>**Distinguished by:** 1) the abundance of fine sand sized lumps of micrite, 2) a crystallitic micromass, dominated by crystallites of calcite. 3) the presence of clay segregation and accumulation features, giving the fabric a 'striped' appearance, and 4) the complete absence of large angular fragments of any rock or mineral.<br>**Geological Associations:** similar mineralogy to local clays but texturally and compositionally distinctive. |

Table 1. Distinguishing characteristics of Group A ceramic fabrics groups that include learner vessels (see also Howie 2012)

resources. However, differences in textural and compositional characteristics and the physical properties of the rock and mineral inclusions in comparison to both the clay samples and the other fabrics in Group A, suggest these derive from compositionally distinct clay deposits, likely in the local area, that were not sampled.

| Fabric Type / Samples | Distinguishing Characteristics |
|---|---|
| \multicolumn{2}{l}{Group B Fabrics: mineralogically incompatible with the natural clay samples from Mantle as they do not contain calcitic inclusions (lumps of micrite, crystalline calcite and fragments of limestone). Rock and mineral assemblages vary. Presence of olivine in the clay components is distinctive. The fabric types, each unique in their own right, derive from compositionally different clay sources.} |
| B-1<br><br>62 | **Occurrence:** 4 typical and 1 learner vessel (untempered variant)<br>**Paste Recipe:** a well sorted, fine-textured, sandy clay containing abundant, rounded fine to very fine sand sized inclusions of monocrystalline quartz and feldspar, and a small quantity of amphibole, pyroxene biotite and olivine, tempered with crushed igneous rock. With one exception, the parent rock is biotite granite.<br>**Distinguished by:** 2) the textural characteristics of the clay component – inclusions are abundant, well sorted, and predominantly the size of fine to very fine sand, resulting in a fine sandy texture, and s) the nature of concentrations features in the clay component – presence of clay pellets present and a greater quantity of iron rich nodules.<br>**Untempered variant:** This fabric is distinguished from the main group by: 1) fewer voids (5-15% of total field of view), 2) the size distribution of inclusions (unimodal); and 3) complete absence of igneous rock fragments (temper).<br>**Geological Associations:** mineralogically incompatible with Mantle clay samples |
| B-2<br><br>47, 55 | **Occurrence:** 7 typical and 2 learner vessels<br>**Paste Recipe:** as poorly sorted, sandy clay containing rounded very coarse to very fine sand sized inclusions of monocrystalline quartz and feldspar, as well as a small quantity of amphibole, pyroxene, biotite and olivine, tempered with crushed igneous rock. In all samples but two, the parent material is biotite granite.<br>**Distinguished by:** 1) the textural characteristics of the clay component – inclusions are poorly sorted and rounded, with a wide range of sizes present, contains common iron rich impregnative clay segregation features; 2) abundant, large igneous rock fragments and 3) the prevalence of inclusions surrounded or partially surrounded by a channel void, reflecting the distinctive shrinkage properties of the clay used.<br>**Geological Associations:** mineralogically incompatible with Mantle clay samples |
| B-3<br><br>46, 51 | **Occurrence:** 8 typical and 2 learner vessels<br>**Paste Recipe:** a comparatively smooth-textured, quartz-rich clay containing abundant, rounded inclusions of monocrystalline quartz, in addition to rounded feldspar inclusions and a smaller quantity of amphibole, pyroxene, biotite, and olivine, tempered with crushed igneous rock. The parent material is granodiorite in most samples.<br>**Distinguished by:** 1) the textural characteristics of the clay component – it contains comparative few inclusions and these are poorly sorted and rounded, with a wide range of sizes present, and 2) the greater quantity of ferromagnesian minerals (amphibole, pyroxene and olivine) present in the clay component.<br>**Geological Associations:** mineralogically incompatible with Mantle clay samples |
| B-4<br><br>45, 52<br><br>44, 48, 56<br><br>48, 50, 61 | **Occurrence:** 8 typical and 9 learner vessels (identical to typical = 3; textural variant = 3; untempered variant = 3)<br>**Paste Recipe:** a mixture of texturally different clay, possibly a lensed clay, tempered with crushed igneous rock (predominantly granodiorite and rarely granite or diorite). One matrix component a well sorted, fine-textured, sandy clay containing abundant, very-fine-sand-sized, angular inclusions of monocrystalline quartz and feldspar, as well as a small quantity of ferromagnesian minerals (biotite, amphibole, pyroxene and olivine); the other is a poorly sorted clay containing comparatively few and predominantly rounded inclusions of the same minerals.<br>**Distinguished by:** 1) a clay consisting of two, texturally different, yet mineralogically similar components; 2) high level of variation among the fabrics with regard to their specific textural, physical, compositional and microstructural characteristics.<br>**Textural variant:** these fabrics contain comparative few igneous rock fragments (temper) and the parent material is granite as opposed to granodiorite in 44 and 56.<br>**Untempered variant:** these fabrics are distinguished by a complete absence of igneous rock fragments (temper)<br>**Geological Associations:** mineralogically incompatible with Mantle clay samples |
| B-6<br><br>53 | **Occurrence:** 1 typical and 1 learner vessel<br>**Paste Recipe:** a well sorted, sandy clay containing rounded inclusions of quartz and feldspar, as well as and a small quantity of ferromagnesian minerals (biotite, amphibole, pyroxene and olivine) and rhyolite, tempered with crushed granodiorite<br>**Distinguished by:** 1) the abundance of temper and the extensive processing of the parent rock to produce a predominance of terminal grades of the constituent minerals, 2) the roundedness of the inclusions in the clay component, and 4) the presence rhyolite fragments in the clay component.<br>**Geological Associations:** mineralogically incompatible with Mantle clay samples |

Table 2. Distinguishing characteristics of Group B ceramic fabrics groups that include learner vessels
(see also Howie 2012)

Roughly two thirds (43/62) of the vessels analyzed are mineralogically incompatible with the natural clay samples (Group B) because they do not contain calcite inclusions and/or carbonate rock fragments. This means that the clays used to make these ceramic bodies are compositionally different from those that occur in the immediate vicinity of the Mantle site. Six compositionally and/or texturally distinct fabrics are evident. Additionally, in each case, the characteristics of the clay component of the fabric, including the physical properties and prevalence of natural rock and mineral fragments are distinct enough to suggest that each derives from a different clay source. Specific mineralogical differences among the fabric types suggest a connection to different, and perhaps geographically separated, geological environments.

It is important to note, however, that although the pottery with Group B fabrics are geologically incompatible with the local clay samples in important respects, we cannot conclude that they all derive from 'non-local' and/or geographically *distant* clay sources. Figure 2 shows the distribution of calcareous (containing calcite and/or carbonate rock deriving components) and non-calcareous soils around the Mantle site. Most of the surrounding area consists of calcareous soils, but non-calcareous soils occur in localized areas (gray areas on the map). These are areas where a mixture of distinct soil complexes occur. It is therefore possible that non-calcareous natural clays do occur in the local area, but have not been identified and sampled. Nonetheless, at least some of the vessels with Group B fabrics most likely derive from a longer distance away, as their mineralogical distinctiveness coincides with non-local decorative elements.

All the fabric types represented by multiple samples contain crushed igneous rock intentionally added as temper, with two main fabric types containing the large majority of the samples analyzed. Although there are differences

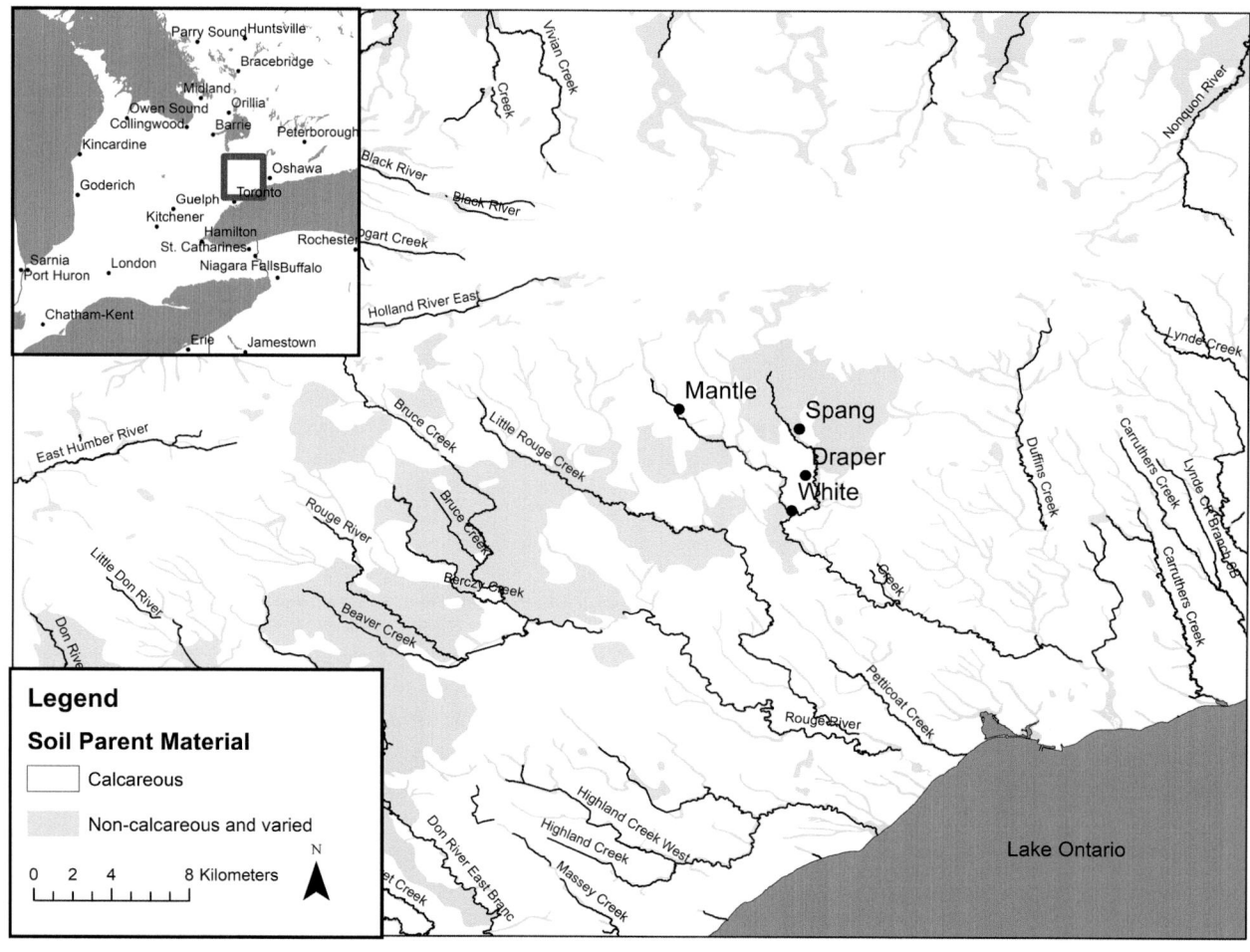

Figure 2. Soil parent material composition of south-central Ontario. Data from soil surveys of York (Hoffman and Richards 1955) and Ontario (Olding, Wicklund and Richards 1956) Counties, Esri, TomTom, and contains information licensed under the Open Government Licence – Canada

among, and less commonly within, fabric types in terms of the specific type or types of igneous rock that was ground up and used, it is significant that potters consistently chose igneous rock – granite, granodiorite, diorite – rather than other available options, such as limestone (a preference also observed by Braun 2015). In an area of glacial till, where igneous and metamorphic rocks, combined, make up less than 20% of deposits, this choice is highly significant; limestone is more abundant and more easily crushed. The identification of crushed rock temper was based on several considerations: a bimodal size distribution of inclusions, with an upper mode consisting of comparatively large-sized, angular, igneous rock and related mineral fragments; an uneven distribution of these clasts across the thin section; and the occurrence of these poorly sorted, angular rock and mineral clasts, alongside well sorted, comparatively rounded, naturally occurring mineral grains. In many instances, the fabric types with crushed igneous rock temper tend to contain either granite – a light-coloured rock – or granodiorite or diorite – both darker coloured rocks. Additionally, only very rarely were multiple types of igneous rock observed together in a sample. The use of granite versus granodiorite or diorite as a tempering material could be interpreted as relating to a selection criteria based on visual characteristics due to the different color of these rocks. The presence of alteration products possibly caused by chemical weathering provides some evidence that the parent rocks derive from unconsolidated rock deposits such as gravel or till.

### Comparing the Learner and Typical Vessel Collections

The learner vessels, as a group, are highly variable in terms of their composition (Tables 1 and 2), which is consistent with Braun's petrographic observations at other local sites (Braun 2012, 2015). Some examples (n=5) are geologically compatible with the natural clay samples from Mantle, but the large majority (n=14/19) are not. Similarly, some learner vessel fabrics are identical to typical vessels (n=7), while the majority are either untempered and sparsely tempered variants or individually unique fabrics within the sample set.

### *Learner Vessel Fabrics Mineralogically Compatible with Mantle Clays (Group A)*

There are four compositionally distinct learner vessel fabric types which are mineralogically compatible with the natural clay samples from Mantle (Table 1). All four of these fabric types are exclusively associated with learner vessels; none of the typical vessels sampled have these fabrics. In three cases (fabric types A-2, A-4, and A-5), a single learner vessel is the only representative of the fabric type, meaning that these ceramic bodies are compositionally unique within the sample set. The natural clays used to make three of the vessels (fabric types A-2, A-3 and A4) are comparable to natural clay samples taken from Mantle and may derive from those specific deposits. In contrast, learner vessel 60 (fabric A-5) is mineralogically consistent with the natural clay samples, but it contains abundant micrite and distinctive segregation features related to soil genesis. These textural and compositional differences indicate that this clay was formed in a different environmental content, but the mineralogical similarity to the Mantle clay samples indicates a broad geological connection to the local raw material sources.

One of the Group A learner vessel fabrics (fabric type A-2) contains crushed bioclastic limestone temper; none of the other Group A learner vessels contain temper intentionally added by the potter. This limestone is comparable to fragments observed in the Mantle clay samples, suggesting that this raw material ingredient is available in the local area. The use of limestone is highly significant as this raw material type is readily available locally, but was only used rarely -- all of the other tempered vessels contain crushed igneous rock.

### *Learner Vessel Fabrics Mineralogically Incompatible with Mantle Clays (Group B)*

An equally complex pattern of highly variable vessel compositions is apparent among the learner vessels that are not mineralogically consistent with Mantle clays (Group B fabric types). Several compositionally distinct fabrics can be distinguished (Table 2). In some cases, (fabric types B-2, B-3 and B-6) the learner vessel fabrics are virtually identical to typical vessels. In three cases (vessels 44, 48 and 56), the learner vessel ceramic bodies appear to represent a comparatively sparsely tempered version of a typical vessel fabric, forming a textural variant, or subgroup, of fabric type B-4.

Vessels 49, 50, 61 (fabric type B-4) and 62 (fabric type B-1), are untempered variants of paste mixtures used to make typical vessels, which contain crushed igneous rock temper. In both cases, the untempered learner ceramic bodies are compositionally similar to tempered examples in all other respects, except for the absence of igneous rock fragments. Accordingly, these learner vessels were made using the same natural clays as typical vessels, but the paste recipe is significantly different as it does not include temper.

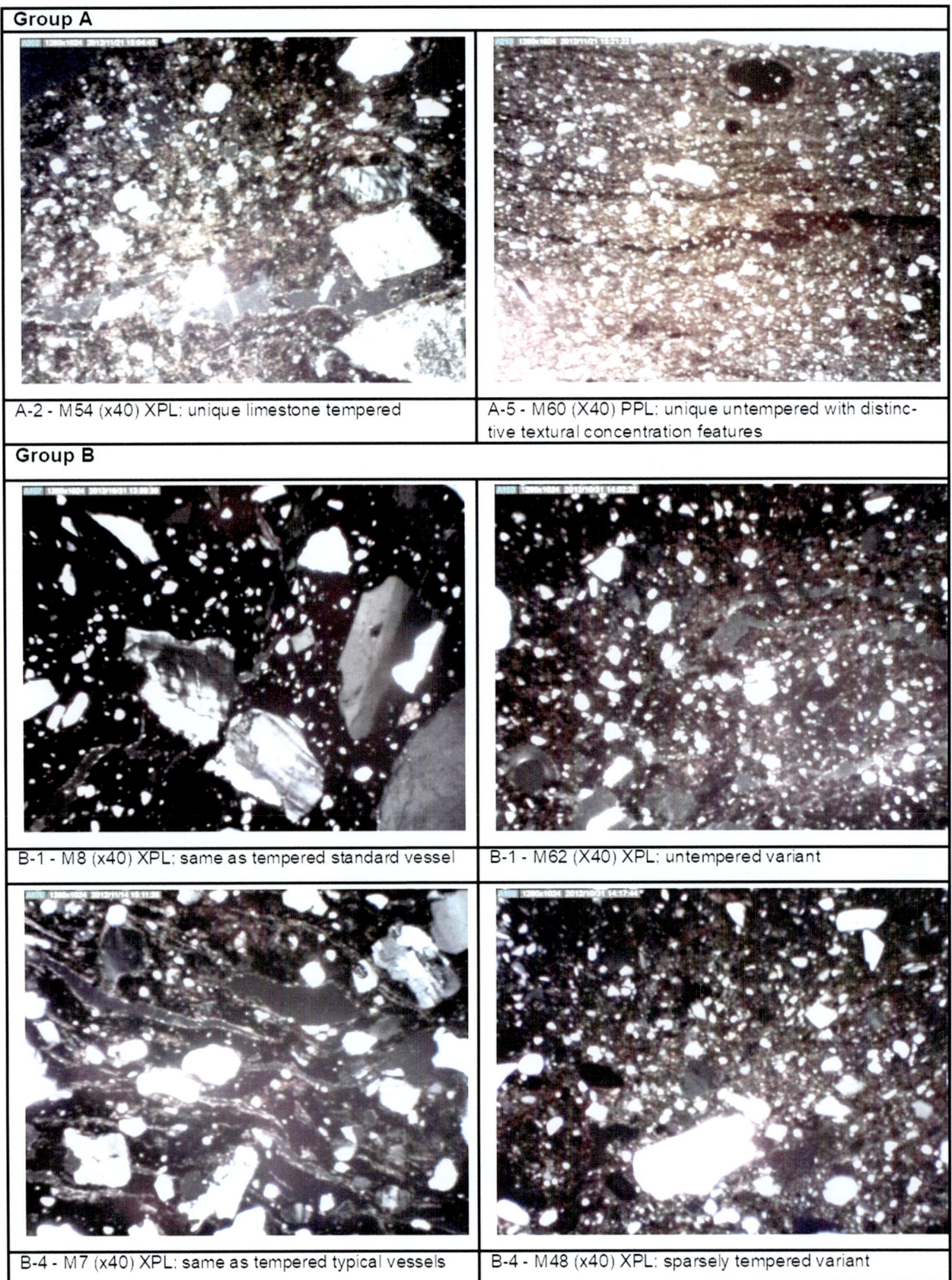

Figure 3. Learner vessel fabrics showing range of compositional variation observed
(see also Howie 2012)

When temper is present in the learner vessels with Group B fabric types, the parent material is always crushed igneous rock, generally of the same type observed in typical vessels with the same fabric type. Interestingly, in the case of vessels 44 and 56 (fabric type B-4), these learner vessel ceramic bodies contain a comparatively small amount of temper and the parent material is crushed granite. This difference is significant as the large majority of the tempered vessels with this fabric type contain crushed granodiorite.

**Pottery and Learning at the Mantle Site**

Considering what we know about the social and geological context of Mantle, the petrographic data suggest a range of different activities that could have been taking place. Rather than thinking of pots as examples of specific junctures in a progressive, accretionary learning process tied into explicit stages of vessel manufacture, it is perhaps more useful to consider what the sum of the compositional evidence tells us about the range of activities that were potentially part of pottery practice at Mantle. Communities of practice are contexts of continuous learning through doing. Therefore, individual vessels could reflect, at once, multiple aspects of both learning and the application of knowledge concerning raw material selection, paste preparation strategies and the desired characteristics of both raw materials and paste mixtures.

*Novices Learning*

Some vessels were made by novice potters. Learner vessels with fabrics virtually identical to typical vessels likely represent learning more focussed on working with pastes and vessel forming skills, perhaps in the context of a group potting session. In this case, we suspect a scenario in which a novice was given some of the prepared paste mixture that more experienced potters were working with and they made their own vessels. However, the evidence suggests that novice potters did not exclusively work with paste mixtures as prepared for the manufacture of typical pottery. Some learner vessels are clearly untempered or sparsely tempered versions of typical vessels. This provides evidence that novice potters were actively involved in paste preparation, or were at least on the scene when this activity was taking place. Sparsely tempered learner pottery could represent a novice's attempt to create a paste mixture, combining raw material ingredients to create a paste from which they, in turn, made a pot. Untempered learner vessel variants of typical vessels are evidence of working with the natural clays that were combined with crushed rock temper to make typical vessels. This exercise would have promoted a familiarity of the behavioral characteristics of natural clays versus paste mixtures, and untempered clay bodies could have provided contrasting examples of desired tactile and behavioral characteristics when compared to bodies made with paste mixtures.

Along the same lines, the occurrence of learner vessels containing crushed granite temper, when typical vessels made from the same natural clay typically contain crushed granodiorite temper, might be interpreted as instances where novice potters, not yet familiar with conventions concerning visual selection criteria, participated in gathering parent material from till deposits and subsequently processed their finds, incorporated the crushed material into a paste mixture, and made pottery out of it.

The image that emerges is one of active learning, where novices acquire knowledge by not only participating directly in various tasks, but undertaking the tasks themselves. Such a learning environment would have created opportunities for novices to directly compare their work to that of more experienced potters. The high level of variability in learner vessel compositions could be interpreted as evidence that such comparisons were central to the learning process, whereby novices learned about how paste ingredients and recipes affect both the workability of ceramic bodies and well as their behavioural characteristics, during the critical stages of vessel forming, drying and firing.

Viewed differently, the learner pottery that is compositionally distinctive in terms of specific raw material ingredients and proportions thereof, and yet overlap with typical pottery in these respects, might be interpreted as instances of play or experimentation by novices. Ferguson (2008, 53-54) notes that since novices tend to waste a lot of raw material, it may be appropriate to hold back preferred raw material resources until more advanced skills have developed. Such learner pottery could also reflect play or learning outside of the context of a typical pottery making session, where the objective is to make a targeted number of vessels to provision a consumer group (e.g., household, lineage or clan). The learner vessels made from natural clays geologically consistent with deposits that occur in the immediate vicinity of the village, and hence readily accessible to children to gather and play with, might be the products of this casual activity. Firing these small objects could have been accomplished on a hearth, without any special preparations.

*Testing Behavioral Characteristics of Raw Materials*

A significant characteristic of the Mantle site, as a social context for craft practice and associated learning, is the strong evidence that the community had moved from a previous location and included people who had moved there from different, and perhaps geographically distant, areas. Whether potters were part of the ancestral community that relocated at Mantle, or complete newcomers to the area, they would have been faced with the task of identifying sources of suitable raw materials, especially natural clays that could be used successfully. The learner vessels made from natural clays geologically consistent with the Mantle clay samples and representing individually unique fabric types within the sample set as a whole might be interpreted as instances of this kind of testing.

As has been discussed, deposits of natural clay are widespread in the area surrounding Mantle and vary considerably in in their textural, compositional and other physical properties that are readily observable. As potters encountered different natural clays that broadly conformed to their understanding of desired characteristics, they would have proceeded to assess workability and the behavioral characteristics of resultant ceramic bodies during forming, drying and firing. The same principle applies to the sole example of use of crushed limestone as a tempering agent, as opposed to igneous rock. Fashioning and firing a simple, hand-modelled, pinch pot would have facilitated this evaluation of general performance characteristics. These expedient test vessels could have been made by experienced potters or novices, and in either situation constitutes an important learning exercise. The occurrence of several distinct fabrics made from raw materials available in the immediate vicinity the site and represented by only one, and in one case, two, learner vessels, suggests that this kind of information was shared among potters within the community, perhaps so that such experiments were not needlessly repeated. The kind of information sharing would have also helped to establish and strengthen relationships between potters with different lineage or clan affiliations.

*Specific Uses*

As discussed by Martelle and others, variability in the size, morphology and quality of learner vessels may relate to differences in function. For example, vessels that are virtually equivalent to typical vessels in all other respects except for their smaller size, might simply be small containers. Some of the comparatively crudely made learner vessels within the sample set could represent expedient vessels made for specific uses. Without a systematic study, it is difficult to distinguish learner vessels from expedient vessels made in a happenstance manner by more experienced potters. Small, expediently made pinch pots, for example, could have been fashioned virtually at any time: alongside typical vessels, using the same paste mixtures, on an as needed basis using clay that could be easily obtained nearby deposits.

**Context and Community of Practice at Mantle**

A community of practice continuously shares and develops knowledge. This knowledge is perpetuated by its members – novices and experts alike. By considering learner vessels as part of the entire technological system of pottery making, the continuous nature of learning and information sharing becomes evident. This approach allows us to avoid to some degree the problem of identifying with certainty vessels made by novices from those made by skilled potters while still considering their value as evidence of learning.

This study illustrates the challenge of archaeological research on technological choices made by potters and the importance of local knowledge. The Mantle potters would have encountered texturally and compositionally diverse clays and it is clear that they experimented with different raw materials. Learning how to evaluate clays and tempering materials based on observable characteristics is an important pottery-making skill, but this would have been especially true for Iroquoian potters of south-central Ontario. Little comparative work exists, but Braun has also identified more petrographic variability in ceramic fabrics among learner vessels than the typical adult assemblage at the thirteenth century Antrex (2012) and Holly (2015) sites, and attributes this variability to the role of these atypical vessels as instruments of learning. With villages typically relocating once a generation, entire communities of potters would frequently move to a new area together. Given the variable geological environment, it is likely that they would encounter new clay resources, even if they only relocated several kilometers away. This suggests that evaluation of clay and temper would have been an important component of community knowledge.

We found that this comparative approach was extremely valuable for uncovering variability in each step of the production process, providing unique insights into the settings in which pottery learning took place. Sometimes novices made pottery with the group and shared raw materials, other times they used different clay sources. This could be evidence of pottery making outside of the group context such as with expedient vessels or play, or simply raw material conservation. If pottery making were an occasional event, we might expect that expedient vessels might be needed occasionally for some immediate use. These could have been made by children, novices, or skilled potters and might be different compositionally from the rest of the assemblage. Thinking through each of these scenarios provides a wealth of testable hypotheses for future research.

## Acknowledgements

Thank you to Andrea Carnevale for collecting clay samples and research support, Alexis Dunlop for assisting with Striker's lab work, and Sherman Horn for a long day of clay survey. Thanks to Jerimy Cunningham, Kathryn Kamp, Kostalena Michelaki, Michelle Hegmon, Stephanie Salwen, and April Kamp-Whittaker for valuable discussions on the content of this paper. Special thanks Sandra L. López Varela and Kostalena Michelaki for the invitation to present at the Ceramic Ecology session at the AAA Annual Meeting associated with this volume, and Sandra L. López Varela for including us in this volume.

## References Cited

ASI. 2012. *The Archaeology of the Mantle Site (Algt-334) Report on the Stage 3-4 Salvage Excavation of Part of Lot 33, Concession 9, Town of Whitchurch-Stouffville, Municipality of York, Ontario*, edited by Archaeological Services Inc. Report on file. Toronto: Ontario Ministry of Culture, Tourism and Sport.

Arnold, Dean E. 1985. *Ceramic Theory and Cultural Process*. Cambridge: Cambridge University Press.

Arnold, Dean E 2015. 'Raw Material Selection, Landscape, Engagement, and Paste Recipes: Insights from Ethnoarchaeology.' Paper presented at the Proceedings of the Workshop of Namur, Belgium May 29-30.

Baldwin, D. J., Desloges J. R, and L. E. Band. 2013. 'Physical Geography of Ontario.' In *Ecology of a Managed Terrestrial Landscape*, edited by David L. Euler and I. D. Thompson, 16-38. Vancouver: University of British Columbia Press.

Biggar, Henry P. 1922. *The Works of Samuel De Champlain*. Toronto: The Champlain Society.

Birch, Jennifer. 2010a. 'Coalescence and Conflict in Iroquoian Ontario.' *Archaeological Review from Cambridge* 25 (1): 29-48.

Birch, Jennifer. 2010b. 'Coalescent Communities in Iroquoian Ontario.' Unpublished PhD Dissertation, McMaster University.

Birch, Jennifer. 2012. 'Coalescent Communities: Settlement Aggregation and Social Integration in Iroquoian Ontario.' *American Antiquity* 77 (4): 646-70.

Birch, Jennifer. 2016. 'Interpreting Iroquoian Site Structure through Geophysical Prospection and Soil Chemistry: Insights from a Coalescent Community in Ontario, Canada.' *Journal of Archaeological Science* 8: 102-11.

Birch, Jennifer, Robert B. Wojtowicz, Aleksandra Pradzynski, and Robert H. Pihl. 2016. 'Multi-scalar perspectives on Iroquoian ceramics: aggregation and integration in precontact Ontario.' In *Process and meaning in spatial archaeology: investigations into pre-Columbian Iroquoian space and place* edited by Eric E. Jones and John L. Creese, 111-114. Boulder: University Press of Colorado.

Birch, Jennifer, and Ronald F. Williamson. 2013a. *The Mantle Site: An Archaeological History of a Huron-Wendat Community*. London: AltaMira Press.

Birch, Jennifer, and Ronald F. Williamson. 2013b. 'Organizational Complexity in Ancestral Wendat Communities: Settlement Aggregation and Community Transformation.' In *From Prehistoric Villages to Cities*, edited by Jennifer Birch, 153-178. New York: Routledge.

Bishop, R. L., R. L. Rands, and G. R. Holley. 1982. 'Ceramic Compositional Analysis in Archaeological Perspective.' In *Advances in Archaeological Method and Theory*, Vol. 5, edited by Michael B. Schiffer, 275–330. New York and London: Academic Press.

Braun, Gregory V. 2102. 'Petrography as a Technique for Investigating Iroquoian Ceramic Production and Smoking Rituals.' *Journal of Archaeological Science* 39 (1): 1-10.

Braun, Gregory Vincent 2015. *Ritual, Materiality, and Memory in an Iroquoian Village*. Unpublished PhD Dissertation. University of Toronto, Toronto.

Boulton, G. S., G. D. Smith, A. S. Jones and J. Newsome. 1985. 'Glacial geology and glaciology of the last mid-latitude ice sheets.' *Journal of the Geological Society* 14 (3): 447-474.

Costin, Cathy Lynne. 2000. 'The use of ethnoarchaeology for the archaeological study of ceramic production.' *Journal of Archaeological Method and Theory* 7 (4): 377-403.

Crown, Patricia L. 2014. 'The archaeology of crafts learning: becoming a potter in the Puebloan southwest.' *Annual Review of Anthropology* 43: 71-88.

Dorland, Steven. 2016a. 'Practicing Informal Apprenticeship: A Study of Learning Landscapes in 15th Century Great Lakes Potting Communities.' Paper presented at the Society for American Archaeology Annual Meeting, April 6-10, Orlando, FL.

Dorland, Steven. 2016b. 'Learning Landscapes in the Great Lakes Region: An Analysis of 15th Century Ceramic Assemblages.' Paper presented at the Ontario Archaeological Society, Toronto Chapter Monthly Meeting, Toronto, ON.

Dorland, Steven. 2017. 'Were Pre-contact Children Really Innovators?' Paper presented at the Canadian Archaeological Association Annual Meeting, May 10-13, Ottawa, ON.

Engelbrecht, William. E. 2003. *Iroquoia: The development of a native world.* Syracuse, NY: Syracuse University Press.

Eyles, Nick. 2004. *Toronto rocks: the geological legacy of the Toronto region.* Markham, ON: Fitzhenry & Whiteside Ltd.

Finlayson, W. D. 1985. *The 1975 and 1978 Rescue Excavations at the Draper Site: Introduction and Settlement Pattern.* Mercury Series Paper 130. Ottawa: Archaeological Survey of Canada, Canadian Museum of Civilization.

Freestone, Ian C. 1991. 'Extending Ceramic Petrology.' In *Recent Developments in Ceramic Petrology*, edited by Andrew Middleton and Ian Freestone, 399-410. Vol. 81. London: British Museum Occasional Paper,

Gosselain, Olivier P. 2000. 'Materializing Identities: An African Perspective.' *Journal of Archaeological Method and Theory* 7 (3): 187-217.

Guillet, G. R., and I. H. Joyce. 1987. *The Clay and Shale Industries of Ontario.* Toronto, Ontario: Report prepared for the Ontario Ministry of Natural Resources.

Guillet, G. R. 1967. *The Clay Products Industry of Ontario.* Toronto, Ontario: Ontario Department of Mines.

Guillet, G. R. 1977. *Clay and shale deposits of Ontario.* Vol. 2358. Toronto, Ontario: Ontario Ministry of Natural Resources.

Hewitt, Donald F., and W. R. Cowan. 1969. *Sand and Gravel in Southern Ontario 1967-1968.* Toronto, Ontario: Ontario Department of Mines.

Herbich, Ingrid. 1987. 'Learning Patterns, Potter Interaction and Ceramic Style among the Luo of Kenya.' *The African Archaeological Review* 5: 193-204.

Hoffman, D. W., and N. R. Richards. 1955. 'Soil Survey of York County.' Guelph, Ontario: Prepared jointly by the Experimental Farms Service, Canada Department of Agriculture and the Ontario Agricultural College.

Howie, L. 2012. *Results of Petrographic Analysis of Pottery and Geological Samples from the Mantle Site (AlGt-334).* HDAS.

Jenkins, Tara. 2016. 'Contexts, Needs, and Social Messaging: Situating Iroquoian Human Bone Artifacts in Southern Ontario, Canada.' In *Theoretical Approaches to Analysis and Interpretation of Commingled Human Remains*, edited by Anna J. Osterholz, 139-183. New York: Springer.

Kowalewski, Stephen A. 2006. 'Coalescent Societies.' In *Light on the Path: Anthropology and History of the Southeastern Indians*, edited by T. J. Pluckhahn and R. Ethridge, 94-122. Tuscaloosa: University of Alabama Press.

Lave, J. 1988. *Cognition in Practice: Mind, Mathematics and Culture in Everyday Life.* New York: Cambridge University Press.

Lave, Jean, and Etienne Wenger. 1991. *Situated learning: Legitimate peripheral participation.* New York: Cambridge University Press.

MacNeish, Richard S. 1952. *Iroquois Pottery Types: A Technique for the Study of Iroquois Prehistory.* Bulletin 124, Anthropological Series No. 31. Ottawa: National Museum of Canada.

Martelle, H. A. 2002. *Huron Potters and Archaeological Constructs: Researching Ceramic Micro-Stylistics.* Unpublished PhD Dissertation, Department of Anthropology, University of Toronto, Toronto.

Muller, Kristin, and Jeff Zamek. 2011. *The Potter's Complete Studio Handbook: The Essential, Start-to-Finish Guide for Ceramic Artists.* Bloomington, IN: Quarry Books.

Neuzil, A. A. 2005. 'Corrugated Ceramics and Migration in the Pueblo III to Pueblo IV Transition, Silver Creek, Arizona.' *Kiva* 71(1): 101-124.

Olding, A. B., R. E. Wicklund, and N. R. Richards. 1956. 'Soil Survey of Ontario County.' Report No. 23 of the Ontario Soil Survey. Guelph, Ontario: Experimental Farm Service, Canada, Department of Agriculture, and the Ontario Agricultural College.

Ontario Geological Survey, 1997. *Quaternary geology, seamless coverage of the province of Ontario: Ontario Geological Survey*, Data Set 14.

Parkinson, William A. 2006. 'Tribal boundaries: Stylistic variability and social boundary maintenance during the transition to the Copper Age on the Great Hungarian Plain.' *Journal of Anthropological Archaeology* 25 (1): 33-58.

Peacock, D. P. S. 1970. 'The Scientific Examination of Ceramics: A Review.' *World Archaeology* 1: 375-389.

Pitelka, Vince 2001. *Clay: A Studio Handbook.* Cleveland, OH: American Ceramic Society.

Sharpe, D. R., P. J. Barnett, H. A. J. Russell, T. A. Brennand, and G. Gorrell. 1999. 'Regional geological mapping of the Oak Ridges Moraine, Greater Toronto Area, southern Ontario.' *Current research* E, Geological Survey of Canada: 123-136.

Sharpe, David R., and Hazen A. J. Russell. 2016. 'A revised depositional setting for Halton sediments in the Oak Ridges Moraine area, Ontario.' *Canadian Journal of Earth Sciences* 53 (3): 281-303.

Shepard, Anna O. 1956. *Ceramics for the Archaeologist.* Washington, D.C.: Carnegie Institution of Washington.

Shotton, F. W. and G. L. Hendry. 1979. 'The Developing Field of Petrology in Archaeology.' *Journal of Archaeological Science* 6: 75-84.

Smith, P. E. 1998. *When Small Pots Speak, The Stories They Tell: The Role of Children in Ceramic Innovation in Prehistoric Huron Society As Seen Through the Analysis of Juvenile Pots.* Unpublished PhD Dissertation McMaster University, Hamilton, ON.

Stark, Miriam T. 1998. *The Archaeology of Social Boundaries.* Washington: Smithsonian Institution Press.

Stark, M. T., Ronald L. Bishop, and Elizabeth Miksa. 2000. 'Ceramic technology and social boundaries: cultural practices in Kalinga clay selection and use.' *Journal of Archaeological Method and Theory* 7 (4): 295-331.

Tomkins, P., P. M. Day, and V. Kilikoglou. 2004. 'Knossos and the earlier Neolithic landscape of the Herakleion Basin.' *British School at Athens Studies* 12: 51-59.

Thurston, P. C. 1991. 'Geology of Ontario: introduction.' In *Geology of Ontario,* edited by P. C. Thurston, H. R. Williams, R. H. Sutcliffe, and G. M. Scott, 3-26, Special Volume No. 4. Toronto, Ontario: Ontario Geological Survey.

Trigger, Bruce G. 1976. *The Children of Aataentsic I: A History of the Huron People to 1660.* Montreal: McGill-Queen's University Press,

Warrick, G. A. 2000. 'The Prehistoric Iroquoian Occupation of Southern Ontario.' *Journal of World Prehistory* 14 (4): 415-466.

Warrick, G. A. 2008. *A Population History of the Huron-Petun, A.D. 500-1650.* New York: Cambridge University Press.

Whitbread, I. K. 1989. 'A proposal for the systematic description of thin sections towards the study of ancient ceramic technology.' In *Proceedings of the Archaeometry: proceedings of the 25th international symposium,* edited by Y. Maniatis, 127-138. New York, Elsevier.

Whitbread, I. K. 1995. *Greek transport amphorae: a petrological and archaeological study.* Fitch Laboratory Occasional Paper 4. Athens: British School at Athens.

Whitbread, I. K. 1996. 'Detection and interpretation of preferred orientation in ceramic thin sections.' In *Imaging the past: electronic imaging and computer graphics in museums and archaeology,* edited by Tony Higgins, Peter Main and Janet Lang, 173-181. London: British Museum.

Williamson, R. F. 2007. 'Otinontsiskiaj ondaon (The House of Cut-Off Heads) The History and Archaeology of Northern Iroquoian Trophy Taking.' In *The Taking and Displaying of Human Body Parts as Trophies by Amerindians,* edited by R. J. Chacon and D. H. Dye, 190-221. New York: Springer Science + Business Media, LLC.

Williamson, Ron F. 2012. 'What Will Be Has Always Been: the Past and Present of Northern Iroquoians.' In *The Oxford Handbook of North American Archaeology,* edited by Timothy Pauketat, 273-285. Oxford: Oxford University Press.

Williamson, Ron F. 2014. 'The Archaeological History of the Wendat to AD 1651: An Overview.' *Ontario Archaeology* (94): 3-63.

Wrong, G. M. 1968. *Sagard's Long Journey to the Country of the Hurons,* translated by H. H. Lagton. Toronto: The Champlain Society.

Zakin, Richard. 1990. *Ceramics: mastering the craft.* Radnor, PA: Chilton Book Company.

# Chapter 6

# Clay Choice: the Impacts of Ceramic Formation Methods and Cultural Behavior

Mary F. Ownby
Desert Archaeology, Inc.; mary@desert.com

**Abstract**
*Although traditionally consider a provenancing tool, petrographic analysis also contributes to clarifying technological processes of pottery making. In areas like the U.S. Southwest, where raw materials are plentiful, examination of thin sections of ceramics can identify the materials choices made by the potter. Such decisions should be viewed within the wider sphere of pottery production including technological and cultural impacts. Two case studies highlight the potters' selection raw materials. The first examines the differences between clays employed for paddle and anvil pottery in southern Arizona and those selected for coil and scrape pottery in northern Arizona. The second case study examines the use of varying clays and tempering material for pottery from Colorado, Utah, New Mexico, and Arizona. Here the technological information is tied to the mobility of people. The presented information endeavors to embed clay choice in the wider context of ceramic formation methods and cultural behavior.*

**Keywords**
*Clay choice, forming techniques, mobility, US Southwest, petrography, experimentation*

## Introduction

The study of ancient pottery has been conducted over decades and includes utilizing many different perspectives from ethnographic to scientific. All of this research and the benefit of diverse approaches have greatly enhanced our understanding of the relationship between people, clay, and culture. In particular, the emphasis on technological choice and ceramic ecology has focused on the raw materials and their properties, embedded in a cultural framework (Arnold 2003; Kolb and Lackey 1988; Lemonnier 2002; Sillar and Tite 2000; Velde and Druc 1999). The *chaîne opératoire* approach considers all of the steps in producing pottery from clay selection to the discard of broken sherds (Gosselain 1995; Lemonnier 1976). This holistic focus has highlighted the numerous choices that potters make and the depth of considerations from technical to social that go into producing a single vessel. The connection among these perspectives on ancient ceramics is the desire to culturally embed this behavior while still viewing pottery as a technological tradition.

The discussion presented here will also take this approach, while additionally considering scientific and experimental evidence. The first part of this study investigates clay selection and forming technique utilizing petrographic data to clarify the types of clay used, i.e., primary or secondary, and how those clays respond to two forming methods, paddle and anvil and coil and scrape. Those techniques were employed prehistorically in two different areas of the U.S. Southwest. Experiential work was conducted to clarify the relationship of clay source and properties to forming methods. The second part of this study examines clay choice and cultural behavior by using petrographic data to suggest where clay and temper were collected. This information is understood in light of the cultural traditions of several groups in Arizona, New Mexico, Colorado, and Utah to suggest that pottery making was part of seasonal movements on the landscape. Other factors involved in producing pottery, such as sources of water and fuel, are also considered. The approach taken here is to examine clay choice from both a *chaîne opératoire*, technological choice, and from a ceramic ecology perspective using petrographic and experimental data to guide the investigation.

## Clay Choice and Forming Method

Within the cultures of southern Arizona known collectively as the Hohokam, paddle and anvil was the preferred method for shaping ceramic vessels (Oppelt 2002). This approach can use a *puki* (small low ceramic bowl) as a mold for creating a rounded base for the pot. Alternatively, clay can be molded over the exterior of an upside-down bowl to form the base (Fontana *et al.* 1962). Once the clay base was somewhat dry it was removed and slabs or coils added to build height. To join the clay slabs/coils to the base and each other, a paddle on the exterior would apply pressure while the anvil on the interior would provide a counter force (see Rye 1981, 71, 84). Using this method additional slabs/coils could be added, integrated, and the vessel shaped and thinned to the desired height and form. For this technique the clays would need to have certain properties to allow for the pressure to move the clay in specific directions, hold the shape, and support additional slabs that could be easily joined.

In contrast, in the northern part of Arizona, including the four corners area, and the length of New Mexico, ancestral and Puebloan pottery was made with the coil and scrape method (Oppelt 2002). Either a flat 'pancake' of clay or a small coil was twisted into a round base. Coils of clay were added, joined, then thinned and shaped by scraping with a tool. An alternative pinching technique was to corrugate the exterior of thin coils using the thumb or a tool (see Rye 1981, 67, 86). Longer coils were used to increase the width of the vessel and shorter coils could bring the width back in. Clays for this method would also need to be stiff to hold the shape and plastic enough for the coils to be joined.

The distinction between the regional employment of these two forming methods raised a question on differences in the clays selected and paste recipes. While both techniques would require somewhat stiff clays that are also plastic, the geological differences between the areas and clay availability suggested closer analysis was needed to determine those clays actually used prehistorically. Extensive petrographic analysis throughout Arizona and New Mexico has provided much information on clay choice and paste recipes for a wide range of pottery over many centuries. Such studies have revealed differences in which clays were used and how they were prepared with links to vessel shape, vessel purpose, and cultural affiliation.

The petrographic analysis of prehistoric southern Arizona paddle and anvil pottery has identified most of the clays as secondary (i.e., formed some distance from the parent outcrop) and likely from small washes or older terraces (Miksa *et al.* 2012; Ownby 2014; Ownby *et al.* 2016). This was determined based on the fine natural inclusions that were mixed in mineralogy and the iron-rich nature of the clay that likely indicates soil weathering (Velde and Druc

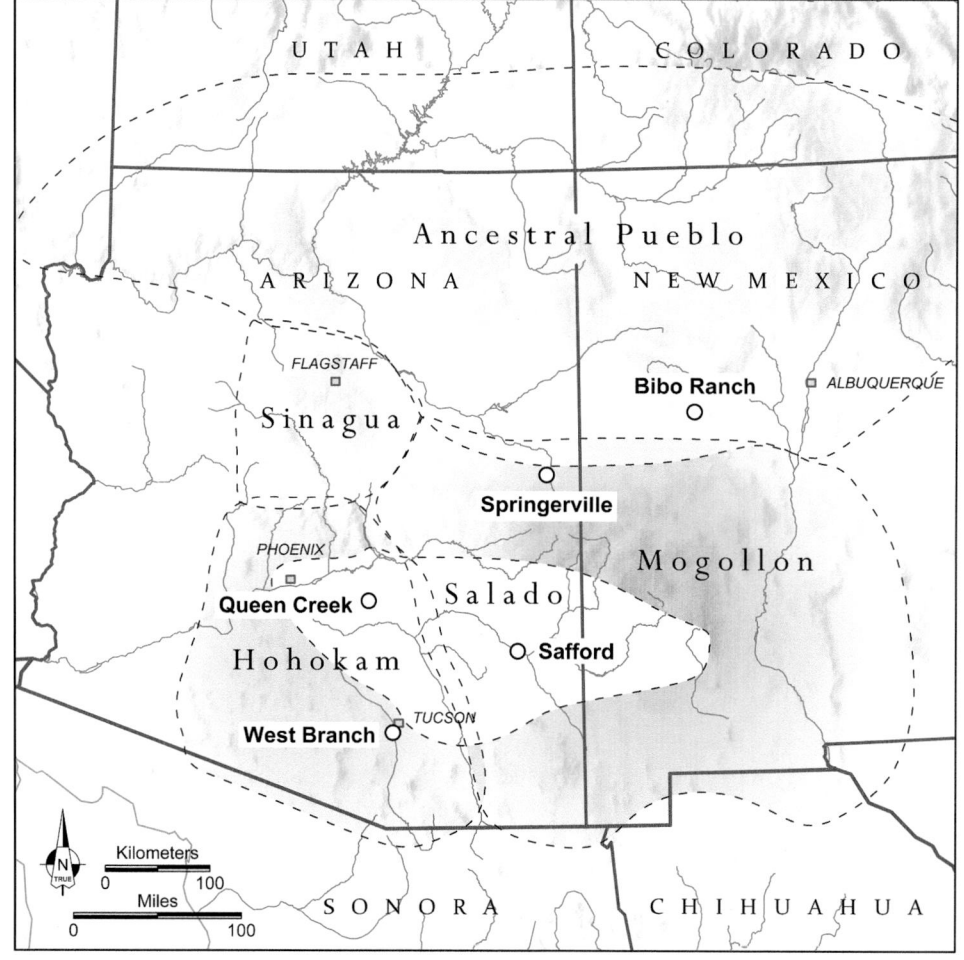

Figure 1. Map showing locations where clay was collected for the experimental vessels. Cultural group areas are also shown. (Map created by Catherine Gilman, Desert Archaeology, Inc.)

| Sample No. | Clay Source | Clay Type | Temper | Forming Method |
|---|---|---|---|---|
| EP-01 | Bibo Ranch | Primary? | Grog | Coil and Scrape |
| EP-02 | Bibo Ranch | Primary? | Grog | Paddle and Anvil |
| EP-03 | Safford | Primary | Grog | Coil and Scrape |
| EP-04 | Safford | Primary | Grog | Paddle and Anvil |
| EP-05 | Springerville | Primary | None | Coil and Scrape |
| EP-06 | Springerville | Primary | None | Paddle and Anvil |
| EP-07 | El Malpais NM | Secondary | None | Coil and Scrape |
| EP-08 | El Malpais NM | Secondary | None | Paddle and Anvil |
| EP-09 | West Branch | Secondary | Sand | Coil and Scrape |
| EP-10 | West Branch | Secondary | Sand | Paddle and Anvil |
| EP-11 | Queen Creek | Secondary | Sand | Coil and Scrape |
| EP-12 | Queen Creek | Secondary | Sand | Paddle and Anvil |

Table 1. Experimental pottery samples. (Table by Ownby)

1999, 59-68). Previous study of secondary clays in the Tucson Basin has indicated they are brown- to red-firing like the pottery (Harry 2000). These clays are naturally sandy, but sand has also been added to create a coarser paste. Typically between 30 and up to 50 percent inclusions are added that are often subangular to subrounded suggesting a source in a wash some distance from the parent rock, but not within a larger alluvial system far from the outcrops.

Petrographic study of pottery in northeastern Arizona and northwestern New Mexico has indicated the use of primary (i.e., formed at the parent outcrop) shale clays for most pottery production using the coil and scrape method (Ownby 2013a, b). These clays are identified as such due to the presence of a small number of shale fragments in the clay and the lack of fine natural mineral inclusion. Experiments firing the shale clays found in northeastern Arizona showed they fire white to gray like the pottery in this area (Geib and Callahan 1987, 103). Similar clays are found throughout the Four Corners area within common sedimentary deposits. In thin section, the clays had few medium-sized mineral grains, while crushed pottery (i.e., grog) was typically the primary added material comprising 10 to 30 percent of the paste. The natural inclusions and grog could range from angular to subrounded.

These observations indicate a possible connection between the type of clay used, primary versus secondary, and the paste recipe and forming method. While undoubtedly some of these choices are culturally prescribed and related to the types of clays available, it was unclear if primary clays would be poorly suited to paddle and anvil methods, and if secondary clays would be unworkable for coil and scrape. In order to test whether the technical properties of the clays correlated with forming methods or cultural preferences, experimental vessels were made with both clay types using both methods (Table 1). Small vessels were created from clay and paste recipes based on petrographic analysis of pottery from several sites. The vessels were fired in an open pit firing and subsequent petrographic analysis examined their fired appearance and firing temperature (no temperature measuring devices were used during the firing). The results were employed to assess the relationship between clay source, paste properties, and forming methods.

## Experimental work

Archaeological excavation of the West Branch Hohokam site in the Tucson Basin identified clay and temper present in a likely pottery-making area (Figure 1; Heidke 2004). Petrographic analysis of the pottery from the site suggested the use of a local secondary clay with the addition of local sand temper (Miksa 2011).

To assess the properties of this clay for paddle and anvil versus coil and scrape techniques, two experimental vessels were made of clay collected from the wash next to the West Branch site (Figure 2). The clay is naturally sandy but additional sand from the wash was added in a mix of one part sand to three parts clay to approximate the ancient paste (Miksa 2011). Water was needed to mix the clay and sand together to form a workable paste that was much stiffer than the clay prepared without additional sand. A small bowl was employed as a *puki* and the semi-dried clay was easily removed from the vessel. Slabs were added to the leather hard clay form by applying a thin layer of water to the vessel and slab before joining. The paddle, a saguaro cactus rib formed into a rectangular shape, and the anvil,

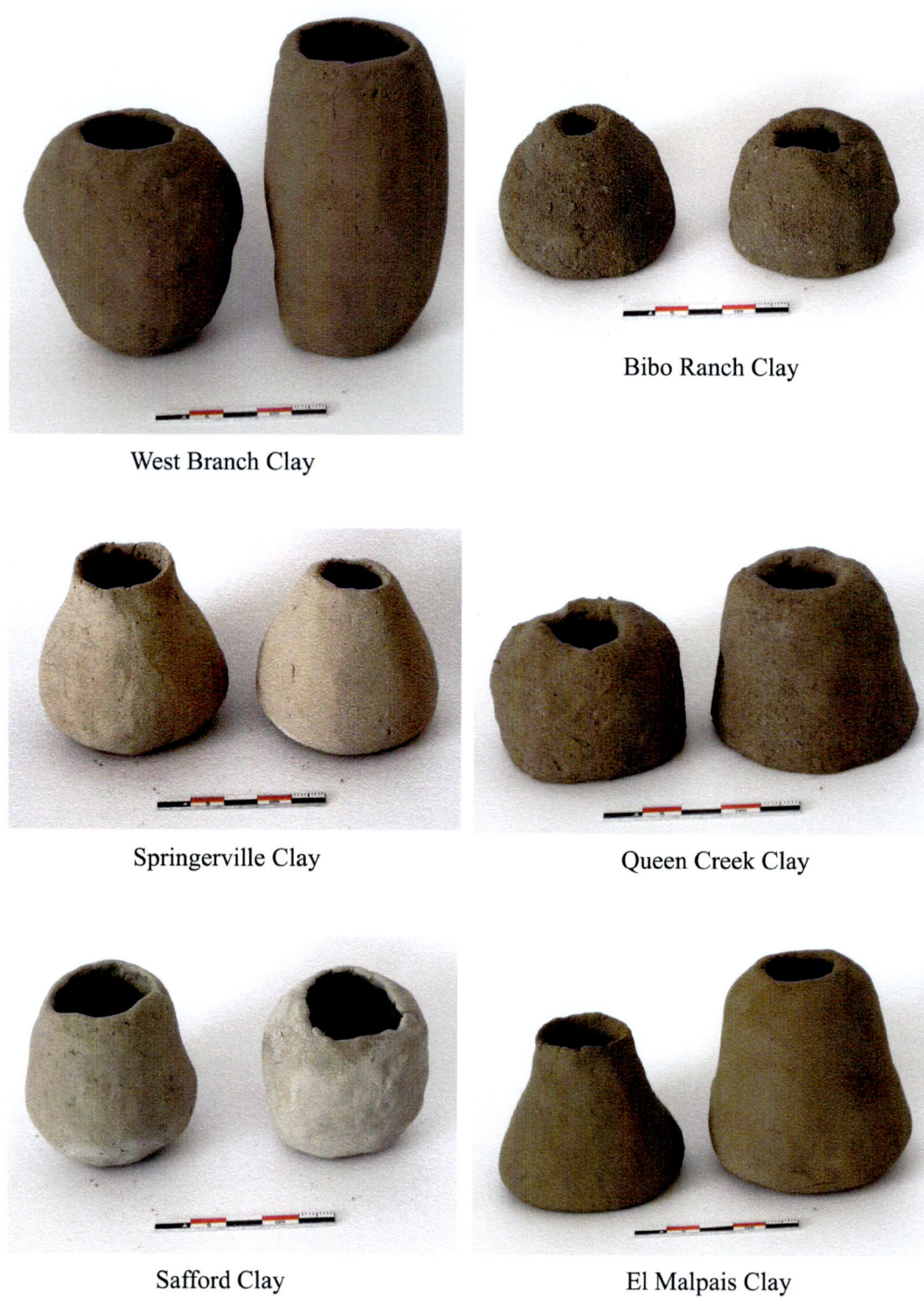

Figure 2. Experimental pots made from several different clays using paddle and anvil (vessels on the left) and coil and scrape (vessels on the right) forming methods. (Figure by Ownby)

a small round stone due to the small size of the vessel, were used to easily join the slabs and raise the height of the vessel. Cracks commonly formed during the paddle and anvil process but were smoothed away with water. After forming, water was used to wet smooth the vessel and to remove any remaining cracks. The clay in general was stiff enough to hold its shape and plastic enough to be formed with the paddle and anvil. A moderate amount of water was needed, a significant consideration in the dry desert of southern Arizona.

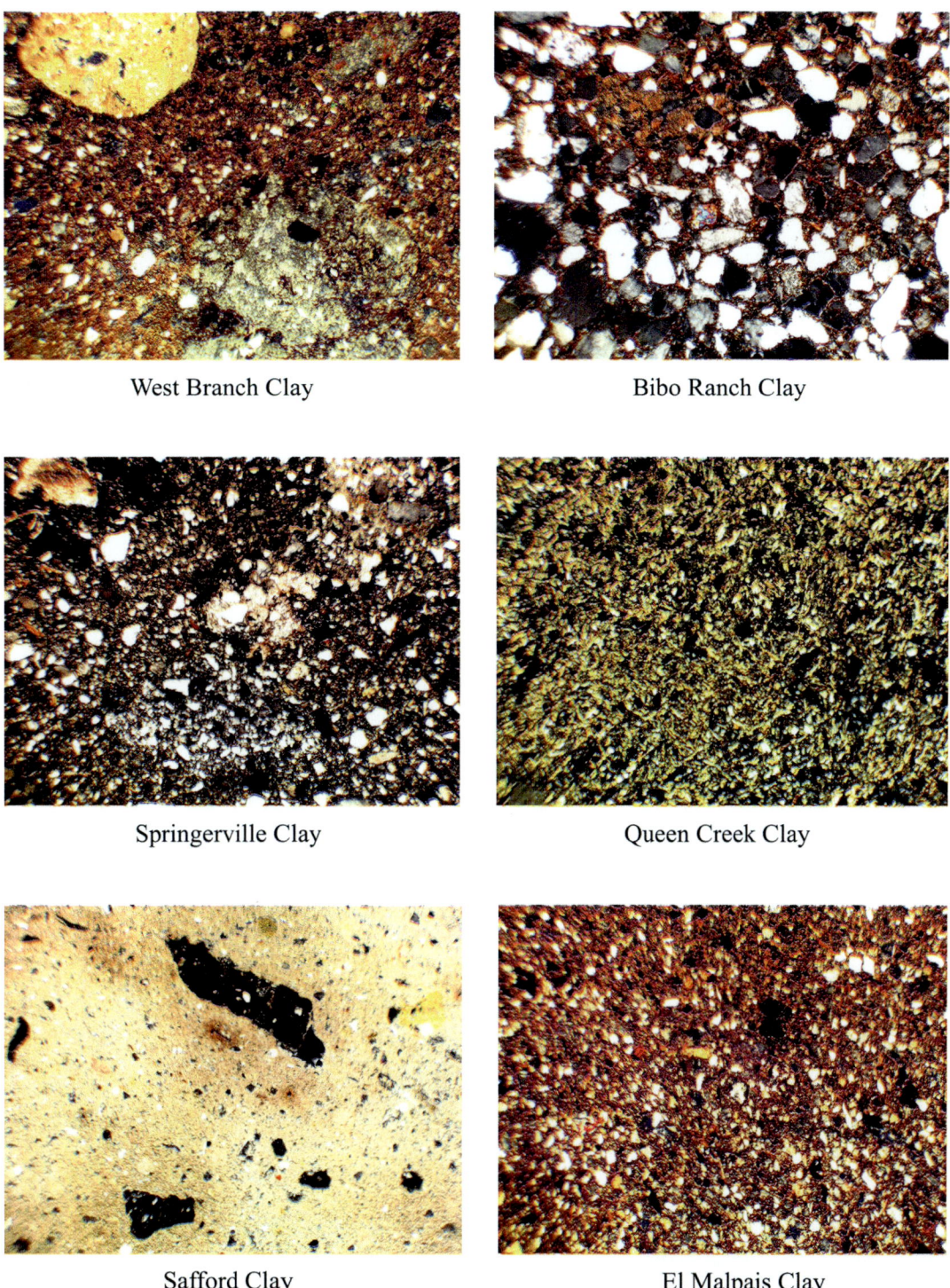

Figure 3. Petrographic thin section images of the coil and scrape pots made from several different clays. Images are in cross-polarized light at 40x magnification. (Figure by Ownby)

This same clay/sand paste was also used with the coil and scrape method to assess if a secondary clay can be worked with this method. While the clay was stiff enough and coils were easily joined, the common sand inclusions caused problems during scraping as they would hinder the scraper and create drag marks in the clay. Again cracks formed and were smoothed away with water. Once the vessel had been complete, water was used to smooth the surface and eliminate cracks. This showed that theoretically a secondary clay with sand temper could be used with the coil and scrape method, but the sand does cause aesthetic issues on the vessel surface.

Both vessels were well vitrified from firing in an open pit firing.[1] The petrographic analysis revealed a paste with very fine to very coarse-sized[2] inclusions that were poorly sorted and angular to rounded in shape (based on Matthew *et al.* 1991 and Powers 1953). The added sand temper comprised mostly rhyolite grains that were approximately 20 percent of the paste (Figure 3). The optical activity of the paste suggested a firing temperature around 800°C with more vitrification on the surfaces (Rice 1987, 431). The clay was iron-rich and argillaceous in appearance in thin section.

In northwestern New Mexico potters to this day use shale clays to create beautiful white vessels with a variety of decoration. Petrographic analysis of a collection of Cibola Black-on-white pottery from several sites in El Malpais National Monument indicated the use of shale clay and grog temper for the majority of the vessels (Ownby 2013b). During the investigation of an archaeological site known as Bibo Ranch, outside of the monument but nearby, a clay was found that was believed to have been utilized for pottery production (see Figure 1; Peeples personal communication). This clay was used to make two experimental vessels. The clay was very rich in fine-sand and quite crumbly; it had to be sieved to remove larger shale fragments. As the typical prehistoric paste in this area included grog, crushed pottery fragments from another vessel (made of a primary clay from Safford, see below) was added at 20 percent to approximate what was observed in the vessels from El Malpais. Water was needed to mix the clay and grog to form a paste.

Both coil and scrape and paddle and anvil methods were poorly successful with this clay. It was crumbly when dry and sticky when wet, and lacked stiffness or plasticity. Coils were difficult to make and water was needed during this process and for joining the coils. Scraping was not possible due to the grittiness of the clay and periods of drying were necessary between adding coils with water. This paste did not work in a *puki* as when even slightly dry it crumbled upon attempts to remove it from the form. Water and the paddle-and-anvil did join coils, but it was not possible to raise the height of the vessel due to the sticky nature of the clay, even with periods of drying before adding slabs. Additional water was needed to smooth cracks and for smoothing the exterior when the shape was complete. Overall, the clay would not have been suitable for pottery production in this area and required more water than other tested clays (see Figure 2). While some vessels were well-fired in the pit firing, the Bibo Ranch clay vessels were poorly vitrified likely due to the common inclusions. Petrographic analysis showed prevalent fine quartz with lesser inclusions of feldspars, chert, and quartzite (see Figure 3). The grog was rare despite the attempt to add a considerable amount. The natural inclusions were subangular to rounded in shape, from fine to medium in size, and comprised around 60 percent of the paste. The clay had a shale and argillaceous appearance and the vessels were fired from 800°C to 850°C.

In light of the poor success with an archaeological clay from the area, a primary shale clay collected near Springerville, Arizona was used instead to examine the forming methods with this type of clay (see Figure 1). This clay was slightly gritty (see below) so no additional temper was added. During the coil and scrape method, the scraper pulled on the clay noticeably so a pebble was employed to join the coils. For the paddle and anvil pot, the clay form was easily removed from the *puki*. Periods of drying were needed for both forming methods between added coils or slabs. Water proved important and was used to attach slabs and smooth the prevalent cracks during the shaping, and for a final smoothing of the vessel (see Figure 2). The vessels fired well in the pit-firing. In thin section, fine quartz was common with some fragments of chert, siltstone, shale, and quartzite (see Figure 3). While very fine to fine-sized natural inclusions dominated, some medium sized grains were present. All were well-sorted and angular to subrounded; comprising 50 percent of the paste. The clay had a shale appearance and was fired to approximately 800°C. This indicates that certain primary clays can be used for paddle and anvil if such clays are available in the area. They are likely rarely used in southern Arizona due to a lack of sedimentary geology (Richard *et al.* 2000).

This brings up an interesting point where cultural preferences for forming methods are affected by changes in clay availability. Such a situation occurred when groups (called the *Kayenta*) from northern Arizona migrated to southern Arizona and southwestern New Mexico (Huntley *et al.* 2016). Petrographic analysis of Maverick Mountain Series (MMS) and Roosevelt Red Ware (RRW), the two pottery wares associated with these migrants, from sites along the Upper Gila River in southwestern New Mexico had identified alluvial clays for these wares based on the

---

[1] A 1ft deep by 1 ft wide and 2 ft long pit was dug for the firing. Small dried juniper branches and sagebrush twigs were placed at the bottom. A slab of sandstone was placed on top of the wood and the vessels placed on it. A tent of juniper wood and sagebrush was placed around the pots. Sandstone slabs were placed around the pit due to wind from the east. The fire burned for 20-25 minutes with some areas reaching higher temperatures than others.

[2] Size categories are very fine (0.0625-0.125 mm), fine (0.125-0.25 mm), medium (0.25-0.5 mm), coarse (0.5-1 mm), very coarse (1-2 mm) (based on the Wentworth [1922] scale).

very fine inclusions in the clay and presence of iron (Ownby 2012, Ownby *et al.* 2014). Fine sand had been added at between 20 and 40 percent to create a paste. Likewise, study of RRW from sites in the Phoenix Basin also suggested the use of alluvial clays from a major drainage, the Salt River, with the addition of fine sand from the same source (files with the author). Such a paste may approximate the fine shale clay with grog used by Kayenta potters in their homeland.

Examination of a large collection of RRW identified most as produced by coil and scrape (Crown 1994, 41-42). This would indicate that the Kayenta groups moving into southern Arizona and southwestern New Mexico continued to employ their ceramic construction technique in the new area (Salado) with different clays. A small percentage of RRW were produced by paddle and anvil, possibly by local groups that were copying the RRW types. Interestingly, where MMS and RRW have been found, unusual Belford brown ware perforated plates have also been identified. These plates were produced by the coil and scrape method typical of groups in the north but in areas in the south (Neuzil and Lyons 2006, 55). These plates are suggested to have been used to produce MMS and RRW pots, serving as pukis (Lyons and Lindsay 2006, 16-20). Petrographic analysis of several of these plates identified secondary clays and coarse pastes similar to the local brown ware vessels (Ownby 2012).[3] The low form and utilitarian nature of these vessels probably meant scraping with a coarse paste was not an issue.

In order to test the utility of such a paste with coil and scrape and paddle and anvil, two experimental pots were made with alluvial clay collected along Queen Creek, a major river in the southern part of the Phoenix Basin (see Figure 1). Fine sand from the river was added to the clay using water to create a paste. The paste was sticky when wet but crumbly when dry. Attempts to create vessels from this paste failed due to the powdery nature of the paste when slightly dry. Instead, two pots were made from the clay alone that did have some natural fine sand (see below). After a two hour drying period, the vessel base was removed from the *puki* and slabs added to build the pot. Water was needed to join the slabs to the form. The paddle could smooth the joins, but the sticky nature of the moistened clay made it difficult to work and impossible to raise the height of the vessel. After adding a slab, the clay needed to dry for two hours before another slab could be added. The Queen Creek clay proved even more challenging for the coil and scrape method. The wet sticky clay meant that scraping was not possible but the coils could be joined with hand pressure. Coils were hard to form and when the clay dried too much between coils, attaching them was not possible as the clay crumbled. Height was not possible to achieve (see Figure 2). Both vessels were poorly fired in the pit firing. Petrographic analysis revealed that the clay was dominated by fine mica and quartz grains with few actual clay particles (see Figure 3). These inclusions were very fine to fine in size, well sorted, mostly round, and comprised 70 percent of the paste. This micaceous clay paste was fired to around 800°C. These results proved interesting given the petrographic evidence for major alluvial clays and fine sand. This may suggest older alluvial clays were used that had weathered more. Overall, paddle and anvil would appear to work better for such clays than coil and scrape.

Finally, the need to further test a primary clay was viewed as necessary and one was located in southern Arizona near Safford, although there is no evidence for its use to make pottery. The fine clay absorbed water with mild difficulty and became sticky if too wet, a typical problem for clays. Grog of the same clay was added with water necessary to fully integrate the paste. The proportion was around 1 part grog to 3 parts clay. This clay works very well with coil and scrape in particular because it does not require water for joining coils. In fact, water created common cracks so was only used at the end to smooth the surface.[4] The plastic clay made joining coils easy and was stiff enough for some height to be achieved. Of note, the grog made drag marks when the scraper was used to join the coils. Surprisingly, the Safford clay paste was not successful for paddle and anvil despite its plasticity and stiffness. The clay cracked in the puki when drying and could not be removed intact. Instead a small base was made by hand. Many cracks formed and water was needed to smooth them. Only some height could be achieved with the paddle as the clay dried quickly.

Both vessels fired well in the pit firing and petrographic analysis showed a calcareous clay that had been fired to at least 800°C. The natural inclusions (mostly quartz and limestone) were only 5 percent of the paste and were mostly very fine in size; they were well sorted and subangular to subrounded in shape. The grog was rare in the paste. Overall, it seemed such primary clays were ideal for coil and scrape but were less suitable for paddle and anvil.

These experiments have provided much insight into the nature of primary and secondary clays and their response to different forming methods. Several other observations are of note, such as the ease of adding water to more

---

[3] Previous petrographic studies also confirmed their local production at a number of sites throughout southern Arizona (Miksa *et al.* 2003; Mills 1998; Stinson 1996).
[4] Joining coils and slabs without water had been tried for the other pastes and proved unsuccessful. Conserving water would likely have been an important consideration for pottery production in the Southwest.

plastic secondary clays but the benefit of needing less water with primary clays. The former are often stickier and more difficult to smooth, while the latter are stiffer and easier to smooth against itself especially when using a scraper. The coil and scrape method works better with stiffer clays lacking temper that would drag on the surface. The paddle and anvil technique is more suited to plastic clays with sand temper to give them greater rigidity. These clays are sticky and sand would also help to alleviate that issue to some extent. Both the clay type and forming method will directly impact the vessel shapes that can be achieved, as seen in the differences in vessel shapes between pottery in southern and northern Arizona. The former often include squat jars and wide bowls, while the latter can be tall ovoid jars and narrower smaller bowls.

The firing showed that a small amount of wood can produce enough heat to vitrify the vessels. Due to the arid nature of this area, using only the amount of wood needed would have been a critical concern. The open pit-firing burned quickly and in thin section the core of the vessel walls showed less vitrification than the surfaces. This confirms the rapid heating of the vessels and the short duration of the firing that did not evenly vitrify the entire vessel.

Finally, a single pot can be made at one time with the coil and scrape method, while using paddle and anvil often required time for the vessel to dry between adding slabs. Thus, many pots could be worked on simultaneously for paddle and anvil, while coil and scrape would produce a single vessel at a time. This provides information on the differences in approaches to pottery production between the two areas. Primary clays would require a trip to the clay source, mining, and transportation back to the village. Once properly prepared by soaking, the clay could be worked and a vessel created at one time.[5] On the other hand, secondary clays could be close to the village (particularly in the case of Tucson and Phoenix Basin pottery), so little time would be required for collecting secondary clays. These clays would also need some time to soak, but once prepared, several vessels could have been made simultaneously.[6] This provides a sense of habitus for the potters in the two areas and how clay choice could affect the entire production process.

**Clay Choice and Mobility**

As just discussed, some potters need to travel to particular locations for the best clay; however, in some cases, clay collection may be part of seasonal mobility (see Arnold 1985 for discussions of resources and mobility). Petrographic analysis of pottery and raw materials compared to geological maps and samples can indicate if the vessel was made near the site or further away. Additionally, the size of sand grains and their angularity can provide information on where along a wash the material was likely acquired. For example, if the sand is round and fine in size, it was likely from some distance from the parent deposits and possibly even within a major river. When sand is collected close to the parent outcrops it can be coarse in size and angular. This general rule also depends on several geological factors, such as the type of rock, the degree and type of weathering, the gradation of the slope, etc. In general, angular and coarse-sized sand grains characterizing a single geological deposit tend to represent raw materials close to the source.

Utilizing these features, petrographic information was employed to assess whether sand and clay was collected close to mountain bases and rock outcrops or within the bajada (an area of alluvial fans extending from the mountain base) areas and river valleys. Four case studies show how this analysis is carried out and the results interpreted in regards to human behavior and raw material choice.[7] Focus was on plain ware pottery (including brown and gray) as this is the most commonly produced ware, typically believed to be locally made, and found in all four areas. Local is defined as within 3 km of a site, the typical distance identified ethnographically for potters to travel for sand temper (Heidke 2011, Table 4.10).

A petrographic study of Fremont pottery from southwestern Utah examined mainly Emery and Snake Valley gray ware (Figure 4; Ownby 2016). Twenty-four samples came from five sites located in the greater Beaver Valley (Table 2). They included 16 Snake Valley Gray ware (Snake Valley Black-on-gray, Snake Valley Red-on-gray, and Snake Valley gray), seven Emery Gray ware, and 1 Emery Black-on-gray ware dated from AD 1000 to 1300 (Watkins 2006). Fourteen samples (from all types) had a sand temper of coarse-sized and angular granite fragments (quartz, potassium feldspar, and rare plagioclase, i.e. syenite) with notable alunite, a hydrated aluminum potassium sulfate mineral. Plutonic deposits in Utah are very uncommon, but to the east of the sites are the Mineral Mountains with

---

[5] Several ethnographic accounts imply this was the case for coil and scrape pottery with a complete vessel made in one sitting, but having a few periods of drying before adding additional coils (Colton 1938: 4-7; Cushing 1886: 501; Kramer 2003: 70-73).
[6] This is attested ethnographically for Papago (O'odham) pottery production where several paddle and anvil pots are in production at the same time (Fontant et al. 1962; Hill 1942). Specifically a number of bases are made at one time and left to dry before coils are added in stages.
[7] In the discussion below it is suggested that sand temper and clay are collected in the same area, which is supported by the petrographic analysis.

CHAPTER 6  CLAY CHOICE: THE IMPACTS OF CERAMIC FORMATION METHODS AND CULTURAL BEHAVIOR

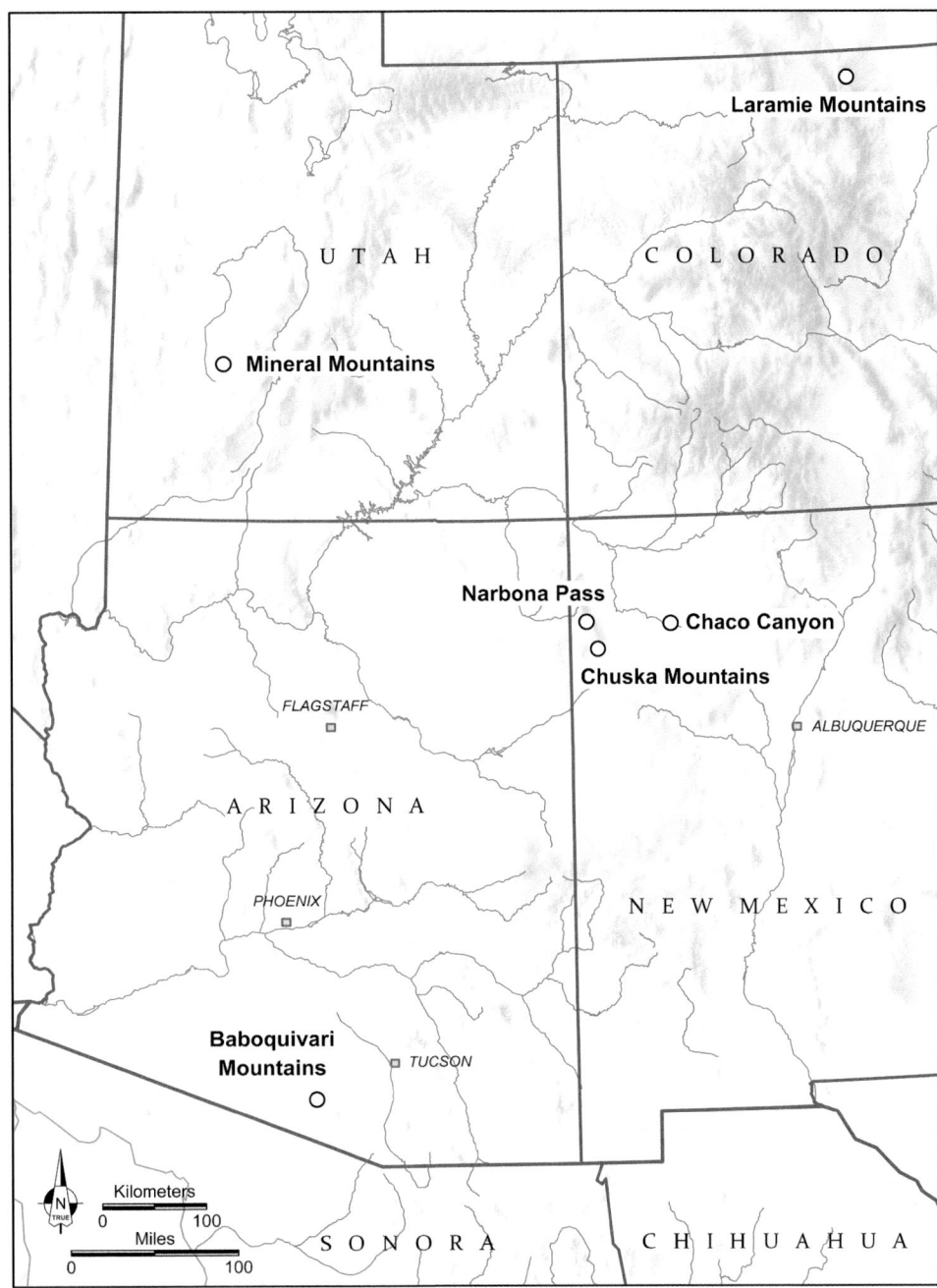

Figure 4. Map showing areas for case studies on clay choice and mobility highlighting the mountains where pottery was made. (Map created by Catherine Gilman, Desert Archaeology, Inc.)

notable monzonite and syenite outcrops (Rowley *et al.* 2005). Based on the composition of the sand and the size and shape of the mineral fragments within both gray wares, the raw materials were acquired at the base of the Mineral Mountains. Likely this area was chosen for several reasons; a stiff clay with the addition of some temper was needed for coil and scrape (Watkins 2009, 145), and an area with water and wood for fuel was also important. The latter is particularly significant as only small trees and shrubs would be in the Beaver Valley near the site, while larger trees would be found in the Mineral Mountains. Further, other resources (animals and plants) could be exploited in these high elevation areas while pottery was produced. The Fremont, a maize-based agricultural society, may have engaged in seasonal rounds timed for when mountain resources were available, there was no conflict with corn agriculture tasks, and pottery production could take place (lack of rain).

A similar situation seems to have occurred for ceramic manufacture in northern Colorado. Petrographic analysis was conducted on 34 samples from seven sites in the greater Fort Collins area (Table 3; Ownby 2015a) and included Early Ceramic Period (AD 150-1150) cord-marked, as well as Middle Ceramic Period (AD 1150-1540) and Late Ceramic

| Site | Sample No. | Ceramic Type | Inclusions | Compatible with Local Geology |
|---|---|---|---|---|
| 42BE1558 | SGC003 | Emery Gray | Andesite+alunite sand | No |
| 42BE1558 | SGC004 | Emery Black-on-gray | K-Feldspar+alunite sand | No |
| 42BE1558 | SGC005 | Snake Valley Gray | Clay with feldspar+alunite | No |
| 42BE1558 | SGC006 | Snake Valley Black-on-gray | Basalt sand | No |
| 42BE1558 | SGC008 | Snake Valley Gray | Plagioclase sand | No |
| 42BE1558 | SGC009 | Emery Gray | K-Feldspar+alunite sand | No |
| 42BE3765 | SGC010 | Emery Gray | K-Feldspar+alunite sand | No |
| 42BE3772 | SGC012 | Snake Valley Red-on-gray | K-Feldspar+alunite sand | No |
| 42BE3776 | SGC013 | Snake Valley Black-on-gray | K-Feldspar+alunite sand | No |
| 42BE3783 | SGC014 | Snake Valley Black-on-gray | K-Feldspar+alunite sand | No |
| 42BE3783 | SGC015 | Snake Valley Gray | K-Feldspar+alunite sand | No |
| 42BE3783 | SGC016 | Snake Valley Gray | K-Feldspar+alunite sand | No |
| 42BE3783 | SGC018 | Snake Valley Gray | Plagioclase sand | No |
| 42BE3783 | SGC020 | Emery Gray | Volcanic+alunite sand | No |
| 42BE3783 | SGC022 | Snake Valley Gray | K-Feldspar+alunite sand | No |
| 42BE3783 | SGC023 | Snake Valley Black-on-gray | K-Feldspar+alunite sand | No |
| 42BE3783 | SGC024 | Snake Valley Black-on-gray | K-Feldspar+alunite sand | No |
| 42BE3783 | SGC026 | Snake Valley Red-on-gray | Plagioclase sand | No |
| 42BE3783 | SGC030 | Emery Gray | K-Feldspar+alunite sand | No |
| 42BE3783 | SGC031 | Snake Valley Gray | Plagioclase sand | No |
| 42BE3783 | SGC032 | Snake Valley Gray | Plagioclase sand | No |
| 42BE3783 | SGC033 | Emery Gray | K-Feldspar+alunite sand | No |
| 42BE3783 | SGC035 | Emery Gray | Plagioclase+alunite sand | No |
| 42BE3783 | SGC036 | Snake Valley Gray | K-Feldspar+alunite sand | No |

Table 2. Ceramic samples from Utah sites in Beaver Valley.
(Table by Ownby)

Period (AD 1540-1730) plain ware and punctate. The vast majority of the analyzed sherds were made with coarse clays and granitic inclusions; however, in some cases, the clay was alluvial (rounded, fine inclusions with coarse subangular sand) and in others it appeared as a residual clay weathering directly from the granite (angular inclusions grading from fine to very coarse). Two types of granite were exploited, Middle Proterozoic Silver Plume granite of quartz, potassium feldspar, microcline, and plagioclase and Early Proterzoic granite gneiss (Braddock and Connor 1988). Both sources of granite are located in the Laramie Mountains to the west of the sites that are situated on low hills (see Figure 4). Populations in this area were highly mobile and pottery production was probably carried out during seasonal rounds when groups were in the mountains (Kornfeld et al. 2016). Coarse clay for construction of large vessels (possibly by a cord wrapped paddle and anvil) was readily available in the mountains along with water and wood for firing. Other resources were probably exploited while the pottery was made. The Middle Ceramic Period (AD 1460-1688) vessels from T-W Diamond are the only example of pottery production using sedimentary shale clays available in the vicinity of the site.

In New Mexico, Chuska Gray Ware (AD 800-1200) is known for its mass production and occurrence at important sites in Chaco Canyon (see Figure 4; Stoltman 1999). Petrographic studies have shown that the pottery was not produced in Chaco Canyon, but came from the Chuska Mountains to the west (Mills et al. 1997; Stoltman 1999). These studies revealed that the clay was likely a primary shale clay with angular to subrounded coarse inclusions of trachybasalt (although other names have been used for this rock type). Previous research suggested the rock was crushed and added to the clay, although a replication experiment showed crushing trachybasalt is difficult (Mills et al. 1997, 276-277). A petrographic study by Ownby (2013a) of 17 samples of Chuska Gray Ware found variable weathering in the trachybasalt and other inclusions besides this rock type, suggesting that the inclusions were a coarse sand (Table 4; Ownby 2013a, 8). Petrographic analysis of 7 Chuska White Ware revealed finer and more rounded inclusions

CHAPTER 6   CLAY CHOICE: THE IMPACTS OF CERAMIC FORMATION METHODS AND CULTURAL BEHAVIOR

| Site | Sample No. | Ceramic Type | Inclusions | Compatible with Local Geology |
|---|---|---|---|---|
| Roberts Buffalo Jump | 1 (4005) | Plain ware – punctate | EP Granite/gneiss | No |
| Roberts Buffalo Jump | 2 (4007) | Plain ware | EP Granite/gneiss | No |
| Roberts Buffalo Jump | 3 (4009) | Plain ware | EP Granite/gneiss | No |
| Roberts Buffalo Jump | 4 (4010) | Plain ware | EP Granite/gneiss | No |
| Roberts Buffalo Jump | 5 (4014) | Plain ware | EP Granite/gneiss | No |
| Owl Canyon Rockshelter | 6 (2015-2) | Plain ware – cord marked | EP Granite/gneiss | No |
| Owl Canyon Rockshelter | 7 (2015-3) | Plain ware – cord marked | EP Granite/gneiss | No |
| Owl Canyon Rockshelter | 8 (2015-4) | Plain ware – cord marked | MP Granite | No |
| Owl Canyon Rockshelter | 9 (2015-6 | Plain ware – cord marked | EP Granite/gneiss | No |
| Owl Canyon Rockshelter | 10 (2015-7) | Plain ware – cord marked | MP Granite | No |
| Kinney Spring | 11 (2015-2) | Plain ware | MP Granite | No |
| Kinney Spring | 12 (2015-3) | Plain ware – cord marked | EP Granite/gneiss | No |
| Kinney Spring | 13 (2015-4) | Plain ware – cord marked | EP Granite/gneiss | No |
| Kinney Spring | 14 (2015-5) | Plain ware – cord marked | EP Granite/gneiss | No |
| Kinney Spring | 15 (2015-6) | Plain ware – cord marked | EP Granite/gneiss | No |
| Kinney Spring | 16 (2015-7) | Plain ware – cord marked | EP Granite/gneiss | No |
| Kinney Spring | 17 (2015-8) | Plain ware – cord marked | EP Granite/gneiss | No |
| 5LR155 | 18 (2015-1) | Plain ware – cord marked | EP Granite/gneiss | No |
| 5LR155 | 19 (2015-2) | Plain ware – cord marked | MP Granite | No |
| 5LR155 | 20 (2015-3) | Plain ware – cord marked | MP Granite | No |
| 5LR155 | 21 (2015-4) | Plain ware – cord marked | MP Granite | No |
| T-W Diamond | 22 (1.1) | Plain ware – punctate | Sedimentary | Yes |
| T-W Diamond | 23 (1.3) | Plain ware | Sedimentary | Yes |
| T-W Diamond | 24 (1.4) | Plain ware – punctate | Sedimentary | Yes |
| T-W Diamond | 25 (1.5) | Plain ware | Sedimentary | Yes |
| T-W Diamond | 26 (2.1) | Plain ware | Sedimentary | Yes |
| Lightning Hill | 27 (284.16) | Plain ware – cord marked | EP Granite/gneiss | No |
| Lightning Hill | 28 (284.17) | Plain ware – cord marked | EP Granite/gneiss | No |
| Lightning Hill | 29 (284.705) | Plain ware – cord marked | EP Granite/gneiss | No |
| Lightning Hill | 30 (284.713) | Plain ware – cord marked | EP Granite/gneiss | No |
| Killdeer Canyon | 31 (1.4) | Plain ware | MP Granite | No |
| Killdeer Canyon | 32 (2.1) | Plain ware | MP Granite | No |
| Killdeer Canyon | 33 (3.1) | Plain ware | MP Granite | No |
| Killdeer Canyon | 34 (3.2) | Plain ware | MP Granite | No |

Table 3. Ceramic samples from northern Colorado sites.
EP=Early Proterozoic; MP=Middle Proterozoic. (Table by Ownby)

indicative of tracybasalt sand (Ownby 2013a, 11). Most of the studies concluded that the source of the trachybasalt was the Narbona Pass area of the Chuska Mountains where rocks with a similar texture and mineralogy can be found. This author investigated the area and found readily available sources of shale clay and sand. However, the sites from which pottery was analyzed (Ownby 2013a) were located at the base of the mountains, while Chaco Canyon is some 75 km east along the Chaco River, providing an easy corridor to move pots from the Chuska area to Chaco Canyon. Therefore, the Chuska wares were not made at the sites, but at Narbona Pass at an elevation of more than 8,700 feet where clay, temper, water, and wood would be available. In particular large trees such as juniper and piñon would be able to supple the fuel for the high amounts of pottery produced. A valuable source of chert is also in this area along with important plant and animal resources only found at this elevation (Cameron 2001). Thus, another case presents itself where pottery is made in the mountains, probably due to the availability of suitable clays, fuel, and abundant water, and the accessibility of other important resources.

| Site | Sample No. | Ceramic Type | Inclusions | Compatible with Local Geology |
|---|---|---|---|---|
| NM-Q-3-72 | 0A0033691 | Indented Corrugated (Chuska Gray) | Mafic volcanic sand | No |
| NM-Q-3-72 | 0A00346AE | Indented Corrugated (Chuska Gray) | Mafic volcanic sand | No |
| NM-Q-3-72 | 0A00346AF | Indented Corrugated (Chuska Gray) | Mafic volcanic sand+sherd | No |
| NM-Q-3-72 | 0A00346BD | Indented Corrugated (Chuska Gray) | Mafic volcanic sand+sherd | No |
| NM-Q-15-29 | 0A0035053 | Indented Corrugated (Chuska Gray) | Mafic volcanic sand | No |
| NM-Q-15-29 | 0A00350D8 | Indented Corrugated (Chuska Gray) | Mafic volcanic sand | No |
| NM-Q-15-29 | 0A0035173 | Indented Corrugated (Chuska Gray) | Mafic volcanic sand | No |
| NM-Q-15-46 | 0A0035176 | Indented Corrugated (Chuska Gray) | Mafic volcanic sand | No |
| NM-Q-15-46 | 0A0035185 | Indented Corrugated (Chuska Gray) | Mafic volcanic sand | No |
| NM-Q-15-46 | 0A003518E | Indented Corrugated (Chuska Gray) | Mafic volcanic sand | No |
| NM-Q-15-29 | 0A0034FEE | Clapboard Corrugated (Chuska Gray) | Mafic volcanic sand+sherd | No |
| NM-Q-15-46 | 0A00339E8 | Clapboard Corrugated (Chuska Gray) | Mafic volcanic sand | No |
| NM-Q-15-46 | 0A0035177 | Clapboard Corrugated (Chuska Gray) | Mafic volcanic sand | No |
| NM-Q-15-46 | 0A0035186 | Clapboard Corrugated (Chuska Gray) | Mafic volcanic sand | No |
| NM-Q-15-29 | 0A002368A | Plain Gray (Chuska) | Sandstone sand | Possibly |
| NM-Q-15-29 | 0A0034D2A | Plain Gray (Chuska) | Mafic volcanic sand | No |
| NM-Q-15-46 | 0A0033982 | Plain Gray (Chuska) | Mafic volcanic sand | No |
| NM-Q-3-72 | 0A0033506 | Newcomb Black-on-white | Mafic volcanic sand | No |
| NM-Q-3-72 | 0A002F590 | Brimhall Black-on-white | Mafic volcanic sand+sherd | No |
| NM-Q-15-46 | 0A0035183 | Chuska Black-on-white | Mafic volcanic sand+sherd | No |
| NM-Q-15-46 | 0A003517F | Crumbled House Black-on-white | Mafic volcanic sand | No |
| NM-Q-15-29 | 0A0035051 | Indeterminate Chuska White Ware | Mafic volcanic sand | No |
| NM-Q-15-43 | 0A0033168 | Indeterminate Chuska White Ware | Mafic volcanic sand+sherd | No |
| NM-Q-15-46 | 0A00339E6 | Indeterminate Chuska White Ware | Quartz/Feldspar sand+sherd | Possibly |

Table 4. Ceramic samples from northwest New Mexico sites along US-491.
(Table by Ownby)

Finally, evidence for such movement of people for pottery making was also identified in southern Arizona. Petrographic analysis of 54 plain ware sherds from 14 sites on the eastern side of the Tohono O'odham Reservation identified clay pastes of secondary clay with coarse-sized and angular inclusions (Table 5; Ownby 2015b, 2017, forthc.).[8] These are mostly granite, though there are subtle differences in the granite in this area, while other samples had distinctive metarhyolite and metamorphic rock fragments. Those sites where plain ware appeared to be made locally were often located at the base of the Baboquivari Mountains (see Figure 4). However, even sites with evidence of local plain ware, such as AZ AA:14:26 (ASM), also had non-local plain ware vessels (Ownby 2015b). The site of AZ DD:1:75 (ASM) is located near Sells Wash, but most of the plain ware was made with raw materials from the Baboquivari or South Comababi Mountains, showing a diversity of sand compositions (Ownby 2017). Analysis of plain ware from several sites along the east side of the Coyote Mountains also confirmed that production was from raw materials at the base of the mountains where some sites are located (author on-going study). In fact, petrographic analysis of Sells Red, an important red ware made in this area, also indicated the manufacture of these vessels in the mountains and using a very specific and consistent paste with inclusions of monzonite and latite (Table 6; Ownby forthc.).

Collectively, the production of plain ware in this area indicates frequent movement of peoples on the landscape[9]. The vessels found at sites often have a range of compositions indicating their production at multiple places, but mostly with coarse raw materials indicative of a source at the base of the mountains. In this area, water would be more common along with some wood resources for firing. Plain ware (mostly jars) may have been made as needed during

---

[8] Dates are difficult as many contexts lacked diagnostic material.
[9] Such activity in the past and present was generously discussed by Jeffords Francisco of the Tohono O'odham Nation.

CHAPTER 6  CLAY CHOICE: THE IMPACTS OF CERAMIC FORMATION METHODS AND CULTURAL BEHAVIOR

| Site | Sample No. | Ceramic Type | Inclusions | Compatible with Local Geology |
|---|---|---|---|---|
| AA:14:38 | SR86-01 | Plain ware | Granite with minor volcanic | No |
| AA:14:26 | SR86-05 | Plain ware | Volcanic with minor granite | No |
| AA:14:2 | SR86-06 | Plain ware | Mix of volcanic and granite | Yes |
| AA:14:2 | SR86-07 | Plain ware | Granite with minor volcanic | Yes |
| AA:14:2 | SR86-08 | Plain ware | Granite with minor volcanic | Yes |
| AA:14:2 | SR86-09 | Plain ware | Granite with minor volcanic | Yes |
| AA:14:2 | SR86-10 | Plain ware | Granite with minor volcanic | Yes |
| AA:14:26 | SR86-13 | Plain ware | Granite with minor volcanic | Yes |
| AA:14:2 | SR86-14 | Plain ware | Granite | Possibly |
| AA:14:26 | SR86-16 | Plain ware | Granite with minor volcanic | Possibly |
| AA:14:25 | SR86-17 | Plain ware | Metamorphic | No |
| AA:14:26 | SR86-18 | Plain ware | Metamorphic | No |
| AA:14:31 | SR86-20 | Plain ware | Volcanic with minor granite | Possibly |
| DD:1:75 | FSS-01 | Plain ware | Schist | No |
| DD:1:75 | FSS-02 | Plain ware | Phyllite | No |
| DD:1:75 | FSS-03 | Plain ware | Granite and rhyolite | No |
| DD:1:75 | FSS-04 | Plain ware | Diorite | Possibly |
| DD:1:75 | FSS-05 | Plain ware | Granite | No |
| DD:1:75 | FSS-06 | Plain ware | Granite | No |
| DD:1:75 | FSS-07 | Plain ware | Diorite | Possibly |
| DD:1:75 | FSS-08 | Plain ware | Granite | No |
| DD:1:75 | FSS-09 | Plain ware | Granite | No |
| DD:1:75 | FSS-10 | Plain ware | Diorite with minor granite | Possibly |
| DD:1:75 | FSS-11 | Plain ware | Diorite | Possibly |
| DD:1:75 | FSS-13 | Plain ware | Rhyolite | No |
| DD:1:75 | FSS-14 | Plain ware | Diorite with minor granite | Possibly |
| DD:1:75 | FSS-15 | Plain ware | Granite, diorite, and volcanic | Yes |
| DD:1:75 | FSS-16 | Plain ware | Diorite with minor granite | Possibly |
| DD:2:54 | SISS-01 | Plain ware | Granite and gneiss | Possibly |
| DD:2:54 | SISS-02 | Plain ware | Granite and gneiss | Possibly |
| DD:2:54 | SISS-03 | Plain ware | Granite and gneiss | Possibly |
| DD:2:54 | SISS-04 | Plain ware | Granite and granodiorite | Unlikely |
| DD:2:54 | SISS-05 | Plain ware | Granite and granodiorite | Unlikely |
| DD:2:54 | SISS-06 | Plain ware | Granite and gneiss | Possibly |
| DD:2:56 | SISS-08 | Plain ware | Granite and gneiss, volcanic and metamorphic rock fragments | Unlikely |
| DD:2:56 | SISS-09 | Plain ware | Granite and gneiss | Possibly |
| DD:2:56 | SISS-10 | Plain ware | Granite and granodiorite | Unlikely |
| DD:2:56 | SISS-11 | Plain ware | Granite and metaquartzite | No |
| DD:2:53 | SISS-14 | Plain ware | Rhyolite and rhyodacite | No |
| DD:2:53 | SISS-15 | Plain ware | Granite and andesite | No |
| DD:2:53 | SISS-16 | Plain ware | Rhyolite and metarhyolite | No |
| DD:1:6 | SISS-17 | Plain ware | Latite and andesite | No |
| DD:1:6 | SISS-18 | Plain ware | Monzonite, andesite, and metaquartzite | Unlikely |
| DD:1:6 | SISS-19 | Plain ware | Rhyolite | No |
| DD:1:6 | SISS-20 | Plain ware | Diorite with minor granite | No |
| DD:1:6 | SISS-21 | Plain ware | Rhyodacite and rhyolite | No |
| DD:1:6 | SISS-22 | Plain ware | Diorite with minor granite | No |
| DD:2:53 | FOS-10 | Plain ware | Rhyodacite and rhyolite | No |

| Site | Sample No. | Ceramic Type | Inclusions | Compatible with Local Geology |
|---|---|---|---|---|
| DD:2:53 | FOS-11 | Plain ware | Rhyolite, monzonite, and latite | No |
| DD:2:53 | FOS-12 | Plain ware | Latite and monzonite | No |
| DD:2:42 | CDA630 | Plain ware | Granite, granodiorite, and diorite | Yes |
| DD:3:97 | CDA633 | Plain ware | Granite, granodiorite, and diorite | Yes |
| DD:3:98 | CDA638 | Plain ware | Granite and granodiorite | Yes |
| DD:3:114 | CDA645 | Plain ware | Granite and granodiorite | Yes |

Table 5. Plain ware samples from southeastern Arizona sites on the eastern side of the Tohono O'odham Reservation. (Table by Ownby)

| Site | Sample No. | Ceramic Type | Inclusions | Compatible with Local Geology |
|---|---|---|---|---|
| AA:14:36 | SR86-04 | Sells Red | Latite | No |
| DD:2:56 | SISS-07 | Sells Red | Latite and monzonite | No |
| DD:2:53 | SISS-12 | Sells Red | Latite and monzonite | No |
| DD:2:53 | SISS-13 | Sells Red | Latite and monzonite | No |
| DD:1:6 | SISS-23 | Sells Red | Latite and monzonite | No |
| DD:1:6 | SISS-24 | Sells Red | Latite and monzonite | No |
| DD:1:6 | SISS-25 | Sells Red | Rhyolite, monzonite, and metaquartzite | Unlikely |
| DD:1:6 | SISS-26 | Sells Red | Latite and monzonite | No |
| DD:1:6 | SISS-27 | Sells Red | Latite and monzonite | No |
| DD:1:6 | SISS-28 | Sells Red | Monzonite, rhyolite, latite, and metaquartzite | Unlikely |
| DD:2:53 | FOS-08 | Sells Red | Latite and monzonite | No |
| DD:2:53 | FOS-09 | Sells Red | Latite and monzonite | No |

Table 6. Sells Red ware samples from southeastern Arizona sites on the eastern side of the Tohono O'odham Reservation. (Table by Ownby)

the course of exploiting plants and hunting animals in the dry winter months in the mountains. The pots were carried to agricultural sites on the bajada in the summer (when monsoon rains are common and preclude pottery making). This correlates with the dual residency of the Tohono O'odham prehistorically with winter residences near mountain springs, and summer residences on valley floors to take advantage of monsoon rains to grow crops. The Sells Red vessels, mostly bowls, show a distinct production with specific raw materials, and a firing regime that allowed for full oxidation of both sides of the vessels. This is unlike the plain wares that are mostly brown, suggesting an incompletely oxidizing atmosphere. Specialized production of Sells Red bowls indicates their unique function in the society and if produced from rare latite/monzonite outcrops near Baboquivari Peak, could relate to the sacred nature of that area (Francisco personal communication). Thus, production of these bowls may have centered on utilizing raw materials connected to a special place, imbuing that importance to the bowls themselves. While little discussed in this paper, clay choice can also be impacted by sacred places on the landscape and the need to carry a part of that within a ceramic vessel.

## Discussion

This paper has attempted to show the utility of petrography beyond provenance. The ability to examine clay type and temper properties means that petrographic analysis can inform on clay choice and temper selection. In the case of work in the American Southwest, this has confirmed a preference for primary clays used with the coil and scrape forming method and secondary clays employed with the paddle and anvil technique. Likely this is due to the clay properties, stiff and only moderately plastic, that allow easy joining of coils and scraping of the surface to smooth those joins. Experiments with a primary clay from Safford, Arizona showed it was the best for coil and scrape while needing minimal water for working. On the other hand, the West Branch secondary clay was ideal for paddle and anvil due to some stiffness and more plasticity for withstanding the pressure of the paddle. Further, in the area of southern Arizona where this method is used commonly, secondary clays are more readily available than sedimentary-based primary clays. The latter are more prevalent in northern Arizona where sand is less common. Secondary clays do exist in the northern area and working those clays is possible, though it requires more water than the primary clays.[10] The secondary clays fire a pink to light gray, whereas the primary clays fire white in oxygen creating the ideal backdrop for black painted decoration.

Undoubtedly, the prehistoric potters in both areas knew well the properties of the clays they chose, both in terms of forming methods, shaping abilities, firing colors, and finished vessel attributes. While there could be many sources of clay on the landscape, ancient experimentation would have identified those with the correct properties for forming method and finished appearance. This leads to the question of which came first: did the method for creating a vessel adapt to the selected clays or were clays chosen that worked well with the forming technique. The latter has a stronger cultural implication, and it should not be overlooked that the different forming methods are particular to distinct cultures; however, the geological distribution of varying clays likely also played a role. During the early stages of pottery development there may have been an interplay between clay and forming method until a suitable match was attained, in other words technological choice. Other aspects (e.g. desired functional properties for the finished vessel) certainly also influenced clay selection and forming technique as these are just two parts to a greater set of choices (i.e., *chaîne opératoire*) involved in producing ceramic vessels.

Another part of the *chaîne opératoire* that is given less consideration is the larger cultural context of group behavior. In this sense, a ceramic ecology approach is more appropriate. This study has presented several cases to highlight how mobility patterns of past peoples probably also influenced clay selection. Further, considerations of water availability along with fuel for firing also played a role. If groups were going into the mountains to exploit plant and animal resources in this area where clay, water, and fuel are plentiful, it may have influenced their decision to produce pottery in this area. Additionally, these coarse clays may have been more appropriate for their forming methods and vessel shapes. Other less noted considerations could be the importance of particular places to past peoples and the timing of pottery production, along with when vessels are needed and when there are opportunities to exchange pots with other groups. Clearly clay choice is heavily imbedded in a multitude of other decisions, some of which are outside the realm of actual pottery production. Though it may be difficult to fully contextualize the process of clay choice, some attempts should be made to highlight the numerous factors at play. This discussion has only focused on clay/non-plastics choices; similar considerations within the cultural context and habits of past people likely affected the multiple other steps in creating ceramic vessels.

## Conclusions

The experimental work and petrographic studies discussed in this paper clarify existing ideas on clay choice, forming methods, and group mobility. They emphasize the importance of using petrographic data to understand such aspects of pottery production in detail and placing them within their cultural context. Ancient ceramic manufacture in almost all cases has proven more complex than expected, so all lines of research and techniques are necessary to elucidate this past technology and its significance to those groups. Petrography can be used as a starting point to lead experimentation, as in this study. The results can then be interpreted in light of other aspects of pottery production and social behavior. Such an approach is not new, see ceramic ecology and technological choice theoretical frameworks, but here the emphasis is on including petrographic data and experimentation with those approaches. Further, the hope is to highlight the significance of the relationship between clay availability and clay choice to forming method and the mobility of past groups. Within a broader context, these considerations should help in illuminating more fully the complexities of past ceramic manufacture.

## Acknowledgements

This project was inspired and greatly helped by participation in the Southwest Kiln Conference in the Fall of 2015 (Safford area) and Fall of 2016 (Springerville area). Invaluable experience and advice were given by the participants, especially Clint Swink and Andy Ward. Further discussions with Joe Hall were particularly helpful and he provided the paddle used. The Bibo Ranch clay was supplied by Dr. Matthew Peeples (Arizona State University). Jeffords

---

[10] A pot made with a secondary clay collected in northwestern New Mexico (El Malpais National Monument) worked well with coil and scrape as it was a fine, untempered clay (see Table 1). However, the clay cracked in the puki and there were many cracks when working with the paddle and anvil. For both methods, the cracks were removed with water, which was also needed to join the slabs and coils. The vessels fired well in the pit firing (see Figures 2 and 3).

Francisco of the Tohono O'odham Nation kindly discussed pottery production and culturally significant locations in southern Arizona.

The petrographic analysis of ceramics from northern Colorado was part of a project with Dr. Jason LaBelle (Colorado State University) who gave permission for discussion of the results here. Likewise, work on pottery from the Tohono O'odham Reservation was part of a larger project by AZTEC Engineering Group, Inc. for the Arizona Department of Transportation. The study of pottery from Utah was part of a project by SWCA Environmental Consultants for Rocky Mountain Power, while the Bureau of Land Management and U.S. Forest Service authorized the use of the Sigurd-Red Butte data for this research. Petrographic analysis of pottery from sites on the east side of the Chuska Mountains was conducted for the U.S. 491 project, which was carried out for the New Mexico Department of Transportation by Statistical Research, Inc. under permit with the Navajo Nation Heritage and Historic Preservation Department. El Malpais National Monument sponsored the analysis of pottery from their area and kindly agreed to its discussion in this paper. I am grateful to all of these projects for the opportunity to work on such interesting and diverse material, and for permission to discuss some of those results here.

Finally, much thanks goes to Suzanne Griset for providing valuable comments on a draft of this report and greatly improving it, though all remaining mistakes are purely my own. Charlotte Ownby and Richard Greene provided important assistance during the experimental pottery firings.

**References Cited**

Arnold, Dean E. 1985. *Ceramic Theory and Cultural Process*. Cambridge: Cambridge University Press.
Arnold, Dean E. 2003. *Ecology and Ceramic Production in an Andean Community*. Cambridge: Cambridge University Press.
Braddock, William A. and Jon J. Connor. 1988. *Geologic Map of the Livermore Mountain Quadrangle, Larimer County, Colorado*. Washington, D.C.: U.S. Geologic Survey.
Cameron, Catherine M. 2001. 'Pink chert, projectile points, and the Chacoan regional system.' *American Antiquity* 66 (1): 79-101.
Colton, Mary. 1938. *Crafts of the Hopi Indians*. Flagstaff: Museum of Northern Arizona.
Crown, Patricia. 1994. *Ceramics and Ideology: Salado Polychrome Pottery*. Albuquerque: University of New Mexico Press.
Cushing, Frank H. 1886. 'A Study of Pueblo Pottery as Illustrative of Zuni Culture Growth.' In *Fourth Annual Report of the Bureau of Ethnography to the Secretary of the Smithsonian Institution*, 467-521. Washington, DC: Government Printing Office.
Fontana, Bernard L., William J. Robinson, Charles W. Cormack, and Earnest E. Leavitt Jr. 1962. *Papago Indian Pottery*. American Ethnological Society, Monograph 37. Seattle: University of Washington Press.
Geib, Phil R. and Martha M. Callahan. 1987. 'Ceramic Exchange within the Kayenta Anasazi Region: Volcanic Ash-Tempered Tusayan White Ware.' *Kiva* 52: 95-112.
Gosselain, Olivier P. 1995. 'Identités techniques. Le travail de la poterie au Cameroun méridional. Description des chaînes opératoires (2 vols.).' PhD Diss., Université Libre de Bruxelles.
Harry, Karen G. 2000. 'Community-Based Craft Specialization: The West Branch Site.' In *The Hohokam Village Revisited*, edited by D. E. Doyel, S. K. Fish, and P. R. Fish, 197-200. Glenwood Springs: Southwestern and Rocky Mountain Division of the American Association for the Advancement of Science.
Heidke, James M. 2004. 'Temper Characterization.' In *Pots, Potters, and Models – Archaeological Investigations at the SRI Locus of the West Branch Site, Tucson, Arizona: Vol. 1. Feature Descriptions, Material Culture, and Specialized Analyses*, edited by K. G. Harry and S. M. Whittlesey, 504-532. Technical Series No. 80. Tucson: Statistical Research, Inc.
Heidke, James M. 2011. 'Prehistoric Pottery Containers from the Julian Wash Site, AZ BB:13:17 (ASM).' In *Craft Specialization in the Southern Tucson Basin: Archaeological Excavations at the Julian Wash Site, AZ BB:13:17 (ASM): Part 1. Introduction, Excavation Results, and Artifact Investigations*, edited by H. D. Wallace, 263-294. Anthropological Papers No. 40. Tucson: Center for Desert Archaeology.
Hill, Gertrude. 1942. 'Notes on Papago Pottery Manufacture at Santa Rosa, Arizona.' *American Anthropologist* 44 (3): 531-533.
Huntley, Deborah L., Jeffery Clark, and Mary F. Ownby. 2016. 'Movement of People and Pots in the Upper Gila Region of the American Southwest.' In *Exploring Cause and Explanation. Historical Ecology, Demography and Movement in the American Southwest*, edited by C. Herhahn and A.F. Ramenofsky, 275-295. Boulder: University of Press of Colorado.
Kolb, Charles C., and Louana M. Lackey. 1988. *A Pot for All Reasons-Ceramic Ecology Revisited*. Philadelphia: Laboratory of Anthropology, Temple University.
Kornfeld, Marcel, George C. Frison, and Mary Lou Larson. 2016. *Prehistoric hunter-gatherers of the High Plains and Rockies, Third Edition*. New York: Routledge.
Kramer, Barbara. 2003. *Nampeyo and her pottery*. Tucson: University of Arizona Press.

Lemonnier, Pierre. 1976. 'La description des chaînes opératoires: contribution à l'analyse des systèmes techniques.' *Techniques et culture* 1: 100-151.

Lemonnier, Pierre. 2002. 'Introduction.' In *Technological choices: transformation in material culture since the Neolithic*, edited by Pierre Lemonnier, 1-35. London: Routledge.

Lyons, Patrick D. and Alexander J. Lindsay, Jr. 2006. 'Perforated Plates and the Salado Phenomenon.' *Kiva* 72: 5-54.

Matthew, Anthony J., Ann J. Woods, and Chad Oliver. 1991. 'Spots Before the Eyes: New Comparison Charts for Visual Percentage Estimation in Archaeological Material.' In *Recent Developments in Ceramic Petrology*, edited by A. P. Middleton and I. C. Freestone, 211-264. British Museum Occasional Paper No. 81. London: British Museum Press.

Miksa, Elizabeth J. 2011. 'Half Million Points and Counting: Two Decades of Petrofacies Modeling in the Greater Tucson Basin and Avra Valley.' In *Craft Specialization in the Southern Tucson Basin: Archaeological Excavations at the Julian Wash Site, AZ BB:13:17 (ASM)*, edited by H. D. Wallace, 553-617. Anthropological Papers No. 40. Tucson: Center for Desert Archaeology.

Miksa, Elizabeth J., Sergio E Castro-Reino, and Carlos P. Lavayen. 2003. *An Actualistic Sand Petrofacies Model for the San Pedro Valley, Arizona, with Application to Classic Period Ceramics*. Ms. on file at Desert Archaeology, Inc. Tucson: Desert Archaeology, Inc.

Miksa, Elizabeth J., Mary F. Ownby, and Carlos P. Lavayén. 2012. 'Petrographic Analysis of Pottery from Honey Bee Village.' In *Life in the Valley of Gold, Archaeological Investigations at Honey Bee Village, A Prehistoric Hohokam Ballcourt Village in the Cañada del Oro Valley of Southern Arizona. Part 1: Introduction, Chronology, Material Culture Investigations, and Summary of Research Results*, edited by H. D. Wallace, 123-181. Anthropological Papers No. 48. Tucson: Center for Desert Archaeology.

Mills, Barbara J. 1998. 'Migration and Pueblo IV Community Reorganization in the Silver Creek Area, East- Central Arizona.' In *Migration and Reorganization: The Pueblo IV Period in the American Southwest*, edited by K. A. Spielmann, 65-80. Arizona State University Anthropological Research Papers No. 51. Tempe: Arizona State University.

Mills, Barbara J., Andrea J. Carpenter, and William Grimm. 1997. 'Sourcing Chuskan Ceramic Production: Petrographic and Experimental Analyses.' *Kiva* 62: 261-282.

Neuzil, Anna A. and Patrick D. Lyons. 2006. *An Analysis of Whole Vessels from the Mills Collection Curated at Eastern Arizona College, Thatcher, Arizona*. Technical Report 2005-01. Tucson: Center for Desert Archaeology.

Oppelt, Norman T. 2002. *List of Southwestern Pottery: Types and Wares: with Dates and References to Descriptions and Illustrations*. Greeley: Oppelt Publications.

Ownby, Mary F. 2012. *Petrographic Analysis of Polychromes and Plain Wares from southern New Mexico and Arizona*. Petrographic Report No. 2012-04. Tucson: Desert Archaeology, Inc.

Ownby, Mary F. 2013a. *Petrographic Analysis of Gray, White, Brown, and Red Wares from the Chuska Slope, New Mexico*. Petrographic Report No. 2013-03. Tucson: Desert Archaeology, Inc.

Ownby, Mary F. 2013b. *Chemical and Petrographic Analysis of Decorated Pottery from Four Sites in El Malpais National Monument, New Mexico*. Petrographic Report No. 2013-01. Tucson: Desert Archaeology, Inc.

Ownby, Mary F. 2014. 'Petrographic Analysis of Pottery from La Villa, AZ T:12:148 (ASM).' In *Excavations at La Villa: Continuity and Change at an Agricultural Village*, edited by M. W. Lindeman, 135-155. Technical Report No. 2012-08. Tucson: Desert Archaeology, Inc.

Ownby, Mary F. 2015a. *Petrographic Analysis of Sand and Pottery from Northern Colorado*. Petrographic Report 2015-02. Tucson: Desert Archaeology, Inc.

Ownby, Mary F. 2015b. 'Petrographic Analysis of Pottery from Six Sites along State Route 86.' In *Phased Archaeological Data Recovery in the Kitt Peak and Santa Rosa Ranch Segments, Mileposts 128.5 to 137.19, State Route 86, Tohono O'Odham Nation, Pima County, Arizona*, edited by P. Cook, 183-200. Technical Report No. 2014-04. Tucson: Desert Archaeology, Inc.

Ownby, Mary F. 2016. *Petrographic Analysis of Pottery from West Central Utah*. Petrographic Report 2016-04. Tucson: Desert Archaeology, Inc.

Ownby, Mary F. 2017. 'Petrographic Analysis of Pottery.' In *Results of Phased Data Recovery at AZ DD:1:75(ASM), State Route 86, Tohono O'odham Nation, Pima County, Arizona*, edited by C. Stone and D. Lundin, 167-187. AZTEC Technical Report No. AZ16-01. Phoenix: AZTEC Engineering Group, Inc.

Ownby, Mary F. forthc. 'Petrographic Analysis of Pottery from Three Sites along State Route 86 and Jackrabbit Ruin.' Phoenix: AZTEC Engineering Group, Inc.

Ownby, Mary F., Deborah L. Huntley, and Matthew Peeples. 2014. 'A Combined Approach: Using NAA and Petrography to Examine Ceramic Production and Exchange in the American Southwest.' *Journal of Archaeological Science* 52: 152-162.

Ownby, Mary F., Carlos P. Lavayén, and Elizabeth J. Miksa. 2016. 'Appendix K: Binocular and Petrographic Analysis of Pottery from the Yuma Wash Site.' In *Excavations at the Yuma Wash Site and Outlying Settlement*, edited by D. L. Swartz, 1-58. Anthropological Papers No. 49. Tucson: Archaeology Southwest.

Powers, Maurice C. 1953. 'A new roundness scale for sedimentary particles.' *Journal of Sedimentary Research* 23 (2): 117-119.

Rice, Prudence. 1987. *Pottery Analysis: A Sourcebook*. Chicago: University of Chicago Press.

Richard, Stephen M., Stephen J. Reynolds, Jon E. Spencer, and Philip A. Pearthree. 2000. *Geologic Map of Arizona 1:1,000,000*. Washington D.C.: United States Geological Survey.

Rowley, Peter D., Garrett S. Vice, Robert E. McDonald, John J. Anderson, Michael N. Machette, David J. Maxwell, E. Bart Ekren, Charles G. Cunningham, Thomas A. Steven, and Bruce R. Wardlaw. 2005. *Interim Geologic Map of the Beaver 30' x 60' Quadrangle, Beaver, Piute, Iron, and Garfield Counties, Utah*. Salt Lake City: Utah Geological Survey.

Rye, Owen S. 1981. *Pottery Technology. Principles and Reconstruction*. Manuals on Archaeology 4. Washington D.C.: Taraxacum.

Sillar, Bill and Michael S. Tite. 2000. 'The challenge of 'technological choices' for materials science approaches in archaeology.' *Archaeometry* 42 (1): 2-20.

Stinson, Susan L. 1996. 'Roosevelt Red Ware and the Organization of Ceramic Production in the Silver Creek Drainage.' Master thesis, University of Arizona.

Stoltman, James B. 1999. 'The Chaco-Chuska Connection: In Defense of Anna Shepard.' In *Pottery and People: A Dynamic Interaction*, edited by J. M. Skibo and G. M. Feinman, 9-24. Salt Lake City: University of Utah Press.

Velde, Bruce and Isabelle Druc, eds. 1999. *Archaeological ceramic materials: origin and utilization*. New York: Springer.

Watkins, Christopher. 2006. 'Parowan pottery and Fremont complexity: Late formative ceramic production and exchange.' PhD Diss., Brigham Young University.

Watkins, Christopher. 2009. 'Type, Series, and Ware: Characterizing Variability in Fremont Ceramic Temper.' *Journal of California and Great Basin Anthropology* 29 (2): 145-162.

Wentworth, Chester K. 1922. 'A scale of grade and class terms for clastic sediments.' *Journal of Geology* 30 (5): 377-392.

# Chapter 7

# Complementary Approaches for Understanding Mazapan Pottery

### Destiny L. Crider
Luther College; cridde01@luther.edu

**Abstract**
*The application of complementary, yet diverse analytical and experimental approaches can provide new perspectives in archaeological ceramic style and technology studies. Here, the exploration is limited to a single pottery type, Mazapan Wavy Line, a unique but abundant Early Postclassic (ca. A.D. 850-900) red painted service ware, distributed across the northern Basin of Mexico and the Tula region. Neutron Activation Analysis (NAA) and Proton Induced X-ray Emission (PIXE) studies provide geochemical evidence for paste and paint recipes and confirm multiple production areas and evidence for exchange. Through observational attribute and stylistic analyses, there is variation in the quality of execution and variety of design. Experimentation in the replication of the fine line designs and brush proto-types demonstrates the importance of apprenticeship in crafting this pottery. Local and regional scales of comparison in these complementary approaches are discussed in the context of the emergence of the expansion of the Toltec state.*

**Keywords**
*Toltec, Early Postclassic, Mesoamerica, Central Mexico, Experimental Archaeology, Ceramic Analysis*

## Introduction

The Central Mexican pottery type commonly known as Mazapan Wavy Line (or Wavy Line Red-on-natural) is easily recognizable by its decoration of parallel red lines commonly applied in horizontal bands with a multi-prong brush on the interior or exterior of service vessels. This diagnostic ceramic and its initial use bridges the chronological and political transition from Epiclassic city-states to Early Postclassic expansion of the Toltec state occurring at least by A.D. 900 (if not somewhat earlier). The capital city of the Toltec state, Tula was located in Hidalgo, Mexico and its influence extended to the rural hinterlands surrounding the city and throughout the Early Postclassic (ca. A.D. 900-1150) expanded its political and economic influence south and into the Basin of Mexico (Figure 1). It is during the Early Postclassic that Tula underwent an urban transformation, shifting focus and monumental architecture to Tula Grande. At its height, the urban center of Tula sprawled across almost 16 km$^2$ with about 50,000 to 60,000 residents with another 60,000 in its immediate hinterland. However, Wavy Line pottery appears to have lost its popularity early on, replaced by a variety of service wares more expedient in decoration and production (Figure 2).

Little attention has been given to the stylistic or technological qualities of this common service ware popular just prior to the rise and expansion of the Toltec state, but it is precisely the unique qualities of its method of application and choices of potters on design that provide an insight into the significance of this pottery. I summarize the outcomes of my various complementary studies over the last decade that have targeted Wavy Line pottery to gain a more nuanced understanding of the production and expression of this seemingly simple ceramic that was popular during the transition from the Epiclassic to Early Postclassic period (ca. AD 900-1000). This discussion explores the potential of combining approaches of stylistic, technological, and chemical characterization analysis to define craft production, economic relations, and socio-political interactions. Compositional study of the vessel clays indicates numerous locales of production. Stylistic analysis documents regional variation in the choice of design. Technological attributes indicate differing patterns of potter techniques in production and design. However, it is through some simple experiments in trying to replicate the decorative techniques and technologies that new insights are explored that indicate that the application of the multiprong brush to ceramic vessels likely necessitated training. Using the attributes of brush width, number of painted lines, and paint quality from archaeological specimens provides framework and guide for experimental objectives in replication. Analyses suggest that the resulting variations in distribution of differing qualities and designs of Wavy Line pottery in Central Mexico may be not only pottery choice, but also access to apprenticed knowledge. Regional patterns in stylistic and technological variation in Wavy Line pottery indicates shifting boundaries in economic activity at an important time of political transition from regional city-state competition of the Epiclassic to the growing influence of a large regional state emergent from Tula, Hidalgo in the Early Postclassic.

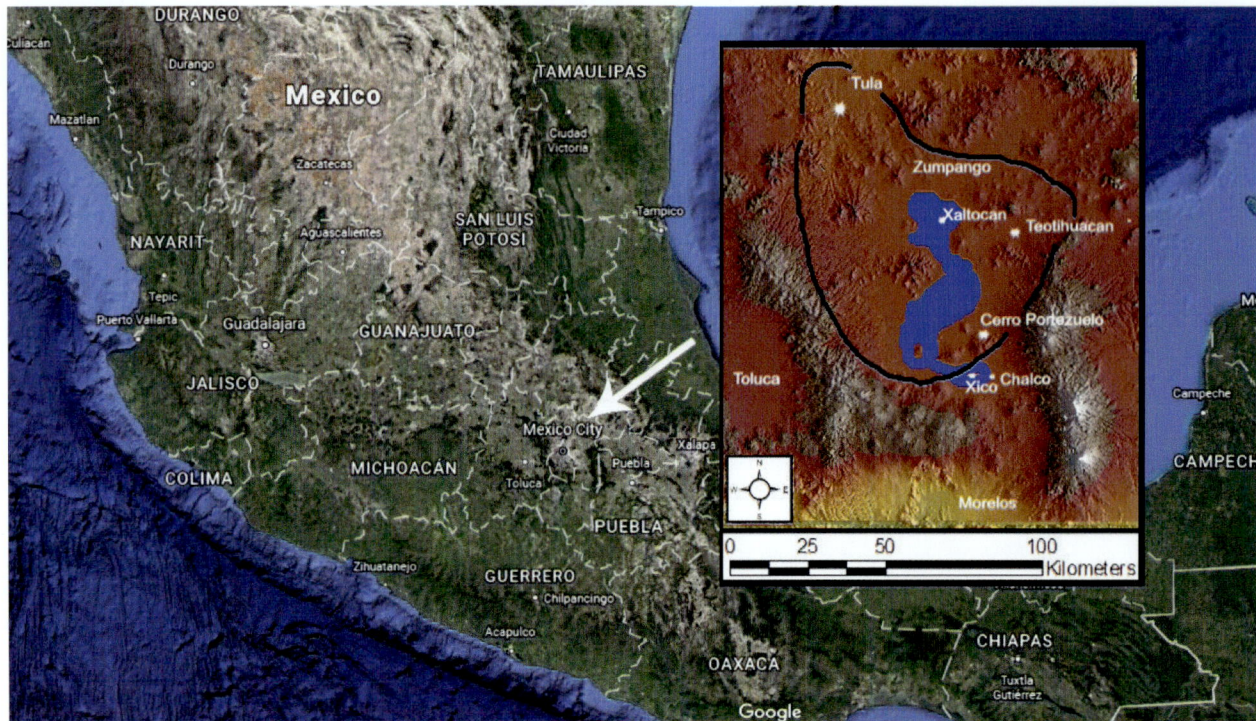

Figure 1. The distribution of Mazapan Wavy Line pottery within the Basin of Mexico. (Figure by Crider)

| A.D. | Period | Tula | | Teotihuacan | | Southern Basin Complex | |
|---|---|---|---|---|---|---|---|
| | | Phase | Types | Phase | Types | Phase | Types |
| 550 | Classic | | | | | | |
| 650 | | La Mesa | CS bowls Coyotlatelco or Proto-Coyotlatelco | Metepec | | Early Epiclassic | CS bowls Tezonchichilco Zone Incised Incised & Punctate stamp simple |
| 750 | Epiclassic | Prado | Guadalupe Incised Ana Maria RB Clara Luz Black Incised | Oxtoticpac | CS bowls resist stamp simple | | |
| 850 | | Corral | Coyotlatelco Jiménez Stamped | Xometla | stamp complex? Coyotlatelco | Coyotlatelco | Coyotlatelco stamp complex? |
| | | Terminal Corral | Wavy Line Blanco White | Mazapan | Wavy Line (Matte) | Mazapan | Wavy Line (Burnished) |
| 950 | | Early Tollan | Joroba Cream Slip | | Joroba Cream Slip Sloppy RN Macana | | Joroba Cream Slip Sloppy RN Macana |
| 1050 | Early Postclassic | | Ink Stamped? Macana Proa Cream Slip Blanco Levantado Sillon incised | Atlatongo | Proa Cream Slip Blanco Levantado Orange Incised Jara Pulido Ira Stamped | Tollan | Proa Cream Slip Blanco Levantado Orange Incised Jara Pulido Ira Stamped |
| 1150 | | Late Tollan | Jara Pulido Ira Stamped | | | Aztec I | Aztec I Chalco-Cholula Polychrome |
| 1250 | Middle Postclassic | Fuego | | Aztec II | | Aztec II / Early Aztec | |
| 1350 | | | | | | | |

Figure 2. Schematic of associated pottery types by chronological periods and phases for Tula and parts of the Basin of Mexico, as used in study of Mazapan Wavy Line pottery. Wavy Line pottery spans the end of the Epiclassic to the early part of the Early Postclassic. (Figure by Crider 2011)

## Distribution and Chronology of Wavy Line Pottery

Due to its highly distinctive design, Vaillant (1932) and Linné (1934) first recognized Mazapan Wavy Line pottery and designated it as a temporal and cultural marker at Teotihuacan and thought its distribution was limited to the Basin of Mexico (Figure 3). In the 1970s, only small amounts were identified in the Tula region and it was hypothesized to be a minor trade ware imported from Teotihuacan (or elsewhere in the Basin of Mexico) during Tula's Terminal Corral phase occupation – a short 50-year phase at the end of the Epiclassic period (Cobean 1978, 1990; Mastache and Cobean 1989, 38; Mastache *et al.* 2002, 218-219). Because of the high amounts of Wavy Line pottery identified in his regional survey, Sanders (1986) hypothesized that the type had its origins in the Teotihuacan Valley. However, despite the early indications of its scarcity in the Tula region, Mazapan Wavy Line was eventually shown to occur in the same proportions in Tula as in Basin sites, at roughly 4-5% of site level assemblages (Bey 1986, 104), especially notable in rural settlements around Tula Grande.

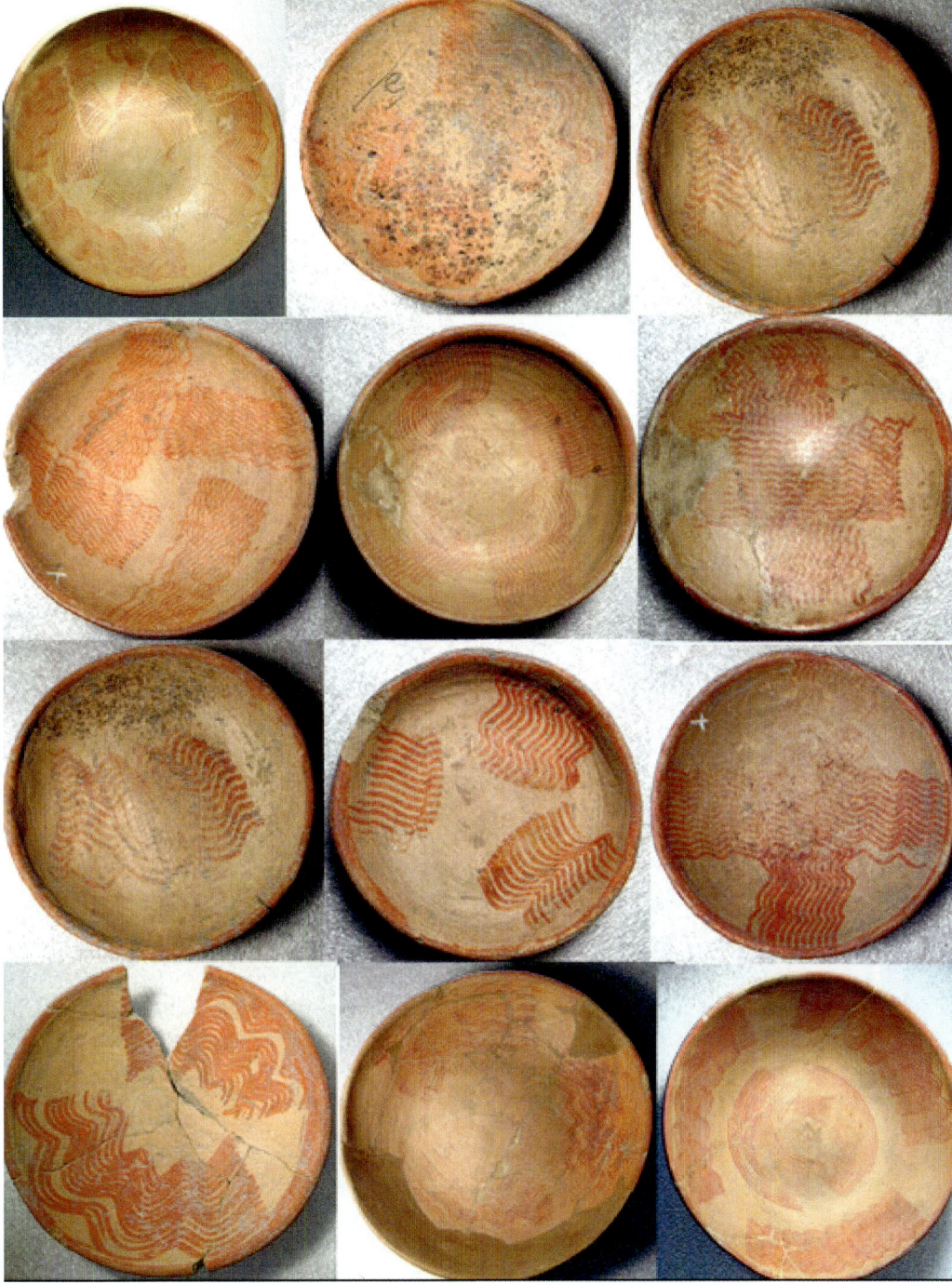

Figure 3. Vessel examples of Mazapan Wavy Line pottery from Vaillant's 1930s excavations at Teotihuacan San Francisco Mazapan (part of the collections at the American Museum of Natural History). Vessels are not shown to same scale, but to highlight the view of interior designs. (Figure by Crider 2011)

Few chronometric dates can be firmly associated to uniquely 'Mazapan Wavy Line' occupational levels in the Basin (Figure 2). Rather, most chronological placement has been determined by association with other known temporal diagnostics – often in mixing with Epiclassic Coyotlatelco and/or Early Postclassic Tollan ceramics. Wavy Line pottery occurs in Tula's Terminal Corral phase (ca. A.D. 850-900) which is characterized as a 'transitional complex' that contains some Corral phase ceramic types like Epiclassic Coyotlatelco Red pottery and 'Proto-Tollan' pottery types, including Wavy Line. Bey (1986, 209-211) suggested that the type was primarily in use in the Early Tollan phase, and occurred in higher frequency in Tula's rural sites as compared to the urban core. Based on Bey's analysis, Mazapan Wavy Line was in the top five most common ceramic types in use at Tula in the Early Tollan phase. He suggested that the type fell in popularity by Late Tollan phase.

In the Valley of Teotihuacan, William T. Sanders (1986) similarly divided the Early Postclassic period into two archaeological phases, the Mazapan phase (which overlaps with Terminal Corral and Early Tollan phases of Tula) and Atlatongo (which corresponds to the apogee of the Tula state). Sanders suggested that it was the latter phase that reflected the *first real* intrusion of Tula-related ceramics into the Teotihuacan Valley and the incorporation of the Teotihuacan Valley into its sphere of influence. Sanders identified the key difference between Mazapan and the later Atlatongo phase as the increased use of a cream slipped ware and a decreased use of the Mazapan Wavy Line pottery. Recall that at the time of his assessment, Wavy Line was thought to be primarily a Teotihuacan Valley product. The recognition of the broader distribution of Mazapan Wavy Line throughout parts of the Basin of Mexico and into Hidalgo suggests that Tula-related influence was earlier than Sanders hypothesized at the time. Given the early temporal placement of Wavy Line pottery in the Tula region, the interactions with the Toltec state into the northern Basin and the Teotihuacan Valley was likely much earlier than suggested by Sanders, and was instead emergent out of the end of the Epiclassic period.

Since the 1980s, Mazapan Wavy Line pottery has been documented throughout the Basin of Mexico (Figure 1). Significant amounts were recovered in Parsons' Zumpango survey (2008) in the northern Basin, an area especially important as the corridor bridging the route between the Tula and into the northern Basin of Mexico. In addition to the Teotihuacan Valley, it also occurs along the western lake shores in settlement areas that include Azcapotzalco (García 2004), and along the east side of the central lake south of the Teotihuacan Valley to include Texcoco area settlements (Parsons 1971). Wavy Line pottery is especially notable at the large center of Cerro Portezuelo (Crider 2011, 2013a; Nichols *et al.* 2013); despite the presence of a handful of Tollan phase style ceramics are present (e.g., cream slipped wares, red painted molcajetes), Mazapan Wavy Line pottery is almost absent in the southern Basin of Mexico around the settlements of Xico and Chalco (Crider, 2011; Parsons *et al.* 1982; Sanders *et al.* 1979, 463), indicating a significant boundary of distribution along the southern shores of the Basin of Mexico lake system during this important era bridging the Epiclassic and Early Postlcassic.

**Production of Wavy Line**

The widespread distribution of Mazapan Wavy Line pottery indicates access and use across parts of the Basin of Mexico and into Hidalgo. Prior to my own study, small samples of Wavy Line that have been submitted to the Missouri University Research Reactor (MURR) for Instrumental Neutron Activation Analysis (INAA); samples were included from Cerro Portezuelo (Nichols *et al.* 2002) and other Basin sites (García 2004) indicated multiple locales of production. As part of a larger regional assessment of Epiclassic and Early Postclassic compositional studies of decorated pottery, I endeavored to systematically sample a range of Epiclassic and Early Postclassic decorated pottery for technological and stylistic attribute analysis and additional INAA. For this summary, I direct the reader elsewhere for greater detail in the goals and methods (e.g., Crider 2011, 2013a) and provide a brief discussion as it relates to this one pottery type.

In order to identify production variation in vessel form, surface finish, decoration, I recorded a series of qualitative and quantitative attributes. Attribute trends were used to compare against compositional results that indicate locale of production and assess exchange patterns across the study region. Given the numerous approaches to the study of regional interaction, for this study I follow the position proposed by Binford (1965), Hegmon (1992), and Lyons and Clark (2008) that artifact style is the product of both conscious and unconscious expressions of identity (Crider 2011, 8). Lyons and Clark (2008) identify two useful approaches to the study of style and the nature of interaction. The 'interactionist' approach privileges the ongoing maintenance of group boundaries, as well as the creation of shared identities, through active and continuously negotiated interaction by human actors. The choice to produce and acquire certain pottery wares and types signify participation in certain networks. While the 'enculturalist' approach favors unconscious, or passive aspect of interaction to account for stylistic variation. Enculturation processes reflect structured learning frameworks in production (Herbich 1987; Hill 1970; Longacre

1970). Reinforcement of specific stylistic attributes and traits occur in day-to-day behaviors of practice. Both interactionist and enculturalist processes can operate together, each contributing to differing indicators of distribution and stylistic variation.

For my regional analysis, I collected attribute analysis of 400 Mazapan Wavy Line sherds and 40 vessels (all from burials at Teotihuacan from the American Museum of Natural History collections) to identify technological and stylistic variation within the type that reflect variation in potters' skill, decorative choices, and quality of paints and surface finish (Figure 4). Collections were selected from regional survey collection blocks established by Sanders, Parsons and Santley (1979). I sampled pottery from numerous (but not all) areas in the Basin of Mexico (Zumpango Survey, Teotihuacan Mapping Project, Teotihuacan Valley Rural Survey, Cerro Portezuelo Project, Chalco Survey) and Tula (INAH Salvage project). A sample of ceramics was selected for attribute analysis from each regional block when available; sherds and were selected based on having sufficient portion of the design space to identify key technological aspects for vessel form, surface finish, and details of decoration and design motif. Cerro Portezuelo (n=161), Teotihuacan region (n=198), and Tula (n=37) are the most represented in my sample; fewer samples were available for study (either based on time or lower amounts present) from other collection areas including Zumpango region (n=36) and the southern Basin (n=12).

In addition, specimens were chosen from multiple survey sections for chemical characterization using INAA and were submitted to the Missouri University Research Reactor (MURR). Samples were selected to represent technological and stylistic variability based upon trends in decorative and technological attributes. Previous compositional studies have shown that geochemical resolution for the Basin of Mexico is such that probable source groups can be distinguished between the areas of the Basin (e.g., Bennyhoff and Heizer 1965; Crider et al. 2007; Garraty 2006; Hodge and Minc 1990; Nichols et al. 2002, Rodriguez-Alegría 2002). Fortunately, geochemical concentrations vary across the Basin of Mexico, which is the essential criterion for the application of compositional methods of clay provenance, such as INAA. As a drainage basin in the interior highlands, sediments from the surrounding volcanic slopes continually accumulate and intermix, creating a continuous amalgam of soils and clays from mixed parent rock sources The Basin is thus best described as a geochemical continuum with east-west and north-south gradients, and boundaries drawn among compositional groups along this continuum are largely arbitrary and for my purposes were selected based on access to specific site collections that were available at the time of analysis.

The classification of the selected Mazapan Wavy Line specimens into compositional groups was examined using a suite of multivariate statistics. The first step was to develop a reference set of compositional groupings derived from previously assayed samples in MURR's Central Mexican datasets. Again, I reference the specific details to my previous study (Crider 2011). The resulting groups generally reflect association to regional quadrants of the Basin (e.g., northeast, southeast, north/northwest) but with large sampling of some sites, I propose some additional composition groups that occur within Basin quadrants. Note that the classification of samples follows a hierarchy of increasingly inclusive groups which facilitates regional comparisons at multiple levels, from the highly localized site

Figure 4. Categories of information collected as part of the attribute study of Epiclassic and Early Postclassic pottery, including Mazapan Wavy Line. (Figure by Crider 2011)

| Tracking Information | Technological Analysis | Decorative Analysis |
|---|---|---|
| Collection/Project | General Form | Interior and Exterior Surface Treatment |
| Specimen Identification | Form Details | Size of Painted Rim Band |
| Temporal Designation | Rim Shape | Decorative Technique |
| Pottery Complex | Rim Angle | Decorative Motif |
| INAA Sample Number | Vessel Measurements | Vessel Color |
| | Wall to Base Angle | Paint/Slip Color |
| | Rim Diameter | Quality of Manufacture |
| | Base Diameter | Quality of Decoration |
| | Length of Support | Quality of Material |
| | Angle of Support | Photograph of Design |
| | Location of support | Line Drawing of Design |
| | Wall Thickness | Vessel Support Shape |
| | Paste Qualities | Line width – between line width |
| | Carbon Streak | Size of decorative zone |
| | Fire Clouding | |

level to the macro-regional level of the Basin of Mexico (Figure 5). Refinement of this schema is ongoing as new sampling occurs in Central Mexico.

Summary of the resulting patterns of group membership for the selected 139 Mazapan Wavy Line specimens supports the premise that there were multiple locales of production across the region, including Tula, the northern Basin, the Teotihuacan Valley, and locally around the site of Cerro Portezuelo (Figure 6). Due to the distribution of Wavy Line in areas not sampled for INAA, it is likely that additional locales of production will be identified on the western shores of the Basin's lake system. The handful of assignments to the southwest Basin quadrant is an additional indicator of this probability. For the northern portion of the study area, most of t the Mazapa Wavy Line pottery was made and used locally, within the designated collection blocks. For example, the Tula collected specimens are almost entirely assigned to local Tula compositional groups (one outlier represented). Tula produced ceramics are represented only in the neighboring area of the Zumpango Survey area in the northern Basin as supplement to locally produced pottery. The adjacent collection areas bridge the corridor between Tula and the Basin of Mexico, and the Zumpango Survey area had been sparsely populated in the

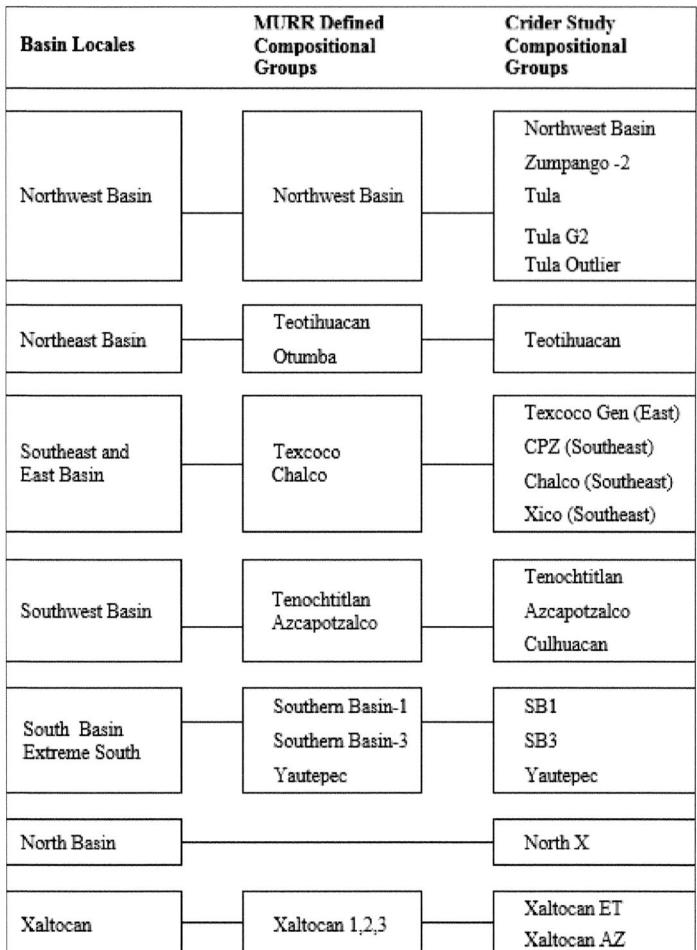

Figure 5. Schematic of the hierarchical organization of the Basin compositional groups by quadrant and the subgroups. (Figure by Crider 2011)

Epiclassic period but underwent a process of 'ruralization' in which small settlements were dispersed throughout the region, presumably an indicator of the increased influence of the Early Postclassic influence of Tula into the Basin (Sanders *et al.* 1979, 140). Widespread access to Mazapan Wavy Line across the Zumpango Survey area suggests that this process began early in the Early Postclassic period.

The Tula-assigned specimens were painted using a multi-prong paint brush in an assortment of design motifs (Figure 7). Based upon attribute study of Tula collected Mazapan Wavy Line (including those not selected for INAA), commonly occurring motifs include design panels with undulating lines and interlocking inter-locking scrolls (similarly observed in the Basin of Mexico collections). However, there are also more complex design motifs in which the layout includes dividing the design space into quartered sections, including connected circles, or intersections of straight and wavy lines. Some similar motifs were observed in the Teotihuacan collections, but were observed more commonly in the Tula collections. Surface finish tends to be matte, although level of burnish and gloss varies. The northern Basin Zumpango collections that I observed were clearly identifiable as Mazapan Wavy Line with multi-prong painted design, motifs were horizontal undulating lines, most in matte surface finish.

The Teotihuacan Valley Wavy Line pottery is well represented in the INAA sampling, selected both from sites within the Teotihuacan Mapping Project and from multiple sites in the Teotihuacan Valley Rural Survey. Similarly, the results indicate a strong pattern of consuming locally produced Wavy Line pottery. Interior decorated pottery is most common in the Teotihuacan collections, and vessel forms range from small saucers to deep open bowls. The most common designs are simple undulating lines in horizontal panels, but there is considerable variation in the execution of this motif. Although the overall layout of the designs tends to be more simplified with few intersections, the technical skill is well-developed – note the vessel in Figure 7I with seventeen parallel lines from

## Chapter 7 Complementary Approaches for Understanding Mazapan Pottery

| Collection Blocks./Type Variant | Tula and North/Northwest | | | | | Northeast | | East-Southeast | Southwest | South | |
|---|---|---|---|---|---|---|---|---|---|---|---|
| | Tula | Tula G2 | Zumpango-2 | Basin NW | North X BL | Teotihuacan | Texcoco | CPZ | Azcapotzalco | South 3 | Grand Total |
| **Tula (Total)** | 29 | 3 | | | | | | | 1 | | 33 |
| Mazapan Wavy Line (Burnished Variety) | 2 | 1 | | | | | | | | | 3 |
| Mazapan Wavy Line (Fine Paste) | 5 | | | | | | | | | | 5 |
| Mazapan Wavy Line (Matte Variety) | 22 | 2 | | | | | | | 1 | | 25 |
| **Zumpango Survey Sites (Total)** | 3 | | 8 | 1 | 1 | | | | | | 13 |
| **Teotihuacan Region (Total)** | | 1 | | | | 39 | 2 | | 1 | | 43 |
| Teotihuacan Mapping Project | | | | | | 19 | 1 | | 1 | | 21 |
| Teotihuacan Valley Rural Survey | | 1 | | | | 20 | 1 | | | | 22 |
| **Cerro Portezuelo (Total)** | | | | | 1 | 19 | 12 | 10 | 1 | | 43 |
| Mazapan Wavy Line (Burnished Variety) | | | | | | 1 | 7 | 10 | | | 18 |
| Mazapan Wavy Line (Matte Variety) | | | | | 1 | 18 | 5 | | 1 | | 25 |
| **Southern Basin Survey Sites (Total)** | | | | | | 1 | 3 | 1 | 1 | 1 | 7 |
| **Grand Total** | 32 | 3 | 9 | 1 | 2 | 59 | 17 | 11 | 4 | 1 | 139 |

Figure 6. Cross-tabulation of the results of compositional group assignments for Mazapan Wavy Line pottery selected for Instrumental Neutron Activation Analysis as compared to the Collection Blocks. For example, three defined variants of Mazapan Wavy Line were collected from the Tula region and nearly all of those samples were assigned to either the Tula or Tula G2 compositional groups, indicating a strong pattern of consuming locally produced pottery. (Figure by Crider)

Figure 7. Mazapan Wavy Line, Matte Variant, Tula compositional group, interior decorated: A) MURR ID DLC026, B) MURR ID DLC027, C) MURR ID DLC039, D) MURR ID DLC035, E) MURR ID DLC038, F) MURR ID DLC032, G) MURR ID DLC037, H) MURR ID DLC028, I) MURR ID DLC032, J) MURR ID DLC030. These examples demonstrate a range of motifs that vary from straight, curved, and interlocking design panels. (Figure by Crider 2011)

a single implementation tool. However, the specific technologies and techniques for producing the distinctive multiple-line motifs are not well understood, a point I will return to shortly. Although not discussed in detail here, in a recent collaborative INAA study focused on the Teotihuacan Valley (Crider, Nichols, Garraty 2017, in press), we pooled MURR project data focused upon the Teotihuacan Valley, spanning the Preclassic through Colonial periods. Using similar statistical procedures as applied to the broader Central Mexican compositional groups, we propose more refined compositional groups within the Teotihuacan Valley. Results indicate multiple compositional groups among the Mazapan Wavy Line pottery, another indication of the 'ruralization' not only of settlement distribution, but also an increase in diverse ceramic production across the Teotihuacan Valley in the shift from Epiclassic to Early Postclassic period.

However, when assessing the trends in the southern portion of the state of Texcoco at the site of Cerro Portezuelo, the Mazapan Wavy Line INAA patterns diverge (see also Crider 2013a for further discussion on Cerro Portezuelo results). A large portion of the Wavy Line used at Cerro Portezuelo and southern Basin is not local, but imported from the Northeast Basin, which includes the Teotihuacan Valley produced pottery. When compositional groups were compared against patterns in stylistic and technological attributes of the pottery, a strong pattern emerged. Broadly speaking, two variants were defined based on surface treatment and technique of applying the painted design. The Matte Variant is distinguished by an even surface finish with minimal burnish marks or glossy finish (Figure 8). A distinctive multi-prong paint brush was used to apply panels of decoration, a common set of traits for Mazapan Wavy Line throughout the Basin and Tula. The Matte Variant of Wavy Line strongly aligns with production of the Northeast Basin, including Teotihuacan and more northerly Texcoco assignment.

Conversely, the Burnished Variant is distinguished by a poorly burnished surface finish, carelessly executed, which often smeared the painted design. There is more gloss to the finish, although it is sloppily executed. In some instances, decorative motifs were painted with a single brush in sets or panels of parallel lines (Figure 9). This Burnished Variant of Mazapan Wavy Line strongly aligns with a local compositional group (Group CPZ) and

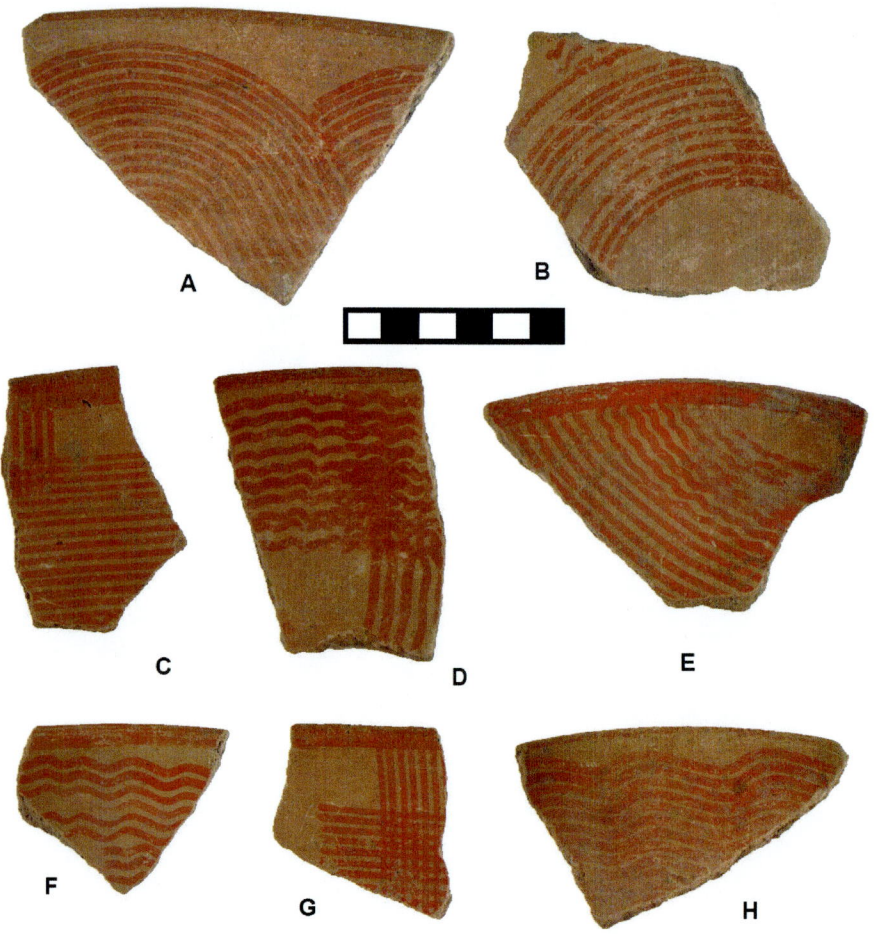

Figure 8. Mazapan Wavy Line, Matte Variant, collected from Cerro Portezuelo and assigned to the Teotihuacan compositional group, interior decorated: A) MURR ID AZC214, B) MURR ID AZC216, C) MURR ID AZC217, D) MURR ID AZC218, E) MURR ID AZC231, F) MURR ID AZC234, G) MURR ID AZC242, H) MURR ID AZC243. These examples have technological and design similarities to those in the Tula compositional group. However, the Teotihuacan produced pottery tends to be less complex in design layout. (Figure by Crider 2011)

# Chapter 7   Complementary Approaches for Understanding Mazapan Pottery

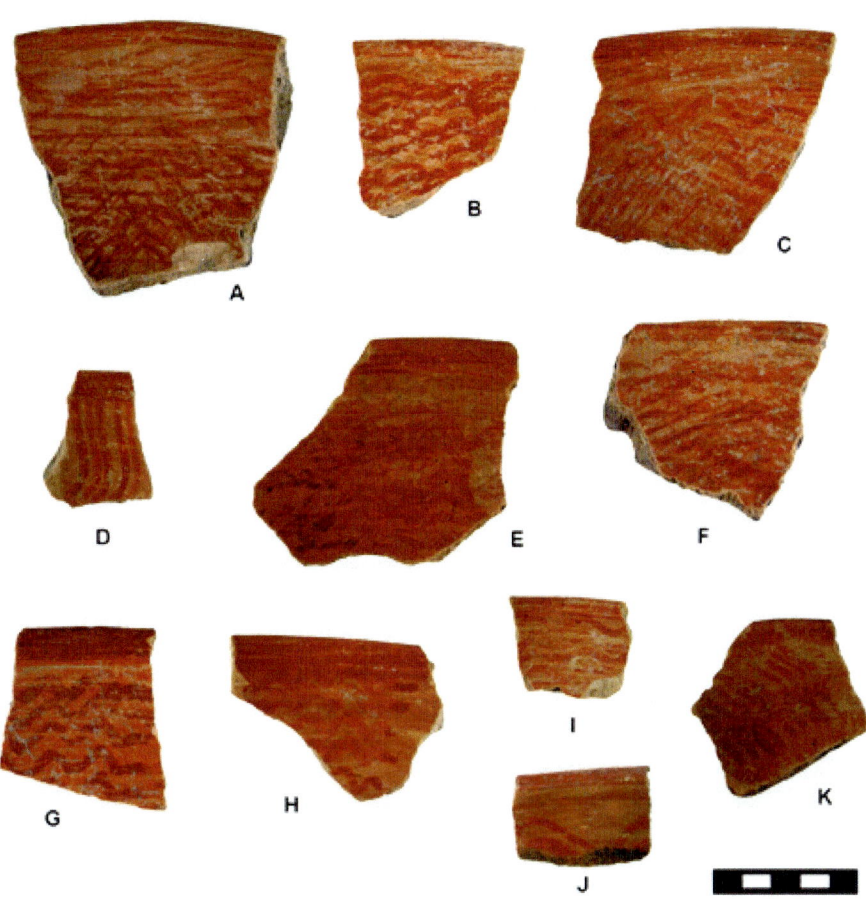

Figure 9. Mazapan Wavy Line, Burnished Variant, CPZ compositional group, interior decorated: A) MURR ID AZC219, B) MURR ID AZC222, C) MURR ID AZC237, D) MURR ID AZC229, E) MURR ID AZC240, F) MURR ID AZC238, G) MURR ID AZC239, H) MURR ID AZC241, I) MURR ID AZC225, J) MURR ID AZC233, K) MURR ID AZC227. Most of these examples are painted with a single brush to create parallel lines, those that might have implemented a multi-prong brush (e.g., D) are not as even and separated of lines as compared to those typical of Matte Variant. The surface is sloppily burnished and streaky, an attribute more typical of Epiclassic pottery, especially low-quality Coyotlatelco Red-on-natural. (Figure by Crider 2011)

some more broadly to a general Texcoco Group, likely local or nearby in southern Texcoco. Given the trend that Wavy Line pottery was largely produced for local consumption, a motif analysis can incorporate a larger sample of vessels (with those for NAA at the core of the analysis). Those vessels from the Tula settlement cluster that are all painted with a multi-prong brush are the most complex in the presentation of design motifs. Commonly occurring are panels of undulating lines and interlocking scrolls. The interior bases show motifs with circles and crossed or quartered designs. There are combinations and intersections of shapes and directions within the same vessel. These examples are among the most complex combinations of design from across the region.

Distribution of the Burnished Variant of the Wavy Line pottery is largely limited to the Cerro Portezuelo settlement cluster. As part of classification analysis of the Cerro Portezuelo Mazapan Wavy Line pottery, I inventoried roughly 200 sherds and found that about 50% can be identified as the Burnished Variant, and extrapolating INAA trends would indicate that at least half of the Wavy Line pottery consumed was locally made, but of a lesser quality than that imported from its northern neighbors. The Burnished Variant of Mazapan Wavy Line exhibits a sloppily burnished surface rather than the matte no-gloss finish of the Matte Variant. The technical qualities for decoration and execution resemble the earlier Epiclassic Coyotlatelco red painted pottery while the designs mimic the Wavy Line Matte Variant, but with simple motifs and design. This provides basis for my current hypothesis that Cerro Portezuelo potters were emulating motifs of the northern Basin tradition, but lacked direct access and training in multi-prong tool technique for decoration. But Cerro Portezuelo may have been a marginal center on the periphery of the expanding Tula-influenced state perhaps only for a brief time. By the close of the Early Postclassic period, Cerro Portezuelo become more closely aligned to Tula's ceramic styles and other material culture (Crider 2013a). Most Burnished Variant designs were executed by painting with a single brush, as indicated by uneven spacing especially visible in the peaks and valleys of the undulating lines. The most common design motif is the horizontal panel of parallel wavy lines decorating the interior of the bowl. These patterns may have been modeled on those of the Matte Variety from Teotihuacan. The paint color is darker and more purplish (or maroon) than the simple red paint on the Matte Variety vessels.

The Matte Variant paint resembles the consistency of ink and has an even appearance in its adherence, while the Burnished Variant paint is less consistent and more like water color where the paint thins and pools on the edges. The CPZ compositional group clays were never used to produce the Matte Variant. This indicates that Cerro Portezuelo was peripheral to production of Matte Wavy Line and the use of the multi-prong brush, but at some point the area became recipient to Teotihuacan produced goods; although one cannot say if they were copying imports (or observing from a distance) or making their own variant to supplement their access to the imports. I believe the import of the pottery to signal an expression of early expansion of northern interaction zones into the southeastern Basin as far south as the Cerro Portezuelo. Preceding the Early Postclassic, Cerro Portezuelo was one of the largest and most dominant Epiclassic regional centers in the Basin. As Tula's power and influence expanded from the north, there may have been direct and purposeful shifts in political boundaries to directly undermine Cerro Portezuelo's regional political role, especially at the time in which Epiclassic city-states cities were transforming into small state administrative centers and the empty zones between centers were becoming settled as small rural communities.

The complementary approaches of compositional analysis and the assessment technological and stylistic attributes of Wavy Line pottery provides a robust method for identifying local and regional boundary maintenance, and shared learning communities in ceramic production. As a quick note, to supplement these methods and gain more information on the paint recipes I selected a sample of 15 sherds to submit for particle-induced X-ray emission (PIXE) at the Arizona State University ion beam analysis of materials (IBeAM) laboratory (Crider 2013b). When compared to other Central Mexican paints, Mazapan Wavy Line has the lowest amounts of iron (Fe), which is significant due to the qualitative difference in the paint and how it is applied with the multi-prong brush. The recipe for this pottery paint produces a thin paint, much like the consistency of ink, that spreads evenly and in narrow lines with crisp edges. This low concentration of iron is likely due to the dilution of the pigment into the mix as compared to the other pottery types typical of the region. The difference is also reflected in the tones of the red color, which can take on a reddish-orange tint as compared to the darker maroon-purplish reds of the earlier Coyotlatelco pottery. This analysis is useful in comparing regional patterns in elemental concentrations within a pottery type, and across pottery types. Both local pigment minerals (especially evidence rare earth or trace elements) and pottery choice in recipe production contribute to the variation (especially dilution and concentration of Fe and Mn). The samples used for the PIXE study include the Matte Variant of Mazapan Wavy Line and were selected from those submitted for INAA. Additional analysis of Burnished Variant would be useful to test the hypothesis of technological continuity in pottery production for Cerro Portezuelo potters from Epiclassic to Early Postclassic.

**How did they do it?**

The technical skill required to create a paint recipe and complex multi-prong brush may have been short-lived, relatively speaking. This popular service ware was widespread and likely found in most households across the Basin and Tula, especially in rural areas. This red-painted dish suite was replaced by more expediently produced bowls which were covered in a thick cream-colored slip and often only painted red on the vessel rims or simple wide line geometric designs. Throughout my many hours of observation and measurement of Mazapan Wavy Line design attributes, especially as I counted row after row of parallel lines across hundreds of vessels, I observed a wide range of skill in their application. The most elegant of examples maintained a clear, crisp line separation for upwards of 15, 16 or more individual parallel lines, placed evenly in symmetrical panels across the interiors of curved, often high-walled bowls. No brush has survived the ages to give us insight into the technology as to how this high-quality design was accomplished.

So, taking advantage of my position at a small liberal arts college, I brought my question to Benjamin Moore, a colleague from the art department at Luther College; and with support from the college we recruited a student, Jayne Cole, to assist in a summer-long experiment. For a few hours, each week we set out to make paint brushes that could accommodate multiple lines of design, hold sufficient paint, lay out even and separated lines, and be applied to the curved surface of a bowl. We had a few successes along the way, as well as many failures to inform our subsequent trials and experiments.

I first introduced my collaborators to the range of variation in attributes and provided them numerous examples of Mazapan Wavy Line pottery from my attribute study (Figure 10). We viewed both the low quality and high-quality archaeological sherds, setting our aspirations to replicate paint quality and brush-line attributes of line thickness and length of line as our first targets. So we developed a set experiment parameters and defined what technical qualities we hoped to replicate. We then began brainstorming and testing brush designs and collecting materials that would have been readily available in Central Mexico, especially the northern Basin from Teotihuacan to Tula, Hidalgo. We surmised that brush handles might include any number of botanicals like soft wood or lake reeds; while

CHAPTER 7  COMPLEMENTARY APPROACHES FOR UNDERSTANDING MAZAPAN POTTERY

* 3 to 12 prongs / individual brush lines per tool
* brushes must maintain line separation
* use of locally available, natural materials
* brush bristles require ability to hold paint for long lines
* narrow line width (1 to 4 mm; 1.5-2.5 most common)
* brush handle/holder design that is easy to use
* brush bristles slightly stiff but also flexible
* clear, strong paint line
* use of slightly watery, thin paint

Figure 10. Selected examples of variety Mazapan Wavy Line from attribute study and the list of goals and parameters set for experiment to replicate brush technology for multi-prong brush. (Figure by Crider)

brush bristles could include hair, maguey or yucca fibers, and we even tried bird feathers (just in case). These items were collected from around the local landscape, or from scrap heaps in the art supplies (with special thanks for a special delivery of maguey leaves from Arizona). Commercially purchased red hematite (iron oxide) pigment was used to prepare our own paint recipe (purchased from art supply store).

We prepared 6 differing combinations of water + solution + binder to test on paper/clay surfaces that best approximated our ideal paint thickness and quality to approximate Wavy Line paint characteristics. Our best paint recipe (2.5 g mineral / 2.5 g clay and 10 ml of water) was used for the duration of our test brushes (Figure 11). We selected a thick, slightly textured, high quality art paper for preliminary assessment on the ability of brushes to make uniform and clean lines, as well as how well brush fibers absorbed and released paint. Clay tiles (unfired) absorbed paints to a much higher degree than the paper. Bowl forms were implemented to test the ability of the brushes to accommodate a curved surface (Figure 12). Each successive step of investigation provided understanding of the unique attributes required of bristle type and length, interaction with clay and paint, and the challenges in maintaining separate and clearly defined lines within the resulting designs. We prepared and tested 37 different brushes with combinations of handle form and material, bristle fiber type, bristle length and bunch quality, and methods of attaching bristles/tines. Brush designs were tested on textured paper, clay tiles, and simple ceramic bowls (Figures 13).

*Summary of Experiment Findings*

First, a comparison of bristle fibers reveals that the choice in fiber directly correlates to the absorption and release of paint from the brush bristles to the medium being painted (Figure 14). *Agave fibers* are thick, coarse and highly absorbent. While bristles were firm and flexible, a needed quality to maintain line separation of very thin brush lines, and accommodate zig-zags and rainbow and spiral designs, we found these brushes resisted the release of paint to the clay – resulting is very short design panels, but performed very well on textured paper. *Human hair* (shampooed and shiny, which we determined may have interfered with our test) easily released the paint, but were difficult to implement in the zig-zag type designs, more suitable for more 'scriptive' type designs common to single prong brushes. In order to have the proper size decorative line, a large bundle of fibers was needed, but in order to hold enough paint to a long design panel the brush bristles needed to be lengthy, which spread the width of the painted line too wide for our purposes. When combined as a set of brushes, the lines spread and created a single block of paint with no line separation (think about the brush used to paint walls). *Deer hair* was selected because it

Figure 11. Selected materials used in creating bristles and paint. On the top row, agave leaves are stripped of outer layer and fibers cleaned and tried for bristles and binding cordage. Center row includes hair for brush fibers: deer fur on left, and donated human hair on right. Bottom row includes mixing and testing consistency of red paint after mineral powder and water mixed. (Figure by Crider)

was less coarse than agave, but more-so than the human hair (and was clear of additives from shampoo). Of the fiber brushes, deer hair more readily absorbed and released the paint, held paint for the longest line, and most fluid of our brushes *when used on clay surfaces.*

Securing the brush bristles to a handle was another creative step in the development of prototypes (Figure 13). The challenge was how to prepare a multi-prong holder that could accommodate dozens of brushes at once. In one iteration, sets of single brushes were tied together with agave cordage in a 'raft' design. The benefit, we surmised, would be ease in replacing a single word or damaged brush rather than scrapping the entire tool after a few uses. In another model, notches were cut along split sticks to set packets of bristle fibers into each one. This model was simple to construct and replace, but required binding the full length of the handle tightly which also keeping

CHAPTER 7   COMPLEMENTARY APPROACHES FOR UNDERSTANDING MAZAPAN POTTERY

Figure 12. Differing media are prepared for testing. Top panels include Jayne Cole preparing bisque bowl forms made in molds, dried, and brush tests on interior and exterior of the bowl forms by Benjamin Moore. Center left panel is a Mazapan Wavy Line sherd with undulating lines in a horizontal design panel, while center right panel is resulting test on texted art paper using stylus brush to replicate common design patterns. Bottom left panel is set of clay test tiles set out to dry, and bottom right panel is Jayne Cole measuring ingredients for paint recipe. (Figure by Crider)

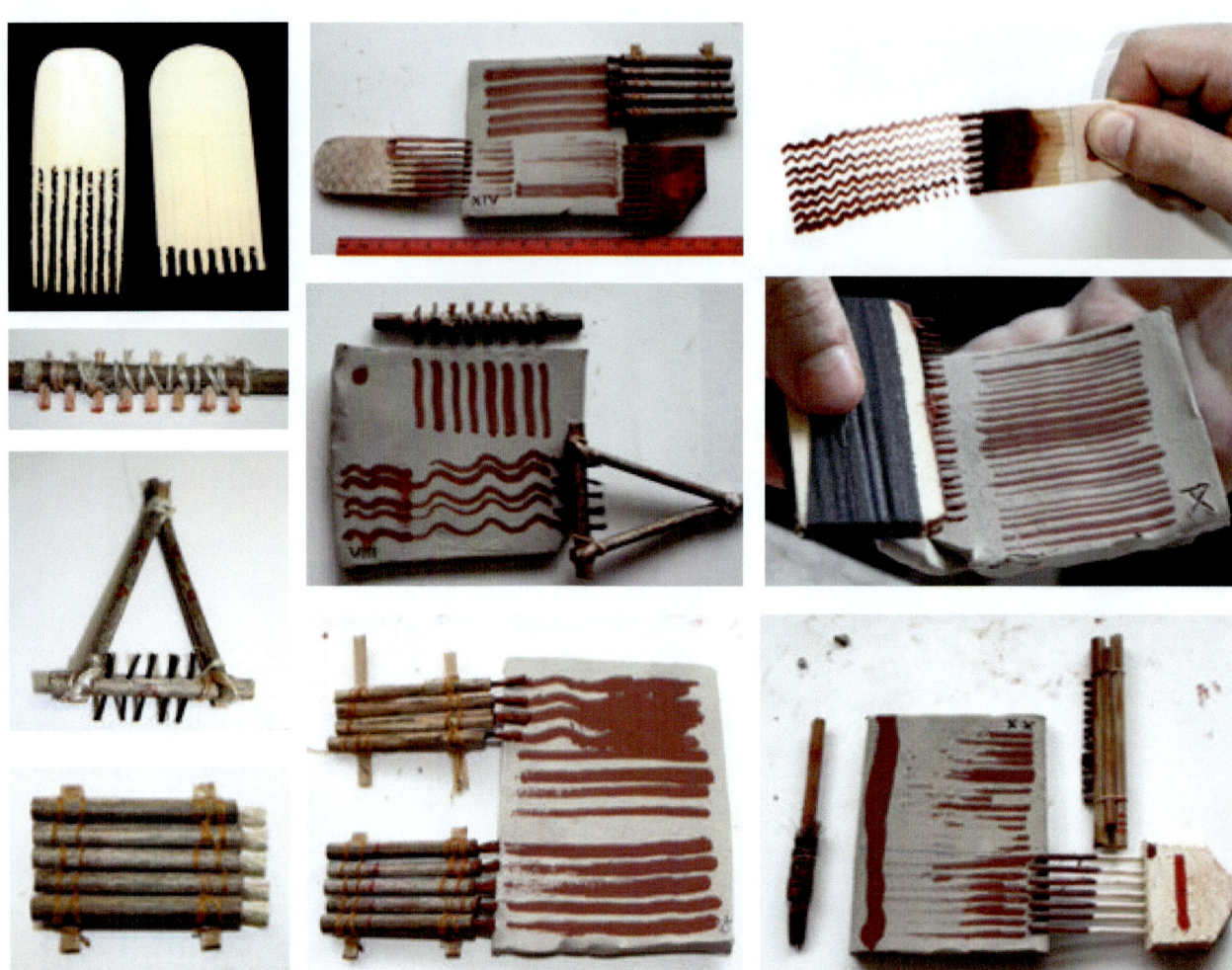

Figure 13. Examples of selected brush prototypes and selected paint tests. Left column from top to bottom: wooden comb stylus cut from balsa wood, Comb style 'split handle with agave fibers, comb style with split stick holder and attached handle with human hair fiber brush bristles, and com raft with five agave fiber brushes. Center column shows clay test tiles to compare results on clay media. Each brush used is set next to results test run. Right column shows additional tests of varying brush prototypes. Top image is a stylus comb on paper, which shows the intensity of paint changes from dark to light as brush releases less paint by end. Center image is a complex brush prototype with a large number of hair bristles in a split comb. Bottom image compares large hair brush (single) with a split comb with hair and a stylus style using toothpicks rather than balsa. (Figure by Crider)

bristles in place during construction. Additionally, a long brush handle with bristles at one end (tooth brush style) was awkward for tile and bowl tests. We also developed a 'stylus' tool that did not use fiber bristles but rather cute prongs into a flat piece of balsa wood. The stylus nibs were cut to the line width and spacing we hoped to achieve. On paper (a flat surface) this tool provided long, clear lines, good line separation, consistent pattern construction with no crossing lines. Unfortunately, once we tried our stylus combs on the interior of the bowls, there were significant challenges in its use. The shape of the brush prevented full contact with the curvature of the bowl wall. Also, it was difficult to prevent paint drips after repeated use, as the wood became completely saturated with paint (Figure 15).

Several observations were made while testing our various brushes. The design of the brush handle became important when testing paper/tile vs. curved bowl surfaces. The primary mechanical kinetic issues include where hand/finger placement occurs and how the arm/wrist motion is constrained during design application. In in the case of the notched sticks, there was no handle to hold and the fingers were always in the way of some of the bristles or by holding the ends would scrape the sides of the bowls. The 'raft' holders did not have this problem (Figure 15).

Creating uniform lines was much simpler on the flat paper and tile media for some prototypes. The arc of the design is controlled by a circular wrist action of moving brush across an even surface. Unfortunately, the same motion was

# Chapter 7 Complementary Approaches for Understanding Mazapan Pottery

not easily replicated on the interior of the prepared bowl forms. Many prototypes were too wide and inflexible to create horizontal design panel on hemispherical bowl form, especially not able to adapt to the curvature of the bowl wall. How the brush is held depends on the shape of the handle and the amount of surface that the artist can hold without getting fingers in the way of bristles. Each successive pass in prototype development was informed by the mechanical and kinetic properties of the previous brush design. For many brush styles, we suspect that there must be a particular method of holding the brush and concurrent method for turning the bowl in a fluid rotation in order to apply a consistent pattern and even design. Since the potters' wheel was not available in central Mexico in Early Postclassic times, a small platform (perhaps a ceramic saucer or large sherd) might have been needed to easily rotate the bowls while applying the multi-prong brush technique.

Figure 14. Comparison of three brush fibers. The top brush is agave fiber, which readily absorbs the paint into the coarse fiber, but does not easily release the paint evenly and consistently for duration of a long line. The center brush is human hair that had difficulty absorbing the paint, but readily releases the paint to the surface medium. Best for more 'scriptive' designs for single brush decoration because the fibers bend easily and do not keep narrow and separate lines. The bottom brush is deer hair, which readily absorbed paint, easily released paint to clay medium. (Figure by Crider)

Figure 15. Methods for holding and using different style brushes. The top row includes the comb split handle which was difficult to dip in paint and not leave paint drips and fingers interfere with motion needed to produce complex motifs. The center row includes the comb raft brush, which is easy to handle and keeps fingers away from paint and clay surface. The bottom row shows handling a single brush, which requires moving both the hand and the bowl to get long line of paint. Finally, the stylus wooden comb requires dipping the entire surface of the stylus in paint and fingers become covered in paint. (Figure by Crider)

These experiments provided useful insights into the challenges of emulating a decorative technique and tradition in the context of having no training or direct observation of a practitioner. It was a creative exploration born from curiosity and from our own expertise. No single brush solution emerged to account for all of the test parameters set out from the Mazapan Wavy Line design attributes. But from this round of experimentation we learned that it is very difficult to emulate the multi-prong tool without prior training, reinforcing the importance of apprenticeship and learning-networks in crafting. We emerged with a few favorite prototypes that could be further refined. For example, our most favorable handle designs allowed for best grip and control without interfering with brushes, especially the Comb 'Raft' Design, Comb Split Handle, and Stylus Comb. The stylus design also has merit, but it must overcome the problem of adapting more readily to bowl curvature in order for the nibs to make consistent contact.

The Mazapan Wavy Line decorative tradition, although seemingly simplistic, was more technologically complex than envisioned. The variation reflected in the archaeological examples reveals a wide range of skill across the Basin, the most highly skilled maintained neat line separation, fluid line placement, symmetry and few errors in paint drips, missing tines, or wayward lines. The most complex designs and highest skilled craftsmen appear to have been practicing in areas around Tula and Teotihuacan. Our own efforts, as non-apprenticed painters of Mazapan Wavy Line pottery approximated those examples at the low end of Basin craftsmanship; perhaps revealing instances of non-trained emulation in some of the archaeological examples.

**New Story of Mazapan Wavy Line?**

Given Bey's (1986) findings of Mazapan Wavy Line pottery at Tula, it is time to put to rest the hypothesis of its Teotihuacan origins. The technique of the multi-prong brush painted decoration may have been introduced by potters originating from areas to the northwest of Tula, as proposed by Braniff (1999). A version of the multi-prong technique with red painted lines on the interior of vessels was used prior to the Early Postclassic in the San Miguel phase of the Classic period in Guanajuato (Braniff 1999, Figure 6.6, 14, 16, 17). These vessels had far fewer parallel lines, and designs included symmetrical panels of straight lines that often overlapped to create cross-hatching and could have additional embellishments of small scrolls. Perhaps a brush proposed in one early experiment for Old World pottery (Braidwood 1939) might have been adequate for these Guanajuato bowls? The Central Mexico Mazapan Wavy Line is distinctly different from The San Miguel Red on Buff pottery in vessel form and overall design layout. However, the uniqueness of the painting technique and some similarity of design motif strongly support a northwestern inspiration of the style. A similar case can be made for the introduction of Coyotlatelco style pottery in the Epiclassic (e.g., Beekman and Christensen 2003; Brambila and Crespo 2005; Braniff 2005; Cobean 1990:174-175; Hirth and Cyphers 1988; López and Nicólas 2005; Manzanilla 2005; Paredes 2005; Rattray 1996, 1998). Certain motifs and techniques of ceramic production and design may have originated to areas north and northwest of the Basin of Mexico, especially from the Bajío, but more local characteristics were solidified during the Epiclassic specific to particular potters and areas within the region (Crider 2011). It is not clear that there is any relationship between the Coyotlatelco pottery producers and those that subsequently became specialists in Mazapan Wavy Line by the close of the Epiclassic. But it does seem that new techniques in painting design emerged and spread across Central Mexico to replace the Coyotlatelco tradition. This spread of a popular style may have been through both emulation or apprenticeship, accounting for the wide variety in skill and quality of the final products. But its distribution to households and communities across the Basin of Mexico, especially in along the northern lakeshores in the Zumpango and Teotihuacan regions, appears to coincide with the process of settling into new open lands as the Early Postclassic political and economic landscape was changing.

**References Cited**

Beekman, Christopher S., and Alexander F. Christensen. 2003. 'Controlling for Doubt and Uncertainty Through Multiple Lines of Evidence: A New Look at the Mesoamerican Nahua Migrations.' *Journal of Archaeological Method and Theory* 10 (2): 111-164.
Bennyhoff, James A., and Robert Fleming Heizer. 1965. 'Neutron Activation Analysis of Some Cuicuilco and Teotihuacan Pottery: Archaeological Interpretation of Results.' *American Antiquity* 30 (3): 348-349.
Bey III, George J. 1986. 'A Regional Analysis of Toltec Ceramics, Tula, Hidalgo, Mexico.' PhD diss., Tulane University.
Binford, Lewis R. 1965. 'Archaeological Systematics and the Study of Culture Process.' *American Antiquity* 31 (2): 202-210.
Braidwood, Robert J. 1939. 'A Note on a Multiple-Brush Device Used by Near Eastern Potters of the Fourth Millennium B.C.' *Man* 39: 192-194.
Brambila Paz, Rosa. and Ana María Crespo. 2005. 'Desplazamientos de poblaciones y creación de territorios en el Bajío.' In *Reacomodos demográficos del Clásico al Posclásico en el centro de México*, edited by Linda Manzanilla, pp. 155-174. México, DF: Universidad Nacional Autónoma de México, Instituto de Investigaciones Antropológicas.

Braniff Cornejo, Beatriz. 1999. *Morales, Guanajuato, y la tradición tolteca*. México, DF: Instituto Nacional de Antropología e Historia.

Braniff Cornejo, Beatriz. 2005. 'Los chichimecas a la caída de Teotihuacan y durante la conformación de la Tula de Hidalgo.' In *Reacomodos demográficos del Clásico al Posclásico en el centro de México*, edited by Linda Manzanilla, pp. 45-56. México, DF: Universidad Nacional Autónoma de México, Instituto de Investigaciones Antropológicas.

Cobean, Robert H. 1978. 'The Pre-Aztec Ceramics of Tula, Hidalgo, Mexico.' PhD diss., Harvard University.

Cobean, Robert H. 1990. *La Cerámica de Tula Hidalgo*. México, DF: Instituto Nacional de Antropología e Historia.

Crider, Destiny L. 2011. 'Epiclassic and Early Postclassic Interaction in Central Mexico as Evidenced by Decorate Pottery.' PhD diss., Arizona State University.

Crider, Destiny L. 2013a. 'Shifting Alliances: Epiclassic and Early Postclassic Interactions at Cerro Portezuelo.' *Ancient Mesoamerica* 24 (1): 107-130.

Crider, Destiny L. 2013b. 'Assessing Mexican pottery paint recipes using particle-induced X-ray emission.' *Open Journal of Archaeometry* 1 (e5): 21-25.

Crider, Destiny, Deborah L. Nichols, and Christopher P. Garraty. 2017 (in press). 'Towards a Micro-Regional Understanding of Ceramic Production in the Teotihuacan Valley.' In *City, Craft and Resilience in Mesoamerica: Papers in Honor of Dan Healan*, edited by Ronald Faulseit. Middle American Research Institute at Tulane University.

Crider, Destiny, Deborah L. Nichols, Hector Neff, Michael D. Glascock. 2007. 'In the Aftermath of Teotihuacan: Epiclassic Pottery Production and Distribution in the Teotihuacan Valley, Mexico.' *Latin American Antiquity* 18 (2): 123-143.

García Chávez, Raúl E. 2004. 'De Tula a Azcapotzalco: caracterización arqueológica de los Altepetl de la Cuenca de México del Postclásico Temprano y Medio, a través del estudio cerámico regional.' PhD Diss., Universidad Nacional Autónoma de México.

Garraty, Christopher P. 2006. 'The Politics of Commerce: Ceramic Production and Exchange in the Basin of Mexico, A.D. 1200-1650.' PhD diss., Arizona State University.

Hegmon, Michelle. 1992. 'Archaeological Research on Style.' *Annual Review of Anthropology* 21 (1): 517-536.

Herbich, Ingrid. 1987 'Learning Patterns, Potter Interaction and Ceramic Style among the Luo of Kenya.' *The African Archaeological Review* 5: 193-204.

Hicks, Frederic, and Henry B. Nicholson. 1964. 'The Transition from Classic to Postclassic at Cerro Portezuelo, Valley of Mexico.' *Actas y Memorias del XXXV Congreso Internacional de Americanistas, México, 1962*, 493-506. Tomo I. México: Instituto Nacional de Antropología e Historia.

Hill, James N. 1970. *Broken K Pueblo: Prehistoric Social Organization in the American Southwest*. Anthropological Papers of the University of Arizona 18. Tucson: University of Arizona Press.

Hirth, Kenneth G., and Ann Cyphers Guillén. 1988. *Tiempo y Asentamiento en Xochicalco*. México, DF: Universidad Nacional Autónoma de México.

Hodge, Mary G., and Leah D. Minc. 1990. 'The Spatial Patterning of Aztec Ceramics: Implications for Prehispanic Exchange Systems in the Valley of Mexico.' *Journal of Field Archaeology* 17 (4): 415-437.

Linné, Sigvald. 2003. *Archaeological Researches at Teotihuacán, Mexico*. Tuscaloosa, Alabama/London: The University of Alabama Press.

Longacre, William A. 1970. *Archaeology as Anthropology: A case Study*. Anthropological Papers of the University of Arizona 17. Tucson: University of Arizona Press.

López Pérez, Claudia M., and Claudia Nicolás Careta. 2005. 'La cerámica de tradición norteña en el valle de Teotihuacan durante el Epiclásico y el Posclásico temprano.' In *Reacomodos demográficos del Clásico al Posclásico en el centro de México*, edited by Linda Manzanilla, pp. 275-286. México, DF: Universidad Nacional Autónoma de México, Instituto de Investigaciones Antropológicas.

Lyons, Patrick D., and Jeffrey J. Clark. 2008. 'Interaction, Enculturation, Social Distance, and Ancient Ethnic Identities.' In *Archaeology Without Borders: Contact, Commerce, and Change in the U.S. Southwestt and Northwestern Mexico*, edited by Laurie D. Webster and Maxine E. McBrinn, pp. 185-208. University of Colorado Press, Boulder.

Manzanilla, Linda R. 2005. 'Migrantes epiclásicos en Teotihuacan. Propuesta metodológica para análisis de migraciones del Clásico al Posclásico.' In *Reacomodos demográficos del Clásico al Posclásico en el centro de México*, edited by Linda R. Manzanilla, pp. 261-274. México, DF: Universidad Nacional Autónoma de México, Instituto de Investigaciones Antropológicas.

Mastache, Alba Guadalupe, and Robert H. Cobean. 1989. 'The Coyotlatelco Culture and the Origins of the Toltec State.' In *Mesoamerica After the Decline of Teotihuacan*, edited by Richard A. Diehl and Janet C. Berlo, pp. 49-68. Washington, D.C.: Dumbarton Oaks.

Mastache, Alba Guadalupe, Robert H. Cobean, and Dan Healan. 2002. *Ancient Tollan: Tula and the Toltec Heartland*. Boulder: University Press of Colorado.

Nichols, Deborah L., Hector Neff, and George L. Cowgill. 2013. 'Cerro Portezuelo: States and Hinterlands in the Pre-Hispanic Basin of Mexico.' *Ancient Mesoamerica* 24 (1): 47-71.

Nichols, Deborah L., Elizabeth Brumfiel, Hector Neff, Mary Hodge, Thomas Charlton, and Michael Glascock. 2002. 'Neutrons, Markets, Cities, and Empire: A 1000-Year Perspective on Ceramic Production and Distribution in the Postclassic Basin of Mexico.' *Journal of Anthropological Archaeology* 21 (1): 25-82.

Paredes Gudiño, Blanca. 2005. Análisis de Flujos Migratorios y Composición Multiétnica de la Población de Tula, Hgo, In *Reacomodos demográficos del Clásico al Posclásico en el centro de México*, edited by Linda Manzanilla, pp. 203-226. México, DF: Universidad Nacional Autónoma de México, Instituto de Investigaciones Antropológicas.

Parsons, Jeffrey R. 1971. *Prehistoric Settlement Patterns in the Texcoco Region, Mexico. Memoirs of the Museum of Anthropology No. 3*. Ann Arbor: University of Michigan.

Parsons, Jeffrey R. 2008. *Prehispanic Settlement Patterns in the Northwestern Valley of Mexico: The Zumpango Region, University of Michigan Memoirs, Number 45*. Ann Arbor: Museum of Anthropology, University of Michigan.

Parsons, Jeffrey R., Elizabeth Brumfiel, Mary H. Parsons, and David J. Wilson. 1982. *Prehispanic Settlement Patterns in the Southern Valley of Mexico, The Chalco-Xochimilco Region. Memoirs of the Museum of Anthropology*. No. 14. Ann Arbor: University of Michigan.

Rodríguez-Alegría, Enrique. 2002. 'Food, eating and Objects of Power: Class Stratification and Ceramic Production and Consumption in Colonial Mexico.' PhD diss., The University of Chicago.

Rattray, Evelyn C. 1966. A Regional Perspective on the Epiclassic Period in Central Mexico. In *Arqueología Mesoamericana: Homenaje a William T. Sanders*, edited by Alba Guadalupe Mastache, Jeffrey R. Parsons, Robert S. Santley, and Mari Carmen Serra Puche, pp. 213-231. México, DF: Instituto Nacional de Antropología y Historia.

Rattray, Evelyn C. 1998. 'El período Epiclásico en México central: una perspectiva regional.' In *Antropología del Occidente de México, XXIV Mesa Redonda de la Sociedad Mexicana de Antropología, vol. III*, pp. 1645-1670. México: SMA/UNAM.

Sanders, William T. 1986. *The Teotihuacan Valley Project, Final Report, Volume 4: The Toltec Period Occupation, Occasional Papers in Anthropology*. No 13. University Park: Department of Anthropology, Pennsylvania State University.

Sanders, William T., Jeffrey Parsons, and Robert S. Santley. 1979. *The Basin of Mexico: Ecological Processes in the Evolution of a Civilization*. New York: Academic Press.

Vaillant, George C. 1932. 'Stratigraphic Research in Central Mexico.' *Proceedings of the National Academy of Sciences*, 18 (7): 487-490.

# Chapter 8

# Sherds of Spartans Past: Ceramics from the Michigan State University Campus Archaeology Program

Lynne Goldstein
Michigan State University; lynneg@msu.edu

Lisa Bright
Michigan State University; brightl1@msu.edu

Jeffrey Painter
Michigan State University; painte15@msu.edu

**Abstract**
*Since its founding in 2005, the Michigan State University (MSU) Campus Archaeology Program (CAP) has conducted surveys and excavations throughout the oldest parts of campus at MSU, the pioneer Land Grant institution. This research requires examining a broad range of material culture from 1855 to 1955, including a wide variety of ceramics. CAP has divided this 100-year period into four eras reflecting broader political, technological, and economic changes. Using these phases, this paper examines the use of ceramics at a Land Grant institution over time. Change in ceramics reflects the development and nature of the university. Initially, students were required to bring their own ceramics from home, often mismatched pieces of varying cost. With increased funding comes institutional ceramics made from durable ironstone with little to no patterning, but a surprising amount of variety. There are also higher end ceramics from faculty homes and for special use, with intricate designs and patterns. The nature of all of these ceramics indicates the kinds of relationships that the early college had, and by examining them spatially it is possible to distinguish between different uses of ceramics and activities, gaining greater insights into campus development.*

**Keywords**
*Historic archaeology, Midwestern U.S. archaeology, Saints' Rest college, Institutional ceramics*

## Introduction

In 2005, archaeologists and students excavated the remains of the first dormitory on Michigan State University's (MSU) campus. The building was constructed in 1856 as the primary housing for the new college's all male student body, and was nicknamed Saints' Rest based on the title of a required Christian devotional. The new college had few financial resources, and Saints' Rest was built with minimal funds. As part of their coursework, students helped with the constant repairs the campus buildings required. During the winter break of 1876, non-student workers left a stove on in the basement, and the building caught fire. The remains of the building, along with other debris, were pushed into the basement and foundations of the structure, and once covered, it was forgotten on the landscape – except for a small stone plaque in the ground noting the building's demolition date and name.

Prior to the excavation of Saints' Rest, many in the university administration believed that none of the historic buildings that first defined the college's landscape in the 19th century could be found under the ground. During the six-week archaeological excavation in 2005, the structure of the basement of the building was uncovered, as well as a diverse range of artifacts, including smoking pipes, toothbrushes, domestic ceramics, test tubes and lab equipment, ink wells, construction materials, and iron stoves that had been imported from Detroit. The site revealed a wealth of information, but most importantly, it demonstrated that the university's campus had archaeological material located just below the surface, and that these cultural heritage resources were being lost or destroyed by construction projects and landscaping. With the success and the publicity associated with the Saints' Rest excavations, MSU changed its perceptions of archaeology and began to realize that they had not been particularly good stewards of their past.

In 2007, the MSU Campus Archaeology Program (CAP) officially began, with the mission to protect and mitigate the archaeological resources of the university's campus, while learning about the past, promoting archaeological outreach, and training students. The program was created and founded by Lynne Goldstein, who coordinated the 2005 excavation of Saints' Rest and has since served as the program's director. CAP is a unique program, and, to our knowledge, the first of its extent at a college or university. Beyond conducting field schools and providing an opportunity for students to learn more about the field, CAP serves the university by working closely with construction crews and the offices of Infrastructure, Planning and Facilities throughout the entire construction process, and is consistently engaged in outreach to promote anthropological work on campus and engage stakeholders in MSU's heritage. The program does much more than compliance work, but it does take compliance work seriously.

The nature of campus development requires rapid, scattered, and often small disturbances to a large landscape. CAP's approach utilizes this apparent discontinuity as a means of conducting regional survey, and to incorporate these disparate assemblages within a research model that examines the campus over time. Often, CAP excavations are only a small shovel test survey or single excavation unit, yielding assemblages that are rarely significant enough to draw substantial conclusions about the past. However, when viewed within a larger context, and compared or contrasted to other sites excavated on the campus, these data become part of a larger concept of cultural development. The ceramic assemblages highlighted here fit specifically into a long-term model of campus development created by CAP, to assess the changes in campus development and higher education between 1855 and 1955. By viewing these assemblages within this framework, archaeologists are able to develop more meaningful conclusions about the material nature of the college campus in the past.

The construction of this model considers the nature of a college or university campus: because maintaining quality standards in education and research, retaining quality faculty, and attracting students requires institutions to stay up-to-date, the built environment is regularly rebuilt, updated, modified, redesigned, and replaced. Such rapid transformation makes campuses a unique cultural landscape, but it also indicates that they are reflections of technological, social, and cultural changes that are occurring throughout the nation and world. This makes the investigation of campuses a vital piece to understanding how broader society is changing over time.

In addition to informing our understanding of broader societal change, the material record of college campuses can also inform us about the way in which institutions encouraged certain types of educational or cultural objectives, and how the students responded to these landscapes. Many universities have distinct approaches to the type of education they hope to provide students, and the built environment is often used as a means of integrating these philosophies into their campus. Over time, these approaches change, often in response to internal changes within the university, or external forces that may shift the university mission or focus. A pertinent example is the passage of the Morrill Land Grant Act of 1862, which provided funding for the development of agricultural colleges in each state. Such funding resulted in either the emergence of new colleges, such as at Michigan Agricultural College, or the expansion of an already existing college, such as at the University of Georgia. Either way, the Act was a reflection of new approaches and demands on agricultural production in the mid-19th century, and had direct effects on the landscape of higher education. Identifying these shifts also plays an important role in understanding how material changes at universities can be identified. Similarly, these educational landscapes had effects on the students and faculty that lived, worked, and studied within them.

Using historical records, maps, architecture and photographs, as well as archaeological data, the CAP model is divided into four phases of development. Since its founding, the Michigan State University (MSU) Campus Archaeology Program (CAP) has conducted surveys and excavations throughout the oldest parts of campus at MSU. The program has examined a broad range of material culture dating from 1855 to 1955, including a wide variety of ceramics. We have divided this 100-year period into four eras that reflect the broader political, technological, social, and economic changes in the campus – not surprisingly, changes in ceramics reflect the development and nature of the university.

We used baseline data to create this four-phase development model, so that we can place any given set of finds into a larger context. Because we have to respond to construction work done on campus, we needed a cultural context to frame our findings. When we have time to conduct independent and intensive excavations, we subsequently focus on specific geographic or chronological areas that will provide additional information and allow us to refine our model. In this way, we can outline what we expect to see in a material record that reflects the series of changes within and between each phase. These changes should be evident in function, materials used, and landscape modification. Our approach to the ceramics combines what we have learned about foodways, economics, technological decisions, and historical records. In the next sections, we outline our expectations for each phase in our model as well as what we have actually recovered to date.

**Phase 1 – 1855-1870**

The Michigan Agricultural College was founded in 1855, and began as six buildings on a 677-acre plot located three miles east of Lansing, Michigan's capitol. The new institution was to focus on the industrialization of agriculture. Graduates of the College were to be trained in a scientific approach to farming, and would return with these new skills to their hometowns. The original campus consisted of six buildings: four faculty houses clustered in one area known as Faculty Row; College Hall – the administrative, library, and teaching building; and Saints' Rest (officially Dormitory No. 1) [Beal 1915, 29]. Students and faculty worked together to build these earliest buildings, clear trees, and plow the fields. Early photographs of both College Hall and Saints' Rest show the amount of ground clearing that was necessary during construction. College President Abbot references these photographs in 1870, when he notes that the College was built through student's work (Beal 1915, 29). An 1870 map (Figure 1A) shows the very limited nature of the college.

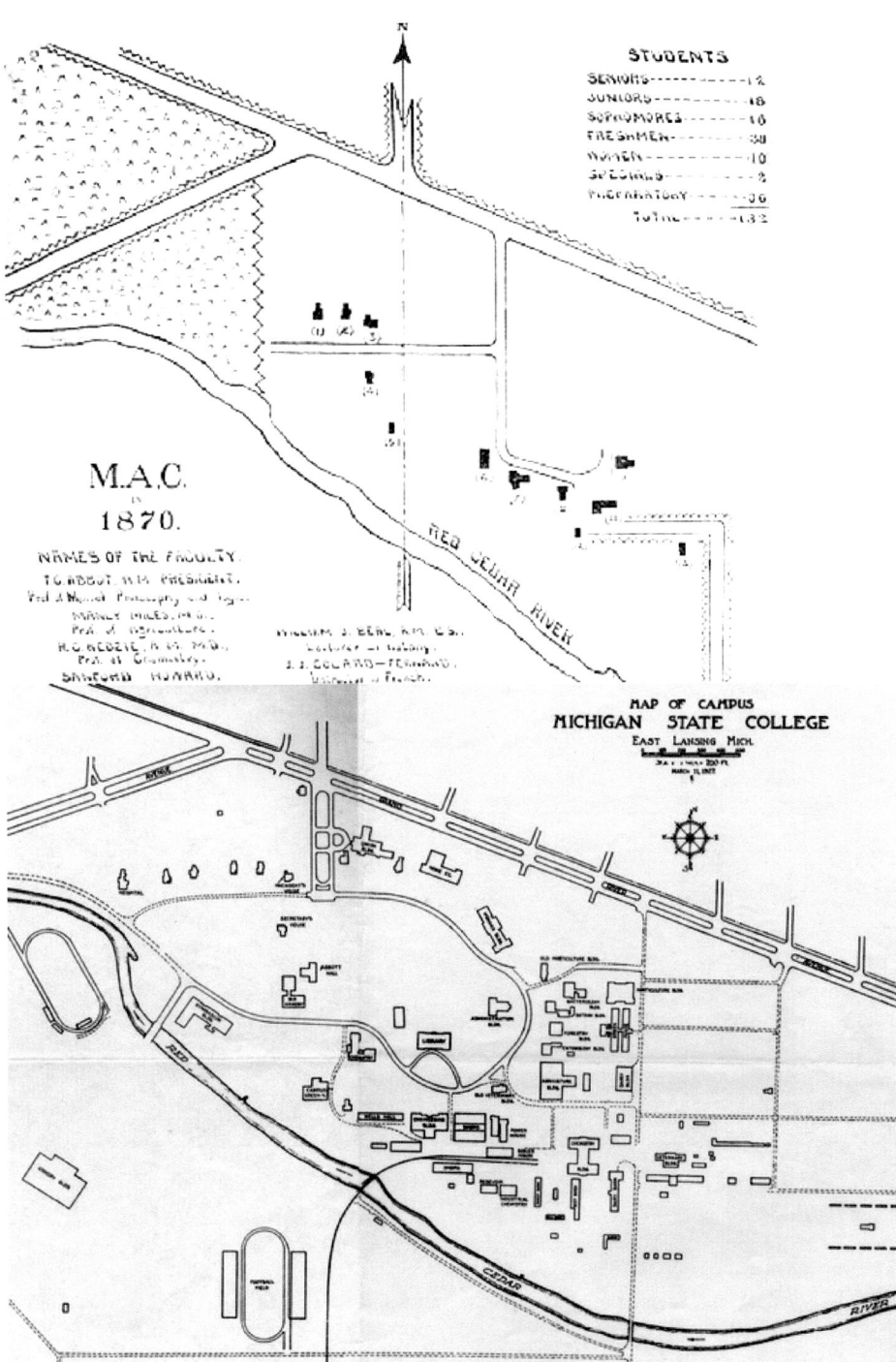

Figure 1. Early campus maps. (A) – upper map. State Agricultural College map, 1870; map by Professor Beal. (B) – lower map. Campus map 1927, showing extent that the college had grown. (Copyright: Michigan State University Archives and Historical Collections)

For Phase 1, we expected to find locally produced materials that reflect the peripheral nature of the earliest college, such as locally made bricks discovered at Saints' Rest, the first dormitory. Artifacts should be minimal in nature, reflecting the very limited and constrained nature of the beginnings of the college. Historians have described this time as the 'starvation period' (Towar 1933, 38), and credit the faculty for keeping the college alive even though there was little interest in the institution's success by the larger public. The small college's close community was an integral element of the campus's survival. Accounts indicate that many fell sick during the earliest years due to the difficult conditions (Beal 1915, 31).

### Institutionally-owned Wares

The ceramic assemblage from this time period is dominated by institutionally-owned dishes, with some other ceramic types that may have been personal items brought to the campus by students or staff. Archival evidence attests to the fact that the college – perhaps expediently – purchased many different types of dishes used in the kitchen and dining room (Michigan State University Archives & Historical Collections: Kuhn Collection).

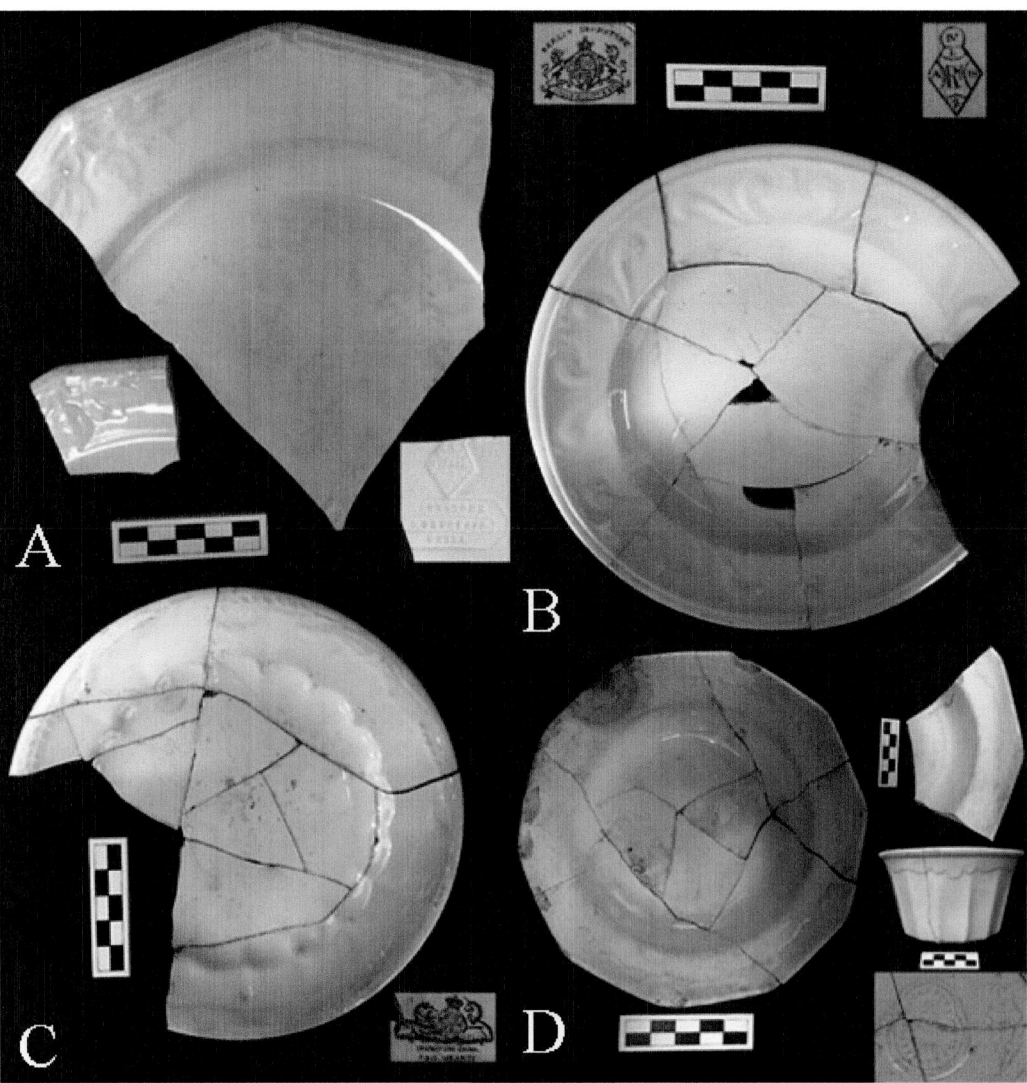

Figure 2. Phase 1 (1855-1870) ceramics. (A) Example of Wedgwood fig pattern. One plate bares a registered design mark indicating a production date of November 27th, 1856; (B) Plate in the 'Berlin Swirl' pattern. Ceramics with this pattern have been recovered produced by Liddle Elliot & Sons (1862-1869), and J. & G. Meakin (Denton 1998); A registered design mark indicates a production date of December 18th, 1856; (C) A wheat pattern plate produced by J. & G. Meakin. J. & G. Meakin produced the wheat pattern from 1860-1930 (Sussman 1985, 8); (D) The scalloped decagon, or Cambridge shape, design (Bev and Ernie 1998) was produced by Davenport. Unfortunately the registered design mark is illegible. We have recovered this pattern in several shapes and sizes. (All photos copyright Michigan State University Campus Archaeology Program)

The institutionally-owned ceramics recovered archaeologically are all white dishes, with many are decorated with different embossed designs (Figure 2). The dishes are generally ironstone, which tend to be stronger and more durable, and they come at a cheaper cost than other alternatives. A number of the dishes recovered are complete or nearly so, and have maker's and registry marks, dating the manufacture of all marked dishes to the late 1850's and early 1860's. Manufacturers all appear to be English, with companies such as Wedgewood, Davenport, Liddle Elliot and Sons, and J. and G. Meakin represented. As to the aforementioned embossed designs, five separate designs were found among the dishes recovered from various excavations related to Saint's Rest, many of them seen on multiple dishes and dish types. These designs include the Wedgewood fig pattern (Bev and Ernie 1995; Holly Lane Antiques; Figure 2A), the Berlin Swirl (Liddle Elliot and Sons, Mayer and Elliot) [Denton 1998; Figure 2B], a wheat pattern (J. and G. Meakin) [Sussman 1985; Figure 2C], a scalloped decagon pattern (also known as Cambridge shape; Davenport) [Bev and Ernie 1998; Figure 2D], and a concave rectangular interior rim pattern.

Alongside numerous different patterns, many dish types are also represented, including plates and bowls of various sizes and different platters. Dishes were found in two overall shapes, circular and decagonal. This variety of dish types is noted in archival documents from the early 1870's. Inventories of college property record the presence of numerous dish types, including soup pans, water and milk pitchers, sugar bowls, pickle dishes, pie plates, soup plates, dinner plates, sauce plates, fruit and jelly dishes, large and small platters, saucers, and cake plates to name a few, each of which was represented by dozens of copies (Michigan State University Archives & Historical Collections, Williams Papers and Kuhn Collection). Unfortunately, the inventories do not document the different styles of ceramics present, so we cannot be certain if different styles represented different functional dish sets, such as tea sets, dessert sets, dinner sets, etc., owned by the college, or if they just mixed the styles of dishes based on what was available at the time of purchase. Dish sets that included numerous, functionally specific dishes were a marker of the Victorian middle and upper classes, and were also seen as an educational tool that prepared individuals for what was considered proper behavior for more 'civilized' people (Williams 1985). As such, the founders of the college must have also supported the educational and social value of Victorian dining, as they spent hundreds of dollars to acquire all of the different types of dishes needed to emulate this style of dining on a large scale.

### Non-institutional Wares

Although the assemblage from this time period is dominated by white ironstone ceramics owned by the university, some examples of decorated ceramics have also been recovered at Saint's Rest. Examples of black transfer print whiteware, black and yellow transfer print pearlware, blue hand-painted whiteware, and porcelain with both blue stippled and green leaf designs have all been found, but in very small quantities, and only in fragmentary pieces (Mustonen 2007). These pieces are in stark contrast to the embossed whitewares used for dining. It is likely that these isolated pieces were not owned by the college, but were instead items brought from home to decorate a room or for private use. Unfortunately, the sherds are too fragmentary to be easily identified, and none possess a maker's mark. The black and yellow transfer printed dish may have been a small pharmaceutical jar due to its heavy curve and remnants of a flat base.

At this time, most things that people needed were supplied and/or rented through the college. To furnish their rooms, students often rented much of their furniture and toiletry items directly from the college, but also brought with them smaller personal items such as photos and other mementos. Many faculty and staff at this time either did not live directly on campus or lived in the residence halls and had access to college-owned goods, so few additional personal effects were present.

### Phase 2 (1870-1900)

Phase 2 represents a gradual change from the small, self-contained, and struggling college to an expanding, more purposeful institution. The emergence of Land-Grant colleges across the country led to a discussion about the best practices for administering, teaching, and designing these places. Landscape architect Frederick Law Olmsted was commissioned by various institutions to prepare a design for these campuses. As Turner (1984, 142) notes, Olmsted believed that a college planned in a park-like setting would instill in students 'civilized and enlightened values.' Olmsted argued that the goal of a Land-Grant institution was to educate students who would be part of the industrial class; they would not become elite members of the scientific community, but would return to their small towns as leaders, revolutionizing the field of agriculture. The space in which they learned, therefore, should correspond to the circumstances in which they would subsequently live. This meant small, two-story buildings that transformed the landscape into a model rural neighborhood. Each aspect of the campus, be it dormitories, labs, or the library, would be in separate buildings, surrounded by shrubbery, trees, and walks. Olmsted refers to this kind of plan as a household ground plan, and he argued that it would emphasize the importance of an education and career in agriculture (Turner 1984, 146).

College President Abbot often described the space as a college park, while Professor Beal called it 'the finest campus...in North America,' and that a student learning in such an environment would 'have his nature materially affected by the beautiful associations' (Beal 1915, 261-262). By maintaining and emphasizing the original, natural landscape, the college developed a more effective educational space and community.

The built environment was also part of this landscape. Faculty Row was gradually expanded throughout this phase, reaching a total of 12 buildings by 1899 (see Figure 1B). These buildings mimicked typical farmhouses, with large front porches and back yards. Each home had a small horse barn. These characteristics provided a small town feel to this area of campus. Just north of the Faculty Row buildings, Dr. Beal added an arboretum. Laboratory Row was built along the eastern edge of the campus, and housed the departments of Horticulture, Bacteriology, Botany, Forestry, and Entomology. These buildings were all small, two to three story structures, mimicking small-town buildings. These 'Rows' encircled the 'sacred space', a green expanse in the center of campus, reflecting Olmsted's vision of a small, rural neighborhood.

Evidence of Phase 2 reflects the adoption of a more explicitly defined approach to the college landscape as defined by Frederick Law Olmsted's household ground plan. The College did not use Olmsted's plan directly, but in 1872 hired Adam Oliver, a student of Olmsted's, to apply these ideas on the campus. Oliver enhanced 'the natural beauty of the existing landscape' and created a space that would 'elicit emotions of tranquility in order to improve the mental and physical health of the members of the community' (Michigan State University Campus Master Plan Report 2001, 6). Oliver maintained much of the original wooded setting, and included winding walks and drives. These decisions may also be reflected in artifacts that would represent an increase in quality of life and a more cohesive infrastructure at the campus.

Excavations conducted by CAP, at and near the Gunson residence, provide excellent examples of the changes in material culture during this beginning of the funded land grant program. Thomas Gunson was brought to the College to take care of the grounds, and he was also the first to teach floraculture (Stuart 1941). Gunson's house was at the edge of Beal Gardens and along the Red Cedar River; he did not live along Faculty Row. Gunson was one of the most popular figures of the College; in addition to acting as a speaker for the institution, he was elected Mayor of East Lansing from 1909-1914 (Lautner 1978, 93).

One example of the ceramics from the Gunson house is Mercer Potter's Trenton New Jersey 'Bordeaux,' (Barber 1904, 57) [Figure 3C], possibly dating to the late 1800s.[1] This pattern came in many different shapes, from platters to dishes. Mercer is part of the Trenton, New Jersey, school of potters, and was founded in 1868 (Barber 1893, 239; Barber 1904, 57). They claim to have been the first to make semi-porcelain ware in America (Barber 1893, 239; Barber 1904, 57).

Another ceramic type found is Adams China 'Fairy Villa' flow-blue transfer print (Figure 3B), which dates to c. 1891-early 1900s (Birks 2004a). It was one of the more desirable flow-blue patterns. Fairy Villa had three distinct runs, with the latest production being in 1917. It was considered an 'Oriental' design category, and in 1955, is classified as the 'Most Popular/Sought After' flow blue pattern (Hogan 2009).

A third pattern is W. T. Copeland's 'Delphi ' pattern in gray. The specific makers mark indicates a production date between 1867-1890 (Birks 2004b). The pattern is a blueish gray floral and scroll design that is a variation of flow-blue, and from our Gunson excavations (Figure 3A), we have flow blue as a soup tureen (with handle), plates, bowls, and possibly a meat trivet.

These patterns represent some of the 'finer' or 'nicer' ceramics from Gunson, and they also represent the earliest dates from this site whose artifacts generally date 1890-1925. Since the building was not constructed until 1891, it's likely that these items were brought into the house from a prior Gunson residence. Our excavations were focused on a garbage dump or fill episode of Gunson items that likely date to a remodeling of his house in 1925 (Michigan State University Archives and Historical Collections UA.4.9.1 37:9). They were expanding the house and adding electricity, and Gunson had recently lost his first wife to illness and married his second (Stuart 1941), who might not have wanted all of the first Mrs. Gunson's belongings.

---

[1] Specific dates for the production of the Bordeaux pattern have not been established.

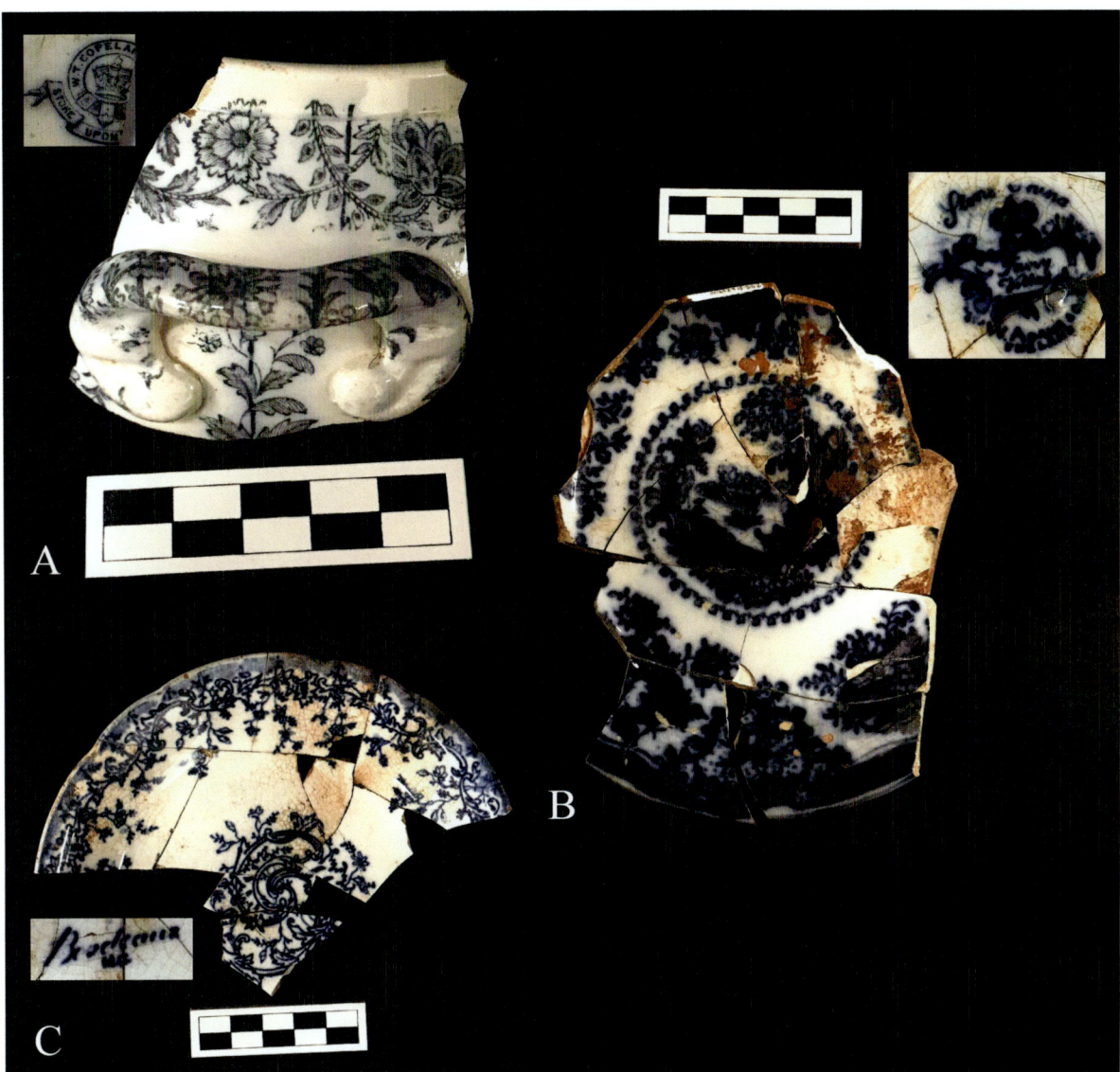

Figure 3. Phase 2 (1870-1900) ceramics. (A) Soup tureen fragment with handle in the Delphi pattern. The W.T. Copeland maker's mark (1867-1890) was found on a Delphi pattern plate fragment (Birks 2004b); (B) W. Adams Company stone china plate in the Fairy Villa pattern, produced 1891-early 1900s (Birks 2004a); (C) Mercer Potter's New Jersey 'Bordeaux' pattern (Barber 1904, 57). (All photos copyright Michigan State University Campus Archaeology Program)

**Phase 3 (1900-1925)**

The financial support provided by the Morrill Land-Grant Act not only allowed for the reshaping of the college landscape, but also made it possible for the college to expand in population, size, and curriculum: the student population tripled between 1885 and 1905, and the number of academic programs increased from five to 13 programs. Program expansion had a direct impact on the landscape of MAC (Michigan Agricultural College). First, the addition of the women's college in 1896 led to the construction of a separate women's building four years later. The introduction of women to the campus significantly diversified the campus population. Co-education was considered a success, despite, in the words of President Snyder, the 'perplexing problems...that the presence of women at this College' brought with it (Beal 1915, 153).

Faculty Row was also affected by this expansion. A trolley line was built in the 1890's, connecting Lansing to the western edge of campus, and expanding into Faculty Row in 1902, where a waiting room was built. The trolley (and later, automobiles) made the horse barns obsolete, and maps indicate that by 1911, only one horse barn remained standing.

The expansion in programming also meant an increase in new faculty. The neighboring town, known then as Collegeville (Towar 1933, 42), increased in size due to the growing college, as many professors began to live off campus. The town became the official municipality of East Lansing in 1907 (Towar 1933, 72). Additionally, since new programs required additional space for teaching, Faculty Row buildings began to change in function from living places to teaching spaces. For example, the President's House became a dorm for senior women and then a campus hospital. Other Faculty Row buildings served as music and home economics practice houses. By the end of Phase 3, most of the Faculty Row buildings were serving non-residential functions, a direct result of the rapid expansion.

Phase 3 represents a significant change in material and building function. The former relates to the expanding access to larger markets, representative of the development of the trolley line and the emergence of East Lansing. The latter is related to the demand for new buildings and programming due to the increasing attendance at MAC. This should be reflected in the archaeological record as well, through changes in materials.

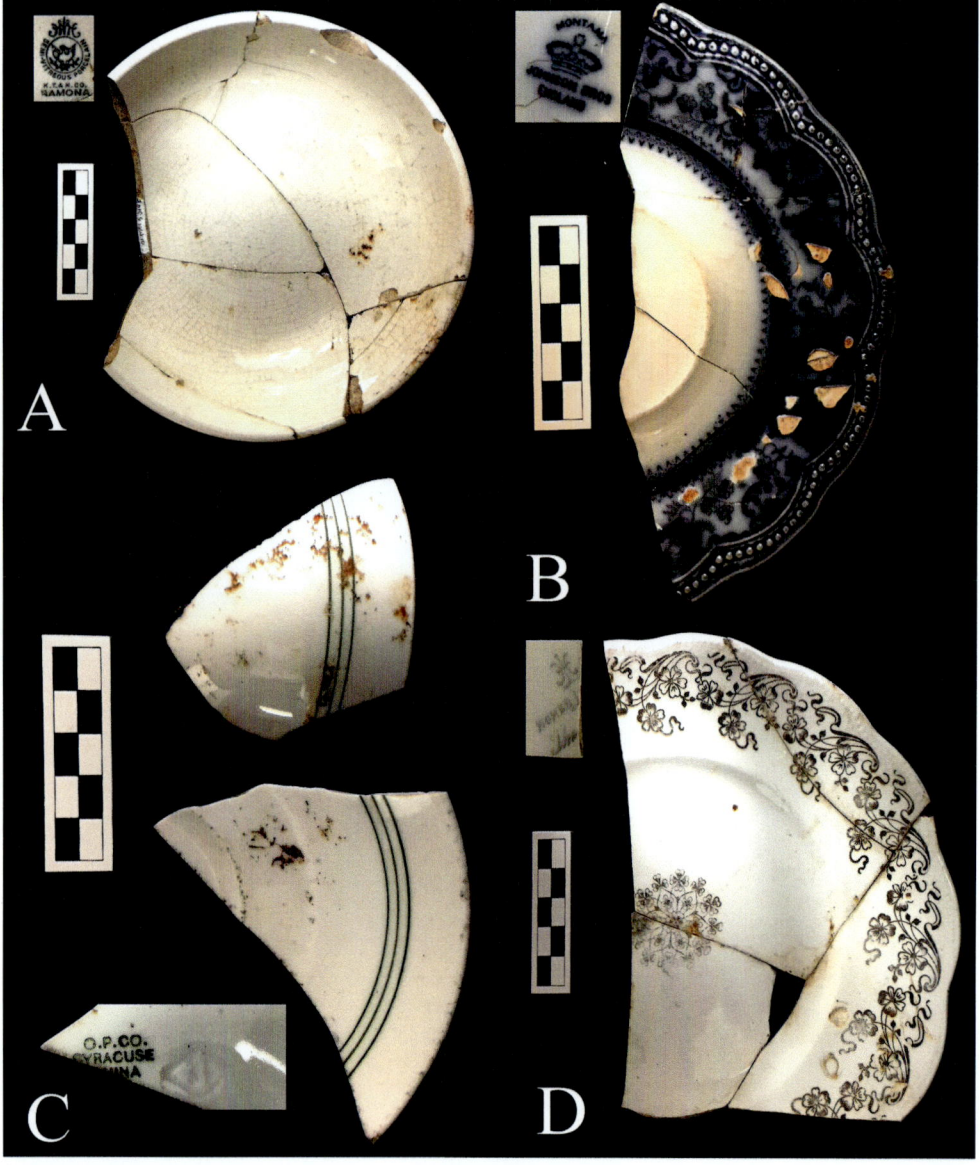

Figure 4. Phase 3 (1900-1925) ceramics. (A) Undecorated whiteware 'Ramona' style bowl produced by Knowles Taylor & Knowles company, circa 1907-1915 (Gates and Ormerod 1982,125); (B) Partial 'Montana' pattern saucer produced by Johnson Brothers post 1913 (Birks 2004c); (C) Onondaga Pottery Company hotelware cup and saucer, white with three green stripes. The maker's mark and date stamp found on one fragment indicate a 1914 production (Nanalulu 2007); (D) Partial gold-leafed shamrock patterned plate produced by Homer Laughlin between 1900-1960 (Gates and Ormerod 1982, 136). (All photos copyright Michigan State University Campus Archaeology Program)

Once again, the majority of examples we have of this period come from our Gunson excavations, and include K.T. & K Co 'Ramona' pattern plain white ware bowl, dating to 1907-1915 (Gates and Ormerod 1982, 125; Figure 4A). Knowles, Taylor and Knowles (K.T. & K) was founded in 1854, in East Liverpool, Ohio (Gates and Ormerod 1982, 115). The Ramona name on the base of the bowl refers to a plain dinner shape line of ceramics, first introduced in 1907. Ramona was available in over a dozen different patterns and decorations (The House Furnishing Review 1908, 13, 49).

Another example from this period is Johnson Brothers 'Montana' ceramics (Figure 4B). The makers' mark indicates a post 1913 production (Birks 2004c). The company was founded in 1883 in Staffordshire, England, with the goal to produce earthenware called white granite. However, the company became most famous for transferware. The mid-range pricing of products made is easy for people to fill their cupboards with Johnson Brothers products. In 1968, the company joined Wedgewood (Birks 2004d).

During Gunson excavations, students were taken with an example of Homer Laughlin gold-leafed shamrock-patterned ceramics (Figure 4D). We have been unable to date this particular pattern, but the maker's mark suggests 1900-1960 (Gates and Ormerod 1982, 136).

Finally, the Gunson excavations yielded a lot of ceramics from the Onondaga Pottery Company. The pieces have a date stamp for July 1914 (Nanalulu 2007) and represent another kind of institutional ceramics. The three green stripes of the pattern represent early 20th century hotel ware (Figure 4C). The chip resistant round-edge shaped hotel ware was introduced in 1896 (Myers 2016). It quickly became the national leader in institutional and hotel ware. Popular patterns include yellow spirals, blue liberty, blue grass, and wood grain.

From these excavations dating from 1900-1925, we have a mixture of plain institutional ware, produced by American manufactures, as well as many examples of expensive fancier ceramics, produced by both American and English manufacturers. Over his nearly five decades of service to the college, Thomas Gunson was a beloved part of campus life and frequently engaged with students, alumni, and local residents. He was known as an outgoing individual with a flair for fashion and life, enjoying his time with students and others on campus. He was typically very well dressed, and his family home served as 'a cosmopolitan haven for undergraduates and graduates alike' (Stuart 1941). Returning alumni would often seek Gunson out in order to reconnect with one of their favorite faculty members. It is not surprising that his home would be stocked with quality ceramics for entertaining his many visitors, with an emphasis on tea service items that would be used during social calls. Also recovered from Gunson excavations and elsewhere on campus are ceramic types associated with the influx of women to the institution. Such gendered items are constrained in their spatial distribution, much as the women were constrained in where they lived, worked, and studied.

**Phase 4 (1925-1955)**

Phase 4 began with a name change. In 1925, the Michigan Agricultural College (MAC) became the Michigan State College of Agriculture and Applied Science (MSC). During the 1930s, 40s, and 50s, MSC embarked on a dramatic building campaign, largely to accommodate the influx of G. I. Bill students returning from World War II. Temporary housing and teaching spaces were erected in a new area, south of the river, to make room for these new students. This expansion also corresponded to an increase in programming, and a more central role of the college to the surrounding communities. For example, the MSU dairy began to bottle and distribute dairy products to surrounding communities, and the increasing size of the athletic department brought residents and alumni to campus on a regular basis. MSC was on its way to becoming a University.

In 1931, Mary Mayo Hall was built just north of the original Faculty Row buildings. This was the first building in a massive construction phase in the Faculty Row area, culminating in the destruction of all but two of the faculty homes. Five women's dormitories replaced these homes. Two Faculty Row buildings remained: one continued to act as the home of the President, and Building 6 remained standing until 1970, serving as the campus' first International Center (Lautner 1978, 135-145).

Phase 4 reflects an increase in artifacts from a larger economic network, due to the integration of MSC into the local economy. Also, campus expansion is evident due to the influx of Depression era funds during the 1930s, and the need for new housing for returning War World II veterans. This is visible through a subsequent change in the material record, in addition to evidence of dramatic changes in the landscape, such as land modification and building demolition. The campus also created more specialized buildings and spatially separated activities, so it is not as common to discover ceramics, unless one excavates a dining hall or residence.

Phase 4 is not well represented by our campus excavations thus far. We have excavated sites dating to this period, but they have been primarily lab spaces and not buildings or areas within which people lived. We have no more than a few very small pieces of ceramics. Given how much ground alteration occurred with the massive increase in building, this is not surprising. In addition, many of the buildings built in this period remain standing and in use.

## Concluding Comments

When the campus was founded, students were required to bring their own ceramics from home, often mismatched pieces representing varying costs. With increased funding comes institutional ceramics made from durable ironstone with little to no patterning. However, we also see evidence of higher end ceramics from faculty homes and for special use, with intricate designs and patterns. The nature of these ceramics reflect the nature of relationships, and by examining them spatially, as well as over time, we can distinguish between different uses of ceramics and activities across the campus.

Historic ceramics are often used to specifically date excavations and buildings. However, when examined in the context of a growing college campus that reflects the many technological, social, economic, and educational changes happening across the country, these same ceramics can provide insight into how people and institutions adapted to an ever-changing landscape.

## References Cited

Barber, Edwin Atlee. 1893. *The pottery and Porcelain of the United States a historical review of American ceramic art from the earliest time to the present day*. New York, NY: G. P. Putnam's Sons.

Barber, Edwin Atlee. 1904. *Marks of American Potters*. Philadelphia, PA: Patterson & White.

Beal, William. 1915. *History of the Michigan Agricultural College and Biographical Sketches of Trustees and Professors*. Lansing, MI: Wynkoop Hallenbeck Crawford Company State Printers.

Bev and Ernie. 1995. "Fig' Shape.' *White Ironstone Notes* 2 (2): 1.

Bev and Ernie. 1998. 'Cambridge Shape aka Scalloped Decagon.' *White Ironstone Notes* 5 (2): 1-12.

Birks, Steve. 2004a. 'North Staffordshire Pottery Marks William Adams.' *The Potteries*. Accessed June 12, 2017. http://www.thepotteries.org/mark/a/adams1.html.

Birks, Steve. 2004b. 'North Staffordshire Pottery Marks W. T. Copeland.' *The Potteries*. Accessed June 17, 2017. http://www.thepotteries.org/mark/c/copelandWT.html.

Birks, Steve. 2004c. 'North Staffordshire Pottery Marks Johnson Bros, (Hanley) Ltd.' *The Potteries*. Accessed June 17, 2017. http://www.thepotteries.org/mark/j/johnson_brothers.html.

Birks, Steve. 2004d. 'A-Z of Stoke-on-Trent Potters Johnson Bros, (Hanley) Ltd.'. *The Potteries*. Accessed June 17, 2017. http://www.thepotteries.org/allpotters/607.html.

Denton, Harriet. 1998. 'Berlin Swirl.' *White Ironstone Notes* 5 (3): 1-13.

Gates, William and Dana Ormerod. 1982. 'East Liverpool Pottery District: Identification of Manufacturers and Marks, 1840-1970.' *Historical Archaeology* 16 (½): 1-358.

Godden, Geoffrey. 1999. *New Handbook of British Pottery & Porcelain Marks*. London, United Kingdom: Barrie & Jenkins.

Groover, Mark D., and S. Homes Hogue. 2014. 'Reconstructing Nineteenth-Century Midwest Foodways: Ceramic and Zooarchaeological Information from the Moore-Youse House and Huddleston Farmstead.' *Midcontinental Journal of Archaeology* 39 (2): 130-144.

Groover, Mark D., and Tyler J. Wolford. 2013. 'The Archaeology of Rural Affluence and Landscape Change at the Clemens Farmstead.' *Journal of African Diaspora Archaeology and Heritage* 2 (2): 131-150.

Hogan, John. 2009. 'Top 10 most desirable flow blue patterns in all four major categories'. *Passion For The Past Antiques and Collectibles*. Accessed June 25, 2017. https://www.passionforthepastantiques.com/articles/item/article/top-10-most-desirable-flow-blue-patterns-in-all-four-major-categories/.

Holly Lane Antiques. 'The Fig Shape Early English White Ironstone.' Accessed June 15, 2017. http://hollylaneantiques.blogspot.com/2011/02/fig-shape-early-english-white-ironstone.html.

Lautner, Harold W. 1978. *From an Oak Opening: A Record of the Development of the Campus Park of Michigan State University, 1855-1969, Volume 1*. East Lansing, MI: Michigan State University.

Meyers, Adrian. 2016. 'The Significance of Hotel-Ware Ceramics in the Twentieth Century.' *Historical Archaeology* 50 (2): 110-126.

Michigan State University Archives and Historical Collections. UA 2.1.7. Joseph R. Williams Papers, College Inventory 1872.

Michigan State University Archives and Historical Collections. University Architect and Chairman of the Building Committee Records. UA 4.9.1. Blue Prints, Faculty Residence – Gunson House 1922, Drawer 37 Folder 9.

Michigan State University Archives & Historical Collections. Kuhn Collection UA 17.107.

Michigan State University Archives & Historical Collections. Kuhn Collection UA 17.107, Box 2523 Volume 91. MAC Account Book, includes Agricultural Boarding Hall Accounts, and Farm accounts 1861-1866.

Michigan State University. *Campus Master Plan Report 2001*. East Lansing, MI: Michigan State University Office of Campus Planning.

Moore, Ted. 2009. 'Creating an Idyllic Space: Nature, Technology, and Campus Planning at the Michigan Agricultural College, 1850-1975.' *Michigan Historical Review* 35 (2): 1-25.

Mustonen, Heather. 2007. 'Public Archaeology and Community Engagement at Michigan State University: The Saints' Rest Archaeological Project.' Unpublished Master thesis, Department of Anthropology, Michigan State University.

Nanalulu, 2007. 'Guide to Date Codes and Backstamps for Syracuse China.' Accessed December 16, 2015. http://www.ebay.com/gds/Guide-to-Date-Codes-and-Backstamps-for-Syracuse-China-/10000000000132854/g.html.

Stuart, Glen. 1941. 'Thomas Gunson 1858-1940.' *Michigan Agricultural College Record* 46 (2): 17.

Sussman, Lynne. 1985. *The Wheat Pattern: An Illustrated Survey*. Studies in Archaeology Architecture and History. National Historic Parks and Sites Branch, Parks Canada, Environment, Canada: Ottawa, Ontario.

The House Furnishing Review. 1908. 29 (1): 1-78. Trade Magazine Association, New York, NY. Accessed on August 21, 2017. https://babel.hathitrust.org/cgi/pt?id=nyp.33433060476102;view=1up;seq=7.

Towar, James. 1933. *History of the City of East Lansing*. Ann Arbor, MI: Mayer-Schairer Company.

Turner, Paul Venable. 1984. *Campus: An American Planning Tradition*. Cambridge, MA: MIT Press.

Wikipedia. 2017. 'Syracuse China.' Accessed on June 30, 2017. https://en.wikipedia.org/wiki/Syracuse_China.

Williams, Susan. 1985. *Savory Suppers and Fashionable Feasts: Dining in Victorian America*. New York, NY: Pantheon Books.

# Chapter 9

# The Ethnoarchaeology of an Abandoned Potter's Workshop in Ticul, Yucatán, México

Dean E. Arnold

Field Museum of Natural History; darnold@fieldmuseum.org

**Abstract**

*By examining the remains of an abandoned potter's workshop on the edge of Ticul, Yucatán, this chapter reconstructs what can be known about it, based upon analogies with the potters' craft and its material signatures in the modern production units of Ticul. This reconstruction identifies some of the activities carried out at the workshop, the materials and fabrication techniques used, and ascertains the length of the workshop's active use-life. Results from this ethnoarchaeological analysis challenge what archaeologists think might be revealed in the ancient material record of pottery workshops.*

**Key words**

*Pottery workshop, ethnoarchaeology, Maya, Mexico*

## Introduction

This chapter describes the remains of a relatively recent abandoned potter's workshop on the edge of Ticul, Yucatán, between 1997 and 2008, and reconstructs what can be known about it, based upon analogies with activities and material evidence. In so doing, this study answers several questions, regarding the potential of an ethnoarchaeological approach to an abandoned pottery workshop. How much can be known and why? What limitations are there? What issues might affect interpretations of ancient production areas?

Largely using participant-observation, this reconstruction is based upon ethnographic data collected in Ticul during 13 field trips that started in 1965. During this time, I recorded hundreds of pages of typed field notes and texts, and question/response interview frames in Yucatek Maya concerning pottery production. Thousands of images of pottery production along with images and maps of the Ticul production units support these data (see Arnold 2008, 2015), including the abandoned workshop features and similar features in modern Ticul.

## Background

In 2002, during a brief trip to Ticul, I noticed what looked like a new pottery workshop located along the highway, west of the city. It had not been there during my visit five years earlier. It consisted of several unattached structures, which except for the kiln, were constructed with perishable materials (such as woven sticks, palm fronds, and cardboard). The structures in this workshop were more like those unattached structures in the household production units in Ticul that I had seen in the previous 40 years than the structures of the other abandoned workshops nearby that were constructed with cement blocks and steel. There was no activity evident in the workshop, but I didn't find that observation out of the ordinary, because Hurricane Isadore had blown through the community six weeks before. Having seen the product of its fury in the destroyed soccer stadium in nearby Muna (Arnold 2015, 254), I thought that the remains of any temporary and fragile structures still standing with no activity was understandable because the hurricane probably had destroyed all the drying pottery and significantly damaged the structures.

In 2008, I returned to Ticul to work on another project, and I was surprised that the only remaining structures of the workshop were the kiln, and a shell of a small structure made of sticks (Figure 1). It had joined a string of four other abandoned workshops along the highway.

## History of the Non-Household Highway Workshops

The establishment of pottery workshops and sales areas along the highway through Ticul has a long history. In the 1950s, a man named Enrique Garma, born in 1916 and died in 1996, began accumulating pots for resale (Arnold 2015, 198). Garma was not a potter, but he lived along the highway that goes through town. By 1965, he had hired potters

Figure 1. Structural remains of an abandoned pottery workshop May-June, 2008 looking Southeast, noting the location of the principal features. (Photograph by Dean E. Arnold)

to make pottery in a workshop behind his house, displaying both drying and fired vessels on the sidewalk in front of it to attract the attention of interested passers-by, who hopefully would buy some of his pots (Arnold 2008, 2015). No potters, or entrepreneurs like Garma, lived along the highway at that time.

In the 1970s, as the number of production units grew (Arnold 2008, 40), some potters realized that they could attract buyers, by acquiring facilities along the highway to display their wares. Most of these facilities were located within Ticul itself, but one was established west of the city along the highway to Muna. The strategy of siting the workshops there was the belief that potential buyers would stop at a workshop outside of town first and attract more customers than if it was sited within the city of Ticul. By the time of my visit in 1984, however, the first workshop established west of the city was abandoned, even before it started making and selling pottery. Its shell remained in 2008.

In 1984, another potter built a traditional Maya house along the highway for his brother to use as a workshop and sales area. He also built a kiln beside the workshop to fire pottery. By 2008, the kiln remained, even though the house that was used as a workshop had disappeared.

Another workshop, established along the highway west of Ticul, was built after my visit in 1994 and was well underway by 1997. It was funded through the Mexican craft organization FONOPAS (Arnold 2008, 141; Arnold 2015, 210-212). This workshop was very large by Ticul standards, and like the workshop built between 1970 and 1984, it was constructed with reinforced cement, cement blocks, fired bricks, with a roof supported by steel girders. It enclosed an immense interior space (Arnold 2015, 210-213) to store raw materials and molds, to make and dry pottery, and to house a small gas kiln in an environment protected from the weather. A traditional beehive kiln was built outside the structure.

Between 2002 and 2008, another small workshop was also constructed on the south side of the highway into town. It was smaller than the two workshops just described, but was constructed of cement blocks with a reinforced concrete roof. By 2008, these workshops appeared to be abandoned.

*Causes for workshop abandonment*

Why were the workshops abandoned? First, there were issues of capital. At least one of the workshops involved the mismanagement of government funds. Because of the collapse of the market for traditional Ticul pottery in the 1970s because of piped water (Arnold 2008, 104-107), and the rise of the tourist center of Cancún, the government of Yucatán wanted to build a workshop along the highway into town to capture the attention of passing tourists.

Because one of the potters was heavily involved in the ruling political party in the State of Yucatán (the PRI) at the time, he was charged with being the manager of the new operation and was responsible for getting the workshop established. In addition to the space constructed to make pottery, which was immense by Ticul standards, additional space for a restaurant was added in front of it. Its walls were covered with beautiful polychrome murals copied from the murals at the Maya site of Bonampak, presumably to attract tourists. Apparently, all the funding was spent on the physical plant, in buying two trucks, and no funds remained to hire potters. Consequently, further government funding was withdrawn and the workshop and the restaurant in front of it never opened to the public.

Second, there were issues of demand that were related to the pattern of highway infrastructure. For many years, the main route from Mérida to Belize went south to the town of Muna and then southeast along the north side of the Puuc Ridge to the city of Peto. This highway route paralleled one of the railroad lines that were built in the early twentieth century to connect the many cities and towns built along the railroad. All vehicular traffic to the Southeast and Belize from Mérida passed through Ticul.

Sometime before 2008, however, another highway route was constructed from Mérida directly to Oxkutzkab, southeast of Ticul, and traffic between Merida and the southeast also by-passed Ticul. Consequently, there were far fewer vehicles that passed through Ticul, and thus, highway traffic resulted in far fewer potential buyers for the pottery workshops located along the highway.

The abandoned workshop, described here, was one of those established for the reasons cited above. Established to provide a competitive advantage for those who traveled to Ticul, like the other workshops, it was far removed from the household of the owner who lived within the city of Ticul.

**The Physical Remains of the Abandoned Workshop**

In 2008, all that remained of the 2002 workshop was a kiln, parts of the standing walls of a pole structure, foundations of at least three small structures that no longer existed, and some associated activity areas (Figure 1). Other structures seen in 2002, no longer remained. Therefore, the remainder of this chapter is organized around the sequence of making pottery, from constructing the workshop to firing the finished vessels. The data are grouped into sections that describe the most obvious features of the site.

*Piles of Raw Material*

On the east side of the surviving pole structure were the remnants of two piles of whitish material (Figure 2). The smaller pile (Figure 2) appears to be a pile of raw material from the temper mines (called *Yo' Sah Kab*) used to make

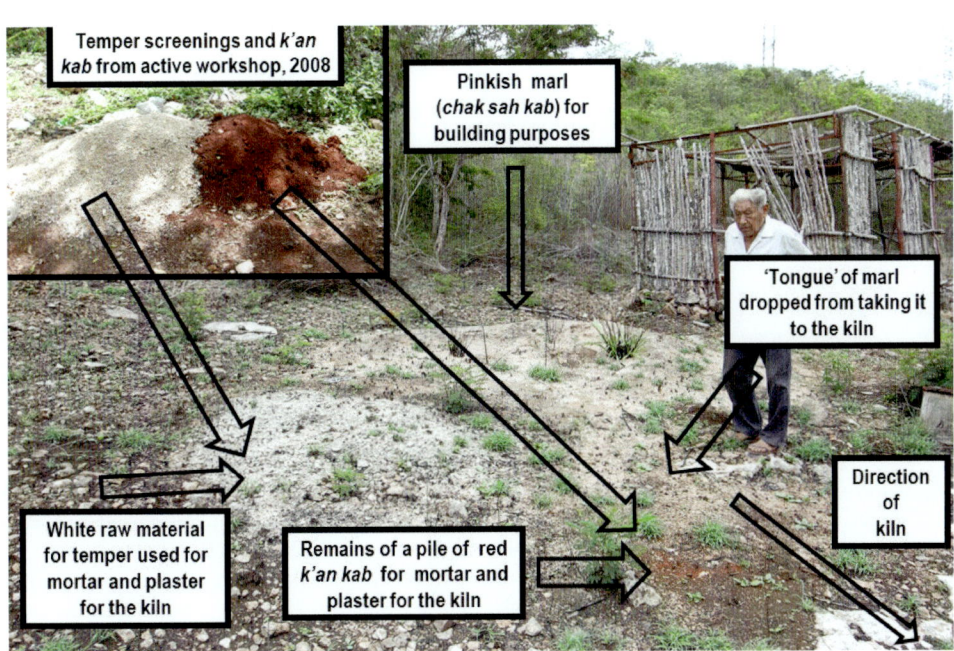

Figure 2. Piles of raw materials at the site and their comparison with an image of piles of raw materials for building and repairing a kiln in a potter's house lot in 2008 (*upper left*). The tongue of marl from the pile towards the *lower right* is likely the detritus falling from moving the marl to the kiln to add its cement facing (Figure 5). It could, however, have resulted from the unloading the marl from the vehicle that brought it to the workshop. (Photograph by Dean E. Arnold)

pottery temper (see Arnold 1971, 2008, 2017). Pottery temper is a mixture of two materials that are marl-based; one originates from marl mines (*nooy*) themselves and the other comes from the screenings (*ta'achach*) of the marl and screenings from previous temper preparation (see Arnold 1971, 2008, 2017). These two materials are crushed, mixed and screened to produce temper. Given the coarseness of the white material used for temper (Figure 2), it appears that owners brought this raw material from the temper mines using a vehicle and unloaded it at the workshop. At the mines, they could have easily scooped up screenings (*ta'achach*) to bring to the workshop or mined the marl (*nooy*) and brought it to the workshop. The small size of the pile suggests that this activity did not occur over a long period of time. This course raw material could also have been sifted to make temper at the workshop rather than buying screened temper from those who prepared and sold it to potters.

More important, this unscreened material from the temper mines was screened and used for the mortar and plaster on the kiln itself by mixing pottery temper and red earth (*k'an kab*, Figure 2). Potters believe that this mixture results in better refractory properties than a mortar and plaster made from a mixture of red earth and red (*chak sah kab*) or white natural marl (*sak sah kab*).

The second pile of raw material with a pinkish tinge was higher and has a larger footprint than the one previously described (Figure 2). This larger pinkish pile consisted of a material called *chak sah kab*, a natural red marl used for construction purposes by mixing it with cement, much like gravel is used to make concrete in North America. After the kiln at the site was built, using mortar and plaster of pottery temper and red earth, it was faced with a mixture of cement and natural marl. This cement surface sheds water from rainfall and prevents it from seeping into the kiln, which could weaken the mortar and plaster, prolonging the useful life of the kiln.

*An Oval-shaped Foundation*

Adjacent to the north side of the surviving pole structure, lay two rows of stones arranged in curved shape, with their open sides facing the other (Figure 3). This configuration appears to be a foundation to anchor the poles of an

Figure 3. The area in front (*north*) of the pole structure (see Figure 1) showing the oval foundation of a structure in the shape of a traditional Maya house. The remains of white material within this foundation appears to be screenings from temper preparation, and indicates that the structure was a location where potters sifted and perhaps stored temper and mixed temper and clay. Insets show raw temper stored inside a house (*upper right*), mixing temper with clay inside a house (*upper left*), and a workshop, (*lower left*), and kneading the mixture outside when weather permits (*lower right*). (Photograph by Dean E. Arnold)

oval structure, like the shape of the traditional Maya house with curved ends and doorways opposite one another on parallel sides. The white material lying between the rows of stones is too course to be pottery temper, but rather, it could be the raw material brought from the temper mines like that used for the mortar and plaster of the kiln, but in this case, was sifted to make temper. If it was used to create temper, it must be stored in a dry location (Figure 3, upper right) to pass through a screen. The resulting temper also must be kept dry before it is mixed with the clay which is most often mixed inside a structure (see Figure 3, upper and lower left). By mixing the dry temper with the wet clay, the potter can control the amount of water and temper added to the paste, and the paste can be mixed more easily. This structure thus appears to be a location where the raw material for temper was stored, where temper was stored, and perhaps where the potter mixed the clay with the temper.

## Discarded Molds

Pottery making, obviously, requires a technique for forming the pottery. Such techniques often do not materialize in the material record. The traditional pottery forming technique in Ticul consisted of drawing up thick coils on a turntable called the *k'abal* (see Thompson 1958, 76-81; Arnold 2008, 232-237). Potters use a gourd scraper to draw up the coils and shape the vessel as the potter moves the turntable with the other hand, or with a foot.

In the late 1940s or early 1950s, vertical-half molding was introduced and once potters learned how make molds, they could produce a variety of sizes and shapes that were not possible to form using the turntable. The great plasticity of the Ticul clay, however, limited the size and shape of mold-made vessels (see Arnold 1999; Arnold 2008, 244-256). Using vertical-half molding to make pottery involves many other advantages and disadvantages (see Arnold 1999; Arnold 2008, 244-256).

Figure 4. *In situ* remains of discarded vertical-half molds at the abandoned workshop site (*upper right*) compared with the outdoor storage of molds covered with a roof (*upper left and lower left*) in 2008, and with uncovered discarded molds at the same household (1997) in the *lower right*. When molds are discarded they are not protected from rainfall, absorb moisture, are subject to the growth of moss, and therefore are difficult or impossible to use again. Molds in active use thus are sheltered from the rain by a roof or stored inside a structure. (Photograph by Dean E. Arnold)

At the abandoned workshop site, the only remnants of vessel forming techniques were two discarded vertical-half molds (Figure 4). Making a vessel with a mold requires very little skill (see Arnold 1999). By using a mold, a potter can only form one vessel of the same exact size and shape, whereas the turntable allows the potter to form almost any vessel of a different size and shape.

## Other structures

Other structures appeared to be placed on raised platforms that provided a foundation for the walls of maize stalks, cane or small saplings. It is difficult to assign a use to these structures, but some of them likely were used to store drying pottery. Because drying vessels must be sheltered from rain and fog in the rainy season, and from excessive heat and sunshine during the dry season, drying vessels usually must be dried indoors for a substantial period before firing. If pottery is not adequately dried before firing, the water in the paste will form steam during firing and break it (see Arnold 1985, 61-98). Potters thus must have adequate indoor space to dry them sufficiently before firing. Consequently, drying requires the largest footprint in the entire pottery making process (Arnold 2015, 243-276).

The structures on the site may also have been used to store molds. When the potter desires to change the size or shape of an object, it is necessary to create a new mold. Using molds to make pottery also requires space to store the molds (Figure 4, upper left). When changes in the demand for new vessels occur, new molds are required, and the number of molds in a production unit can increase over time. Molds also must be sheltered from the weather to maintain the integrity of the object coming from the mold. Stored molds not sheltered from the weather will deteriorate (Arnold 1999, Figure 4).

## The Kiln

The kiln was the principal material evidence of pottery production at the site (Figure 5). Without the presence of the kiln, the oral history of the site, and the existence of other abandoned pottery making workshops nearby, this site probably would not be identified as a pottery making workshop.

Figure 5. The kiln at the abandoned workshop site (*below*) showing the lack of wasters around it compared with abandoned kilns in Ticul in the *upper left* (in 1984) and *upper right* (in 2008). Compare the lack of wasters in these images with four active kilns from 1984 (Figure 6) that show wasters on the sides and front of the kilns. (Photograph by Dean E. Arnold)

Kilns last about 30 years if they are properly maintained and protected by covering them with palm fronts, metal sheeting, or branches of *huano* palm (Figure 6). Even so, potters must inspect both the interior and exterior of the kiln regularly, and replace its plaster and mortar as needed, so that water will not seep into it from the heavy downpours of the rainy season. Kilns collapse when they are not properly maintained.

To prolong the kiln's useful life, it was faced with cement, a practice that reduces future maintenance. Such a practice, however, adds more capital costs to construction, but such costs must be weighed against the projected costs and labor of future maintenance. This enhancement of the kiln suggests that the person who established the workshop intended to produce pottery there for a long time. Why the owner went to the expense of constructing such a well-built kiln, relative to the lesser durability of the other structures of the workshop, is puzzling.

The kiln had no wasters beside it (Figure 5). When the potter loads the kiln, he uses larger wasters to hold smaller items of pottery inside, and uses smaller wasters to wedge into the stack of pottery to keep it stable, when the vessels shrink because of the loss of the water in the clay during firing. Small wasters are also used to separate pottery in the kiln to allow the carbon deposited on the vessels during the first phase of firing to oxidize in the last part of the process. To create a waster of appropriate size, the potter trims it by selectively breaking it, and then discards the unused portions on the floor of the kiln. When the vessels are unloaded from the kiln after firing, the larger wasters are placed outside the kiln so that they can be used and trimmed again during the next firing event. Small trimmed fragments of wasters remain on the floor of the kiln.

Abandoned kilns in Ticul, however, generally do not have large wasters beside them (Figure 5). Apparently, there are not enough wasters to use for firing so that when kilns are abandoned, wasters beside them are moved to the sides of active kilns. Active kilns on the other hand, have piles of wasters near them.

Figure 6. Active kilns in 1984 that show wasters beside them. These kilns use branches of *huano* palm (*upper right*), tar impregnated cardboard (*upper left and upper right*), sheet metal (*upper left*) and boards (*upper left and upper right*) to protect the kiln from rainfall and keep it from deteriorating. Facing the exterior of the kiln with cement prevents this problem. (Photograph by Dean E. Arnold)

## Charcoal Scatters and Length of Use

Since the workshop did not exist at the time of my 1997 visit, and appeared to be unused in 2002, the workshop had a tentative use-life of at least five years. It is unclear, however, if it was in operation after my 2002 visit given what little remained of it in 2008. Given its state at that time, it was obvious that it had been abandoned for some time, perhaps even for the entire period since 2002. Nevertheless, the absolute maximum use-life of the workshop could have been eleven years. Its actual use-life was probably much less.

The duration of the pottery making activity can be ascertained by the relationship of the production cycle to its material signatures. Pottery production occurs within a minimum of a two-week cycle from obtaining clay and temper to firing. Inclement weather extends the length of this cycle because rainy weather and periods of high humidity put constraints on mining clay and temper (Arnold 1985, 61-98; Arnold 2008, 153-220), and extend the amount of drying time to so that the pottery will not break during firing (Arnold 2015, 249-276). During a period of intense rains, cool temperatures, and/or cloudy weather, the production cycle may be extended more than two weeks to as much as one month. The cycle is shorter in the dry season when such constraints do not exist, but by way of contrast, drying may have to be slowed so that the vessels do not crack because of rapid shrinkage due to low humidity.

One production cycle can be marked by the removal of charcoal from the kiln after firing (Figure 7). Potters use wood for firing, and to cool the kiln as quickly as possible and avoid over-firing at the end of the process, the potter may remove the burning coals from the kiln using a scraper made of a board attached to a long pole. A few potters may also throw water on the remaining embers to cool the kiln, but this behavior shortens the kiln's use-life. Even so, potters may still remove the smoldering embers with a scraper. Once dampened with the embers removed, the potter can enter the kiln as soon as a few hours after the completion of firing. Without cooling the kiln with water, however, the potter cannot enter it for at least 24 hours. It is still very hot, however, but it is tolerable to go inside and unload it.

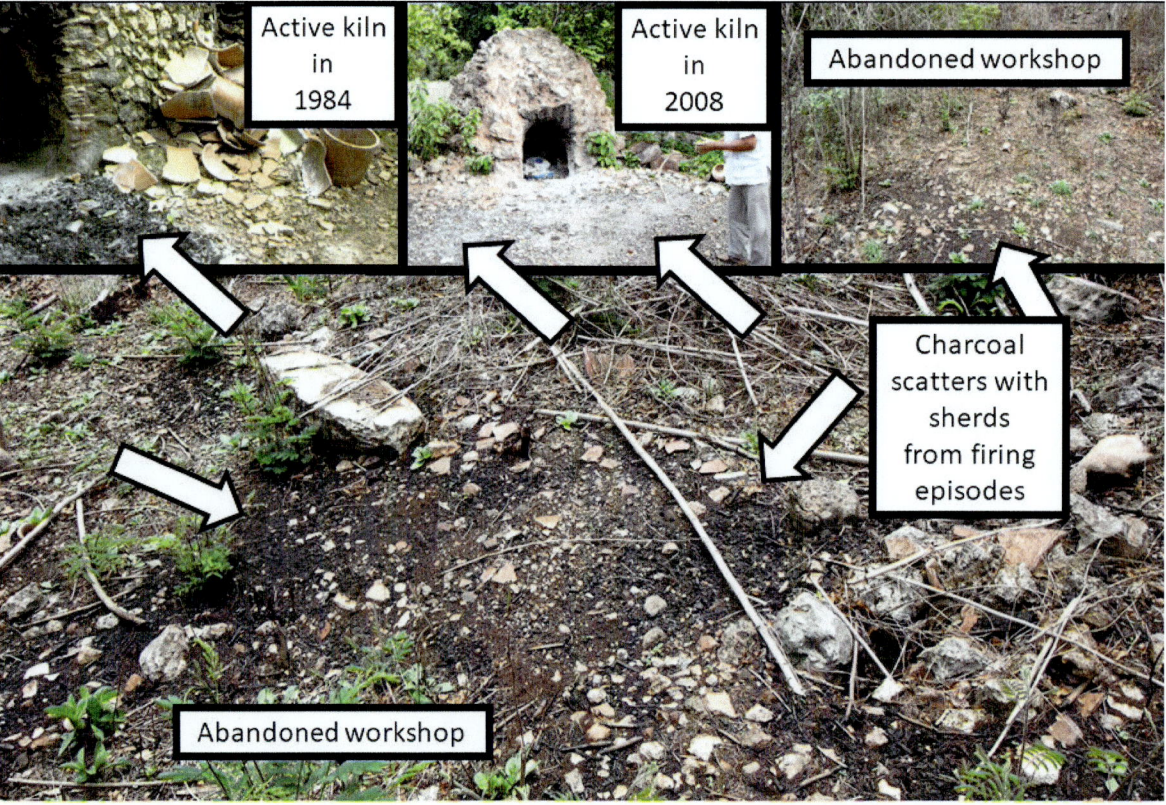

Figure 7. Charcoal scatters around the abandoned workshop site in 2008 (*bottom and upper right*) compared with charcoal scatters in front of active kilns in Ticul in 1984 (*upper left*) and 2008 (*upper middle*). (Photograph by Dean E. Arnold)

Using the number of charcoal scatters around the abandoned workshop site, it is possible to infer the amount of time that the workshop was in operation. The charcoal pulled from the kiln also contains potsherds that are discarded fragments of the trimmed wasters. After rainfall, the ash from the kiln washes into the ground. So, the ash, charcoal, and sherds removed from the kiln soon become a scatter of charcoal and sherds. Each charcoal scatter thus is a material index of at least one firing event, but may indicate more than one event if the charcoal is not removed from the inside of the kiln after each firing, or if the amount of charcoal in a scatter was large.

These charcoal scatters are usually left near the kiln, but potters' house lots often have spreads of charcoal around them in locations more distant from the kiln. In house lots with limited space, the charcoal may be dumped in the same location, but workshops may also remove such accumulations to areas outside of Ticul if they own a truck.

Around the kiln in this abandoned workshop, there were eight such charcoal scatters (Figure 7). If each is the result of at least one firing event, then the elapsed time for the use-life of the workshop was eight firing events. Since firing events occur at the end of the production sequence that is usually two weeks long, amount of time that the workshop was used was at least sixteen weeks. The probable total elapsed time for production activity at this workshop thus was probably less than one year.

**Discussion**

The most puzzling aspect of the material remains of this workshop is that there is so little evidence of pottery production. Even the material analogs with potters' house lots in Ticul are limited. Except for the kiln, the structural remains of this workshop were difficult to attribute to pottery making without the analogical ethnoarchaeological evidence from Ticul. There were few wasters or broken pots. Why?

Several decades ago, Michael Schiffer (1983, 1985) pointed out that archaeological sites (particularly ancient households in his discussion) do not reflect the systemic context of the relationship of the household's material residues to the behavior of its members as if the occupants just walked out one day and left everything behind. This 'Pompeii Premise', Schiffer argued, is probably seldom true. Rather, Schiffer argued that what archaeologists see in ancient households are not material residues that are frozen in time when occupants suddenly left the site, but rather were the result of a series of site formation processes that were largely cultural in nature.

In this case, one formation process that left so little in this site can be ascertained from the brief oral history that I elicited from my informant. From his account, the workshop was established by the daughter of a traditional potter and her husband. After pottery was no longer made there, the owner had wanted to sell him the kiln for 5000 pesos. The only reason that this offer to sell made sense was that it was made with cement and a special kind of rocks (*sakel bach tuunich*) that were uniquely suited to building kilns (see Arnold 2008, 285; Arnold 2017). This kind of rock occurs infrequently and are not always available. The seller thought that either the kiln could be dismantled and the rocks reused, or the buyer could transport his pottery to the site to fire it. It is, however, always risky to move dried pottery more than a little distance because it is so fragile.

This brief narrative indicates that everything useful and valuable in the workshop was removed or sold when it was abandoned and moved to another production unit. Except for the kiln that the owner tried to sell, only the useless items remained. Because the kiln was both permanent and expensive, it is not surprising that the owner wanted to sell it, but it is not surprising that no one wanted to buy it.

**Conclusion**

This reconstruction of the abandoned workshop outside of Ticul provides a cautionary tale about the material signatures of pottery production units and shows the importance of site formation processes that limit inferences about the production of ancient abandoned workshops. A firing area is the most obvious indication of pottery production as it is in highland Guatemala where kilns are not used, and the only remains of firing are fire-hardened areas near pottery making households (Arnold 1978, 377-379). In the case of the workshop described here, except for the kiln, the structural remains are difficult to attribute to pottery making.

So, one is left with foundations of structures, highly fragmented wasters from the kiln, useless molds that either were damaged or were missing their other half, and the remains of raw materials used to construct the kiln and make the pottery. No clay remains as that would hydrate and disappear with the intense rains of the rainy season.

Although the natural marl and the raw material for pottery temper also contain clay (palygorskite and smectite), they mainly consist of calcite and dolomite and would not disappear as quickly.

By comparing the material remains at the site, and with those of pottery production in the household production units in Ticul, it is possible to make the following inferences. First, an oval paste preparation area appears to exist inside the remains of a structure used to store and sift temper, and to mix temper and clay. Second, discarded fragments of two molds indicated that potters used vertical-half molding to form at least some of the pottery at the workshop. Third, the pile of the raw material that appears to be from the temper mines suggested the kiln was constructed in the traditional way using the ingredients of *sah kab* temper and the red earth (*k'an kab*) for its mortar and plaster. Fourth, wasters, thought to the normal material signature of production units, may not be present at a workshop site because they can be reused by potters elsewhere. Finally, scatters of charcoal removed from the kiln after firing allows an estimate of the duration of the workshop activity that was probably less than one year. These observations suggest that, interpretations of what might be pottery production units can be enhanced by studying the materials signatures of modern traditional production units in the same community.

What does this mean for the archaeology of pottery production areas in the Maya area and elsewhere? These data suggest that abandoned production units like this one, and the neighboring abandoned workshops that are spatially removed from households, have a relatively short life. By way of contrast, pottery production that takes place in households can persist for many decades (see Arnold 2008, 2015). This same observation also conforms to data about pottery making workshops attached to tourist hotels in Uxmal (Arnold 2015, 231-241), and is probably also true for ancient workshops that were attached to elites.

## Acknowledgements

The data for this paper was collected during research in Yucatán in 2008 and was funded by a grant from the National Geographic Society (No. 7433-08) for another project.

## References Cited

Arnold, Dean E. 1971. 'Ethnomineralogy of Ticul, Yucatan Potters: Etics and Emics'. *American Antiquity* 36: 20-40.
Arnold, Dean E. 1978. 'The Ethnography of Pottery Making in the Valley of Guatemala'. In *The Ceramics of Kaminaljuyu*, edited by Ronald K. Wetherington, 327-400. University Park: Pennsylvania State University Press.
Arnold, Dean E. 1985. *Ceramic Theory and Cultural Process*. Cambridge: Cambridge University Press.
Arnold, Dean E. 1999. 'Advantages and Disadvantages of Vertical-half Molding Technology: Implications for Production Organization'. In *Pottery and People: A Dynamic Interaction*, edited by James M. Skibo and Gary M. Feinman, 50-80. Salt Lake City: University of Utah Press.
Arnold, Dean E. 2008. *Social Change and the Evolution of Ceramic Production and Distribution in a Maya Community*. Boulder: University Press of Colorado.
Arnold, Dean E. 2015. *The Evolution of Ceramic Production Organization in a Maya Community*. Boulder: University Press of Colorado.
Arnold, Dean E. 2017. *Maya Potters' Indigenous Knowledge: Cognition, Engagement and Practice*. Boulder: University Press of Colorado.
Schiffer, Michael B. 1983. 'Toward the Identification of Formation Processes'. *American Antiquity* 48 (5): 675-706.
Schiffer, Michael B. 1985. 'Is There a 'Pompeii Premise' in Archaeology?'. *Journal of Anthropological Research* 45 (1): 18-41.
Thompson, Raymond H. 1958. 'Modern Yucatecan Maya Pottery Making.' *Memoirs of the Society for American Archaeology*, No. 15, Salt Lake City.

# Chapter 10

# Making Traditional Pottery Sustainable Today: Three Case Studies in Akita Prefecture, Japan

### Cara L. Reedy
Rensselaer Polytechnic Institute; reedyc@rpi.edu

### Chandra L. Reedy
University of Delaware; clreedy@udel.edu

**Abstract**

Handmade ceramics are an important cultural heritage of Japan, yet by the late 19th century traditional workshops were disappearing in favor of factory mass production. Many studies focus on national and international programs that support traditional potters. We investigate preservation efforts originating with craft practitioners themselves. Three case studies in Akita Prefecture represent three different approaches. Naraoka kiln was established in 1863 and has operated continuously. At Waheegama kiln, operations established in 1770 ended by 1900. In 1975, a descendant of an original potter began to rediscover traditional practices. For both kilns we examine raw materials, fabrication, firing, products, and marketing strategies, highlighting what remains original and what was changed so that the kilns could continue to thrive. The third site is a small shop (*Kurashi no Utsuwa Mike*) in a residential area selling affordable pottery. They sell some products from Akita kilns and many from kilns in other prefectures where they have family ties and can obtain objects inexpensively. The owner produces some pottery himself, and holds workshops in the store for local residents. These three sites demonstrate connections to past materials and processes that transform pottery into meaningful objects for both makers and users of pottery in Akita today.

**Keywords**
*Japanese pottery; Intangible cultural heritage; Akita; Naraoka kiln; Waheegama kiln*

Introduction

A central part of the human experience shared by people and societies throughout the world is a desire to feel ties with past traditions. Community identity is often united around tangible material culture with local connections to the past and associated intangible cultural heritage (such as meanings, rituals, knowledge, and skills). Traditional pottery is integrally connected to many aspects of a community. These include aspects of the environment, such as the location of raw materials and fuel sources; technological skills, like fabrication and decoration methods, firing techniques, and kiln design; and sociocultural variables such as the organization of production, gender roles, learning and apprenticeship practices, form and decoration in design of products, and marketing and sales strategies including range and locations of markets. These ties to the past can be a source of pride and can enhance the sense of having long-term roots in the community. Yet, in many communities, traditional crafts have partially or wholly disappeared as one of the effects of widespread mass production in factories, with modernized methods and new materials, and globalization, which brings easy availability of inexpensive mass-produced objects from all over the world into almost any community. In response, programs intended to help preserve traditional crafts and their associated knowledge and skills have emerged at both the international and national levels.

Most programs aimed at preserving traditional craft skills and methods are top-down, with governments or international or national organizations and panels of non-craftspeople enacting legislation or promoting and supporting craftspeople. While these programs have had many beneficial effects, it is worth noting the success achieved through local individual efforts originating with craft practitioners themselves. We highlight three case studies of such efforts in Akita Prefecture of northeastern Japan, which is located well outside of the famous Japanese 'pottery villages' or major production centers mainly found in central and southern Japan (such as Mashiko, Tokoname, Seto, Mino, Shigaraki, Bizen, Arita, and others). These local people in Akita have pursued various strategies that are helping to preserve traditional Japanese pottery products and techniques in their home prefecture.

**National Programs for Preservation of Traditional Pottery Technology in Japan**

Pottery holds a very elevated place in the history of material culture in Japan. The craft dates back to 10,000 BC (Moes 2003). Pottery workshops and entire villages where a large number of inhabitants were involved in pottery production developed throughout the country wherever good clay deposits were found in abundance, with many regional styles and specializations. While influenced at various times by Korea and China, these regions developed their own unique materials, fabrication methods, and decorative techniques (Crueger *et al.* 2004; Sanders and Tomimoto 1967; Wilson 1995). Upon the end of isolation from the West in the 19th century, Japan became increasingly conscious of the uniqueness of its own culture, including craft skills, and preservation of these was considered important for maintaining a sense of national identity and pride (Akagawa 2016). With the end of the feudal system that had provided patronage to pottery workshops, and the emergence of industrialization from the late 19th century onward bringing mass-produced factory objects, often influenced by Western styles and tastes, onto the market, traditional handmade Japanese pottery was considered to be in danger of dying out (Japan Folk Crafts Museum 1991).

The term 'traditional craft' usually refers to handmade objects using traditional raw materials, forms, and designs (Xu 2013). The value in preserving traditional craft technologies is recognized by many international and national programs directed towards that goal. For example, the UNESCO Convention for the Safeguarding of Intangible Cultural Heritage explicitly incorporates traditional craftsmanship within the domain of intangible cultural heritage (Smith and Akagawa 2009; UNESCO 2003, 2007). This is recognition of the fact that while preserving craft products themselves in a museum environment may be important, preservation of the necessary skills and knowledge is crucial for the continued production of those crafts. This UNESCO convention is rooted in many ideas that originated in Japan about the need to preserve traditional skills, expressed and debated during development of the 1994 ICOMOS (International Council on Monuments and Sites) Nara Document on Authenticity (Akagawa 2016).

Programs of a national or regional scale aimed at preserving traditional crafts emerged in many countries at the end of the 19th and beginning of the 20th centuries as a reaction to increased industrialization. In the West, many of these programs were connected to the ideals of the Arts and Crafts movement. In the United States, for example, new philanthropic foundations emerged in the early 20th century with the goal of providing support for 'handicrafts' for social purposes, focusing on the idea that making and viewing crafts could help reconnect people to their cultural traditions (White 2004).

In the late 19th century, the Japanese government established both the Department of Industrial Craft, at Tokyo Imperial University, and the Imperial Technical Craft Scheme to protect some of Japan's unique craft traditions (Akagawa 2016). In the 1920s, the government established additional craft training institutes. As the issue of preservation of cultural heritage gained increasing importance in Japan, the Cultural Property Law was enacted in 1950, and included the idea of intangible cultural heritage. Craft works were included as tangible cultural heritage alongside monuments, works of art, books, and historic documents. Intangible cultural heritage incorporates distinguished individuals and institutions who contribute to development of professional skills in performing and visual arts.

National efforts to support traditional crafts included establishment in the 1950s of an annual Japan Fine Arts Exhibition (*Nitten*) and the first Japan Traditional Handicrafts Exhibition held in 1954 at the initiative of the Cultural Properties Protection Committee (now Agency for Cultural Affairs) (Kida 2012). During this post-war period, the cultural category of 'traditional crafts' received a variety of new systems for recognition and preservation, and the work of potters engaged in recovery of lost traditional techniques or reviving traditional forms received more positive response both within Japan and outside of it than they had in the pre-war period (Kida 2012). For pottery, the Japan Ceramics Promotion Association, founded in 1947, focused on promoting the production of traditional crafts, primarily for export. Internally, reviving traditional Japanese crafts was seen as a way to connect back with the past and to unify the country, while externally engaging other parts of the world with positive aspects of Japan's culture and to communicate original aesthetic ideas of long-term cultural importance.

In the mid-1950s, the Japanese government revised the cultural properties laws to establish the Living National Treasures award (Holders of Important Intangible Cultural Assets), as a means of highlighting and supporting the continuing work of traditional 'applied' artists and craftsmen, reviving craft techniques of the past which had either died out or were in danger of doing so, and publicizing the intangible aspects of these crafts. The program was intended to protect traditional crafts, in the same way that preservation programs had long been enacted for the protection of works of art, buildings, and other tangible cultural heritage in Japan (Fontein 1982). The legal changes of the 1950s also included instituting a system for documenting intangible folk materials; this turned the focus onto preserving the objects and skills of ordinary people, not only for building national pride but also 'to nurture the love of one's hometown' (Akagawa 2015, 2016; Kurabayashi 1997).

In the 1950s, Japan was a global trailblazer in the establishment of programs to register and preserve intangible cultural properties, which included applied arts and crafts. In addition to registering endangered or important crafts, Holders of Important Intangible Cultural Properties, known as 'National Living Treasures', can be nominated if highly trained and able to represent a tradition to a high degree. The award comes with financial support to ensure continuation of the tradition, as well as full documentation of the craft and exhibitions to publicize it (Fontein 1982). One of the highest honors in the arts in Japan is to be appointed a Living National Treasure, and more than 30 ceramicists have been included (Creuger et al. 2004; Faulkner 2003; Hamaka and Ohmi 1999). For example, one of the most famous Japanese potters of the 20th century, Hamada Shoji (1894-1978) was accorded that honor (Carter 2008). This institution itself, and the publicity it gains for the honorees, reflects a national interest in preserving traditional crafts in Japan. Its emergence in the 1950s is a response to the concern at that time about the potential loss of Japanese cultural traditions due to greater Western and global influence and interactions. Yet, national programs such as this one can only highlight and support the most well-known craft traditions of a country.

Further Japanese government help in preserving traditional pottery methods came with a 1974 law supporting craft companies that use mainly traditional materials and methods to adapt craft products for current markets. Other programs that help to support and preserve traditional pottery workshops in Japan are administered by prefectures and municipalities (Crueger et al. 2004). Preservation of traditional crafts is often connected to tourism and the economic incentives it brings (Pryor 1988). Unique local crafts are seen as important for attracting tourists (Israr et al. 2010) and tourism may be perceived as a means of supporting the existence and continuation of local traditional crafts. The intangible cultural aspects connected with making and using crafts are recognized as important draws for heritage tourism, while at the same time the expression of that intangible heritage for tourists can help to renew a community's sense of pride, identity, and place (Bowers and Corsane 2012).

Economic development initiatives, administered by international, regional, or national programs, often focus on supporting traditional crafts by providing training, materials, and access to markets for craft products, as a means of economic support for poor urban or rural citizens (Szala-Meneok and McIntosh 1996). While providing that economic boost, it is seen as an added benefit that these programs can also help preserve traditional craft technologies and products (Graburn 2004; Kreps 2012). However, it is also recognized that some crafts will tend to fade away if they serve primarily local utilitarian needs, while those that appeal to tourists, or can be adapted and changed so that they do appeal to them, will be more likely to continue (Pryor 1988).

One of the most famous national efforts of the 20th century to preserve traditional crafts is the Japanese folk craft movement. One of Hamada Shoji's colleagues, the scholar Muneyoshi (Sōetsu) Yanagi (1889-1961) worked with him and the potter Kanjirō Kawai in the late 1920s on the development of *mingei* (people's art, or folk crafts, movement). Their movement, along with the Japan Folk Art Association, was devoted to the documentation, promotion, and preservation of the traditional 'hand-crafted art of ordinary people' that was disappearing due to competition from mass-produced industrialized products, with many parallels to the Arts and Crafts movement in the West (Kikuchi 1997; Moeran 1989). Movement leaders were instrumental in helping many kilns to revive their diminishing production (Mizuo 1981; Okamura 1981). This movement was successful in helping to preserve many traditional Japanese craft technologies, including pottery. Indeed, the *mingei* movement and the help and inspiration of Hamada are directly credited by the Waheegama kiln owners in Kakunodate (see below) for the re-establishment of their kiln and revival of traditional *Shiraiwa* wares. Yet, the effects of this movement are actually complex; it has also been noted that many communities that found their traditional pottery elevated to folk art status changed their original production technologies to better cater to tourists and other folk art connoisseurs (Moeran 1997). Tensions within the movement also arose between purists who wished to preserve their idea of a traditional simple lifestyle that would lead craftspeople to maintain the 'essence' of traditional crafts, versus those who sought to interact more with the modern world and make changes as needed (Faulkner 2003).

The national *mingei* movement promoted some ideals (Muraoka and Okamura 1973; Yanagi 1972) that were limiting and not sustainable. The idea that part of the beauty of folk crafts comes from the fact that they are functional and use locally-obtained natural materials may apply to many traditional pottery workshops. However, the ideal of using only traditional methods of production does not always apply, as will be seen in the case studies below. Limiting, too, is the movement's ideal that crafters should maintain pure, spiritual, or 'humble' intentions during fabrication; such an ideal may not be shared by all craft producers. But most importantly, the *mingei* ideal that works should be made by unknown crafters working cooperatively but without regard for financial gain is simply not economically sustainable. Hence while this folk art movement helped in the preservation of traditional crafts in Japan through exhibitions, publications, and media promotion of handmade crafts, such a national movement on its own is not sufficient to ensure preservation of a craft technology and its intangible aspects.

It has been noted (Xu 2013) that any efforts to preserve traditional crafts can benefit from starting with a good understanding of the reasons for their longevity and success in the past. For a traditional craft to continue to be sustainable, it must be seen by those who make, purchase, and use it as an item of value. Zhang (2012) noted that handicrafts that are ascribed values of tradition, cultural authenticity, or connections to a specific place tend to be seen as more valuable. In order to help preserve a craft tradition, governmental or national programs may use various strategies in order to emphasize or enhance the prestige of the craft objects, especially as they relate to cultural or national association. One problem is that 'romanticizing the pre-modern glosses over realities of historical continuities' (Zhang 2012). Revitalization and continuity of traditional crafts requires that they not be fossilized, but that they must be able to evolve and change while still retaining the core of what makes them a traditional craft (Akagawa 2016). In the past, the creativity and innovation of traditional craftspeople led to periodic changes in materials and design. Such changes responded to changing markets and consumer taste. To be healthy and sustainable, any traditional craft as practiced today must also continue to innovate and evolve. Bottom-up preservation efforts initiated and carried out by actual practitioners, in this case local potters, are much more likely to embody this concept of 'traditional but able to evolve and adapt'.

**Traditional Pottery in Akita Prefecture, Japan: Three Case Studies of Practioner-Led Preservation**

While the international, regional, and national craft technology preservation efforts discussed above have positively impacted the survival of traditional Japanese pottery skills and knowledge, other, more local approaches initiated by individual practitioners can also be found and are of crucial importance for the widespread preservation and continued diversity of traditional Japanese pottery. It was already noted decades ago that in spite of the existence of some traditional pottery kilns and villages that provide a link to Japan's past, these persisting traditions of long-standing indigenous technological developments are rare and vulnerable (Rhodes 1970). In other countries where pottery traditions have been revived and saved, local practitioner-led actions were primarily responsible, in bottom-up rather than top-down efforts (Arnold 2015; Reedy et al. 2017). These quiet, but effective, local practitioner-directed efforts can also be found in Japan. Here we focus on three examples in Akita Prefecture.

Figure 1. Map showing location of Akita Prefecture in the northeast of Japan. The three pottery sites are found in the central part of Akita Prefecture. (Map by authors)

Akita Prefecture is located in northeastern Japan, in the Tohoku region of northern Honshu (the main island of Japan) [Figure 1]. Famous for rice farming and sake brewing, Akita's primarily rural economy relies heavily on agriculture, fishing, and forestry. The prefecture does not appear among the usual lists or descriptions of the most famous traditional pottery regions or towns of Japan (for example, http://www.explorejapaneseceramics.com/towns/list.html). Yet, we found three locations where local efforts have led to continuation or revival of traditional pottery production and consumption: Naraoka kiln, Waheegama kiln, and *Kurashi no Utsuwa Mike*, a shop in a residential area of the prefecture capital, Akita *shi* (Akita city) [Figure 1].

## Naraoka Kiln, Daisen City

Naraoka kiln is located on the outskirts of Daisen, Naraoka district, in central Akita Prefecture. The kiln was established in 1863 by Seiji Komatsu, and has operated continuously as a family-run operation since that time. It has been designated an intangible cultural property of Daisen city. A small shop located adjacent to the pottery studio displays and sells a variety of the kiln's products (Figure 2A). Small signs found throughout the shop help potential customers to understand the history of Naraoka kiln and its products, and highlight the traditional aspects of the pottery made and sold here. For example, one sign reads:

Traditional ceramics
Naraoka ware
  Beginning at the end of the Edo Period, in the verdant land of Naraoka, we have continued to make items that are attached to people's daily lives.
  Even now, by such things as using local clay and firing in a climbing kiln, we value tradition while aiming to create pottery that pleases everyone.
(Translation by Cara L. Reedy)

Behind the shop are rooms housing the clay processing equipment, the production studio itself, and the original four-chambered *noborigama* (or 'climbing') kiln (Figure 2B). The clay is collected nearby, from a location about a five minute walk from the kiln. They have considerable clay reserves, enough for the next 100-200 years at least, in their estimation. The clay is now machine-excavated and brought back to the studio by the truckload. After being allowed to weather for several years, to improve the working properties of the clay, sand is added (to increase porosity and thus improve drying and firing properties) and it is mixed with water and machine-processed to grind, blend, homogenize, remove air pockets, and bring to the best working consistency. While much effort is required to make the clay usable, they would rather expend the effort instead of purchasing clay from elsewhere, since they 'believe that we can inherit tradition by using local clay and make things with Naraoka personality' (Komatsu 2017). All products are made individually by hand, using both moulds/slab building and wheel building techniques. As objects await firing, they are stored on wooden shelves with good air circulation on all sides to facilitate complete drying (Figure 3A).

Figure 2. (A) Shop at Naraoka kiln; (B) Naraoka's original 1863 four-chambered climbing kiln, still used once per year.
(Photographs by Cara L. Reedy)

Figure 3. (A) Fabricated objects drying on wooden shelves in the workshop, with enhanced air circulation to facilitate drying; (B) Burnt rice straw for glaze being prepared for elutriation on the workshop patio. (Photographs by Cara L. Reedy)

The workshop is small, employing five people. In the past, assistants used to come into the business through an apprenticeship system. Today, most potters are trained by university art departments. According to the studio, the reason people come to this sort of difficult work is because they like making things with their hands. They particularly like seeing other people enjoy the items they make – when people buy their things, they feel like saying, 'Thank you.'

Naraoka ware is especially known for its blue 'sea cucumber glaze' (speckled and mottled like the surface of a sea cucumber, an effect called *namako*) over a dark brown clay substrate. The workshop collects and prepares all of their own glaze ingredients. These mainly include straw ash, prepared by collecting straw from the rice fields surrounding the kiln and burning it (Figure 3B), followed by elutriation and grinding; oak ash, also prepared from locally-collected wood; and a feldspar-rich weathered volcanic ash (called 'white clay'), which they collect locally as well. The potters say that the volcanic ash produces the speckled blue-white glaze that is reminiscent of the surface of a sea cucumber, the oak ash helps the glaze mix together more easily, and the rice straw ash produces a glass-like brilliance and translucency. After initial bisque firing at 800°C, the glaze is applied in preparation for the final firing.

Modern gas and electric kilns are used two to three times per month. These work well for special orders that require fast turn-around times, and for bisque firings; they are inexpensive, stable, and easy to use. Once a year, the original 1863 four-chambered climbing kiln is fired for the production of regular products of the workshop. One of the potters noted that there used to be many climbing kilns in the region that have now disappeared. For example, near the current Naraoka pottery, there used to be *Naraoka Rokubee* kiln but 'the fire of that kiln vanished quite a while ago' (Komatsu 2017).

The climbing kiln at Naraoka can hold up to 2000 items, depending on their size, and is rather difficult to use and keep stable; the firing also produces much smoke and they consider it environmentally problematic. The temperature needed for the sea cucumber glaze is high; following the traditional manner, wood fuel is burned in the firebox at the base of the kiln, and hot air moves upward into each of the chambers. Approximately five tons of wood are required for a firing. The kiln must be watched at all times to maintain the fire at the correct temperature, adding wood as need to bring the temperature up to the required level. It takes three days to gradually achieve the maximum temperature needed (near 1300°C, cone 10) in all chambers, which is then held steady for one hour. A slot with removable bricks along the kiln sides providing a view of the cones mounted into clay chunks allows the temperature in each chamber to be monitored during the firing process. Depending on the products, either reducing conditions (excluding, or blocking off air into the kiln) or oxidizing conditions (allowing air to enter the kiln) may be used. The kiln is then allowed to cool for another three days, before the pottery is removed. After this intense firing regime, the historic kiln requires a significant amount of repairs each year.

There are many types of goods for sale in the shop attached to the studio. The focus of the goods available in the shop is not 'works of art' that would be used only for display, or items used only for special occasions such as tea ceremony, but rather on things such as flower pots, plates, bowls, and cups that can be used in daily life. The pottery is displayed in a variety of aesthetic ways throughout the store: lined up on shelves or spread out on a low *tatami* platform in the middle of the store. Petal-shaped ceramic chopstick rests are arranged in the shapes of flowers, and small groups of objects are isolated on stands and displayed together as they might be used in the home. There are photographs of the potters at work on the walls, reminding the visitor that the wares were made right there, and giving a sense of the long history of the kiln.

There is much variety in price of objects. While there are expensive items, there are also simpler or smaller items which are inexpensive, so that all visitors can find something to purchase. One workshop employee said that many people buy Naraoka ware as gifts or souvenirs, and he worried that few people buy them to actually use in everyday life anymore. He noted that if people want pottery to eat from, they can buy cheap items in a store very easily, so most people do that instead. The way Naraoka appeals to customers is that its items are unique to that particular kiln, not just that its items are traditional. Many of the products display the Naraoka kiln mark on the underside center. Purchasing items unique to this kiln appeals to visitors from other parts of Japan, and to local customers who want to display or use Akita products in their homes or send them as special local gifts to friends and relatives living outside of Akita.

The kiln's signature blue and white glaze (Figure 4A) is highlighted in particular. One sign notes:

> Naraoka ware
> *Namako* [sea cucumber] glaze
> The characteristics of *namako* glaze are a beautiful blue color and subtle changes.
> It uses local ingredients, and its charm is drawn out to the greatest extent.
> (Translation by Cara L. Reedy)

To encourage purchases, signs posted around the shop provide multiple examples of how various products can be used. The sign next to a bowl shaped like a three-leaf clover (Figure 4B) indicates this product is called a 'three-colored delicacy holder'. The sign goes on to suggest that while of course this object can be used as a condiment holder, one can also put in tea bags or *konpeitou* (star-shaped sugar candies), or jam or cream, for use at tea time. Another sign guides customers as to how they might use some of the small bowls for sale:

> Guide to lipped bowls
>   Kitchenware used since long ago when pouring things such as sake, oil, or soy sauce into small containers. Now, it has come to be used as small bowls or serving dishes, or many other such things.
>   The standing type doesn't take up space, so it is suitable for holding *mentsuyu* [a type of dipping sauce] or dressing.
> (Translation by Cara L. Reedy)

Figure 4. (A) The shop highlights the kiln's signature mottled blue 'sea cucumber' glaze (namako-yu); (B) Signage accompanying this 'three-colored delicacy holder' suggests uses for it. (Photographs by Cara L. Reedy)

Figure 5. (A) This grouping of objects displays how they could be used together, encouraging more purchases; (B) A sign informs potential customers that these plates are in the shape of Akita's prefectural flower, the giant butterbur, and provides local lore about the plants. (Photographs by Cara L. Reedy)

Groupings of objects display how several items could be used together (Figure 5A). These exhibits further encourage purchases by giving customers ideas of how they could use multiple objects as an ensemble. Other small signed displays help visitors to understand how particular object forms are a local specialty related to Akita Prefecture in particular. For example, one sign (Figure 5B) indicates that peculiarly-shaped plates in front of it are called giant butterbur plates. The sign informs potential customers that:

> These are plates modeled after the leaves of giant butterburs, Akita's prefectural flower. Akita giant butterburs are famous for being large, with leaf stalks 2 meters long and leaf diameters of up to 1.5 meters, to the point of being sung of in Akita Ondo [Akita March]:
> 'In the land of Akita
>   even when it rains you don't need an umbrella,
>   lightly hold up a handy butterbur leaf
>   and go on out.'
> (Translation by Cara L. Reedy)

In addition to selling to visitors who come to their pottery workshop, the kiln markets its products through many local stores, especially ones focusing on souvenirs of Akita Prefecture. These include five in Daisen, in addition to their own store; six in Akita city; five in Senboku District, four of which are in Kakunodate near the Waheegama kiln discussed below; and various roadside stations in the prefecture. They also sell products at seven stores located outside of Akita (Komatsu 2017).

### Waheegama Kiln, Kakunodate

Waheegama kiln is located outside the town of Kakunodate. While it makes a variety of products, one specialty of this family-run kiln is *Shiraiwa-yaki* (*Shiraiwa* ware). It is characterized by brown iron-rich clay that, like at Naraoka kiln, has a graduated blue and white speckled glaze called *namako-yu* (mottled sea cucumber glaze) (Figure 6). This glaze was featured in many historic products from the Kakunodate area. First established in 1771 by Unshichi Matsumoto, *Shiraiwa-yaki* potters once flourished in the Kakunodate area with six family-run kilns. However, the kilns had all been shut down by 1900, never fully recovering from the earthquake of 1896 that heavily damaged the kilns (Crueger *et al.* 2004; Mizuo 1981).

In 1975, Sunao Watanabe, a descendant of *Shiraiwa-yaki* potters of this region and who received training in ceramics at Iwate University, revived this ware at Waheegama. Her husband, Toshihara Watanabe, a ceramics artist who has taught at a number of universities in Japan and exhibited his works widely, joined in these efforts. During 1992-1993 he designed and built the traditional four-chambered climbing kiln at Waheegama (Figure 7), by consulting historical descriptions of the kilns in books and photographing the details of one still in use. This is the only kiln in the Kakunodate area that has been revived.

CHAPTER 10   MAKING TRADITIONAL POTTERY SUSTAINABLE TODAY

Figure 6. (A) The main specialty of Waheegama kiln is Shiraiwa ware, a graduated blue and white speckled/mottled glaze over a brown iron-rich body; (B) The kiln sells many variations on Shiraiwa ware, as well as a white-glazed ware. (Photographs by Cara L. Reedy)

Figure 7. (A) Traditional four-chambered climbing kiln at Waheegama that was reconstructed in 1992-1993; wood fuel is stacked alongside it; (B) Zigzag-shaped white paper streamers on and above the kiln are used in Shinto ceremonies to bless the kiln and its operation; (C) Netting over kiln openings prevents entry by birds, since there are ventilation openings below the rafters. (Photographs by Cara L. Reedy)

The Watanabes say that their main inspiration for the building of this kiln and the revival of traditional *Shiraiwa* wares was the *mingei* movement. Shoji Hamada (1894-1978), a Living National Treasure of Japan, was one of the collaborators in this movement who inspired them. Sunao Watanabe says that she was greatly supported by him in her wish to revive *Shiraiwa* pottery in her birthplace of Kakunodate.

For fire safety, the kiln is housed in a separate building (Figure 8A), with the studio and a small shop (Figure 8B) located nearby. The couple and their daughter (Aoi Watanbe) run the family business, with everyone participating in all steps of pottery production. Clay is collected adjacent to the workshop. Prior to establishing the kiln at this location, the Watanabes conducted experiments with the clay; while it had been used in the past for local pottery production, they wanted to ensure that they fully understood its working properties. The iron-rich clay will turn red under oxidizing firing conditions and gray to black under reducing conditions. They add a small amount of sand to the clay to improve its drying and firing properties. Some types of objects are given a rougher surface, such as some of their teacups; they add coarse sand in these cases. Fine sand is added if a smooth surface is needed, such as with ink stones and chopstick holders. Like the Naraoka kiln, they use wheels to help shape the clay, but there are some items which are built with moulds. The clay is allowed to dry indoors prior to firing.

Figure 8. (A) For fire safety, the kiln is housed in a separate building, with ventilation openings between the walls and rafters; (B) Many customers travel to the shop located at the kiln site to make their purchases. (Photographs by Chandra L. Reedy)

The potters also gather and prepare their own glaze materials. The traditional *namako-yu* pottery had long since ceased being produced in this region before the 1975 re-establishment of the Waheegama kiln. Hence, reproducing it required much experimentation with local glaze ingredients and with firing processes until they could adequately reproduce the traditional historic glaze appearance. They burn rice straw from the local harvest for ash and collect and grind local sodic feldspathic stone.

In addition to the blue sea cucumber glaze, the kiln also specializes in wares with a white glaze (Figures 6B, 9) over the same brown iron-rich clay. For this white glaze they collect, grind, and combine local limestone with the feldspar.

The climbing kiln here is slightly smaller than the one at Naraoka. In the shed that covers the kiln are tall stacks of cut wood lining the walls for use in the next firing (Figure 7A), as well as stacks of saggars for housing smaller pottery items during firing to protect them from exposure to ash from the fire, which would change the color of the glaze. Netting hanging over the openings to the kiln chambers prevents birds from flying in (Figure 7C) since there are open spaces for air to enter between the walls and the rafters. On top of the lowest chamber, above the opening where firewood is fed into the kiln, and hanging from the roof of the kiln shed, are *shide* paper tassels (Figures 7A, 7B). These are zigzag-shaped white paper streamers used in Shinto ceremonies; they help to bless the kiln and its operations.

The traditional kiln here, as at Naraoka, is fired only once per year. That firing requires a large amount of wood. They fill the main fire box with Japanese red pine wood first, as it has oils that are good at achieving a high temperature quickly. Then, one by one, they fill the side chambers using regular pine wood. During firing, smoke fills the kiln house. Sand is stored directly in front of the kiln to put out any fires that might start as a result of the heat of firing. It takes three days to achieve the peak temperature; they then cool the kiln for about one week before removing the pottery. Items with different glazes need to be fired at different temperatures, and so they are arranged in the kiln accordingly. The items needing the lowest temperatures are placed at the back and in the top chamber of the kiln, the areas furthest from the intense heat of the fire. After firing, the kiln does not need much repair work, unlike the one at Naraoka, perhaps because the Waheegama kiln is so much newer in construction.

In addition to the climbing kiln, Waheegama uses a kerosene kiln. While it is more difficult to control the temperatures in the wood-burning climbing kiln and kerosene one versus electric or gas kilns, they believe that better results come from using more traditional methods. However, they do much experimentation and innovation in forms, designs, and types of products.

The kiln emphasizes many ordinary household items such as cups, bowls, and plates. However, they also make some additional traditional products such as a *furo* (a portable stove used to heat water during a tea ceremony) (Figure

9B), hibachi heating devices, inkstones, and chopstick rests (Figure 9C). An unusual product of this kiln is a ceramic *Ojizou-sama* statue for the nearby Buddhist temple (Figure 10A). Since this type of statue (intended to commemorate a deceased child) is usually carved from stone, this is an intriguing way for the kiln to branch out and serve the local community. A sign in front of a display of such statues ties the history of these objects into local history and local pottery traditions:

The Ojizou-sama of Shiraiwa
A long time ago, one hundred and seventy years before now.
   This land, known for its fertile fields of Michi-no-ku [a poetic name for the Northeast region], was struck with an unprecedented poor harvest.
   The grains on the ears of rice were small, there was no grass for oxen and horses to eat, and people could not raise children.
   The impoverished people of Shiraiwa, as a memorial service for their lost children, offered hundreds of figures of Ojizou-sama as a prayer.
   Those who made them were the people of the old Shiraiwa Pottery.
   Time passed, and everyone's worries about tomorrow's meal went away.
   However, people's wishes once again changed shape, and the Ojizou-sama of Shiraiwa continued on as a support for prayer.

Figure 9. (A) A second specialty of Waheegama kiln is a white glaze over brown iron-rich clay; (B) A traditional Waheegama kiln product is a portable stove used to heat water during a tea ceremony. C. Chopstick rests are another traditional product. (Photographs by Cara L. Reedy)

Figure 10. (A) Ojizou-sama statues commemorate deceased children and are usually made of stone; ceramic versions are a specialty of Waheegama kiln; (B) In addition to its traditional products, the kiln also sells some modern art pottery. (Photographs by Cara L. Reedy)

Those wishing for their children to grow up healthy, those doing prayers [or making a wish to a Kami or Buddha], those putting their hands together during their daily lives….
Now, in the lineage of Shiraiwa ware that has continuously created the Ojizou-sama, we have added the name of Waheegama.
They have the distinctive gentle appearance of clay items, but if they could become talismans for everyone's hearts, we would know the highest form of happiness.
(Translation by Cara L. Reedy)

To more of an extent than at Naraoka, besides the colors of the glazes being used to make patterns on the ceramics, images are drawn. For example, one rectangular plate had an interesting variegated white-tan glaze, but also featured rabbits frolicking across it where the glaze had been blocked from the surface of the plate in a resist technique (Figure 9A). There are also pieces where glaze had been painted on. The design methods are quite varied and creative, and include some pieces that could be categorized as 'modern art pottery' (Figure 10B), as well as ceramic jewelry. One stated goal of Waheegama kiln is to continue to use traditional handmade methods and local glaze materials, but to produce pottery that is suitable for modern uses and which fits the aesthetics of modern consumers.

According to the owner, while they have one other location where their wares are sold, most customers come to the small shop at the kiln to see items in person and purchase them on site. The owner says that many people buy the pottery to use themselves, as well as purchasing it to give as gifts. They also recently started selling through a website (https://www.waheegama.com/) operated by the daughter, who is fluent in English and created an English version of the site as well. She is pleased that while in the past people mostly came because the pottery is famous in the local area, they now also have the website as a form of wider advertisement in addition to word of mouth.

### Kurashi no Utsuwa Mike Pottery Shop, Akita shi

This family-run pottery shop in Akita *shi* (Akita city), called *Kurashi no Utsuwa Mike* (暮らしの器 ミケ), is located in a residential area, surrounded by homes. It is situated in a small neighborhood set back from a main road, across the street from a park, and most of the surrounding buildings are apartments and small houses. It is not in a location that would be seen or sought out by tourists, but instead caters to those who live in its residential quarter. The small shop was established 20 years ago and is operated by an amateur potter, his wife, and their daughter. It sells affordable utilitarian pottery like bowls, tea cups, and plates that would be used in an everyday context. They estimate that their customers are about 95% female. The shop reports that many of these customers are local housewives who have an interest in cooking, and are seeking out interesting pottery to use in serving their meals and teas. They usually buy the pottery sold at the store for their own use, rather than as gifts, and to use either as ordinary kitchenware or tableware or for special occasions.

While they do sell wares from the local kilns, most of the pottery sold in the shop is not made in Akita, but instead comes mainly from three other locations: Kasama, in Ibaraki prefecture; Mashiko, in Tochigi prefecture; and Shigaraki in Shiga prefecture. Some pottery from other locales is also represented, mainly Kyoto and Fukushima. The owners chose these areas to buy from because there are many potters there, they have some family ties in those areas, and they can obtain pottery from those locations relatively inexpensively. They note that if they sold only local Akita products, many of these are more expensive for them to purchase and so would have to sell for higher prices, and their local customers are seeking more lower-priced utilitarian wares. The pottery sold in the shop includes a variety of forms, designs, glaze colors, and textures (Figure 11). Also popular with their customers are unglazed objects, colored naturally and randomly by ash during wood firings; where the ash lands on the surface, the clay turns glassy and become different intriguing colors.

The store itself is small, and pottery takes up most of the display space. However, the shop also sells other handmade craft items, mainly local glass and local Akita lacquerware products. One small section of the store is devoted to unique but affordable women's fashions and accessories, including locally-made jewelry, which would appeal to the mostly-female customer base. A small selection of homemade food items is available near the check-out area. Pottery and other craft workshops are also held in the store, at a table located in the back (Figure 11B).

The husband is a talented self-taught potter. He says that he read technical books and observed other potters in order to learn the craft. In his spare time he produces a small amount of pottery, mainly coarse-grained ash-glazed ware. He fabricates the pieces on the table in the back of the shop, and later takes them for firing to a shared kiln located outside of town in the hills near the border between Akita and Yamagata Prefectures. His wife makes all of

Figure 11. (A) Kurashi no Utsuwa Mike pottery shop is located in a residential neighborhood, and sells a variety of inexpensive handmade utilitarian products; (B) This table in the back of the store is used for craft workshops; the owner himself made most of the objects displayed here. (Photographs by Chandra L. Reedy)

the food items sold in the shop, in the kitchen area at the back of the shop where the craft table is located. These items are often seasonal; for example, she makes and sells small packets of Christmas cookies in December. On the 10th of every month the shop features sweets from their kitchen. A website (http://www.mike-craft.com/) illustrates the types of objects they sell, and provides photographs and a map to inform potential customers who do not live in the adjacent area how to find their shop.

## Conclusions

Both Akita Prefecture kilns use a variety of strategies to help ensure the sustainability of traditional ceramics. Both incorporate a shop at the kiln and workshop site. This on-site shop is intended to attract tourists and visitors to the prefecture who wish to feel that they are purchasing unique local products. While tours of the actual workshops and the traditional climbing kiln are given only upon request, simply by arriving at the rural kiln locations and visiting the on-site shop, visitors feel that they are seeing and purchasing authentic and unique Akita souvenirs.

Within the shops, signage helps the visitors understand which products are particular local specialties, and which are unique to a specific kiln. The signs also help explain local history and how the kiln products are connected to it. Other signs impart ideas about how to use certain products in the home, encouraging more purchases. A variety of price points ensures that all visitors will find something to buy, whether they are a student at one of the local universities seeking inexpensive but beautiful and useful souvenirs of Akita, or a collector seeking unique art pottery.

Both kilns retain connections to their history by using local clay, local traditional glaze raw materials that they collect and prepare themselves, hand-building techniques, and by maintaining a traditional wood-burning climbing kiln, even though it is used only once per year. At the same time, they have incorporated modern innovations in order to be competitive. For example, they have moved from a traditional apprenticeship system to relying on university art department graduates to find new workers. Mechanized clay extraction and processing methods are used. Kerosene, gas, and electric kilns are used on a regular basis. And, in both kiln shops, they sell a mix of traditional items, with some forms unique to each kiln, and some innovative modern designs and product types. In addition to the on-site shops at the kiln location, they also sell their products through other venues both within and outside of the prefecture, although the two kilns vary in number and location of these venues.

While one kiln has had an unbroken tradition since 1863, the other experienced a 75-year break in production. A descendant of one of the pottery families reconstructed a traditional climbing kiln in the same location where one had existed before, and uses the same local raw materials. This potter specifically credits the *mingei* movement as her inspiration.

The *Kurashi no Utsuwa Mike* shop, by establishing a location within a residential area and selling affordable utilitarian pottery, helps to strengthen the local market for traditional Japanese pottery, rather than supporting a tourist market or catering to visitors seeking Akita souvenirs. In addition to local wares, they emphasize objects purchased from other prefectures where family ties enable them to obtain relatively inexpensive handmade products from kilns in those locations.

They maintain a consistent and regular customer base by also selling other local Akita craft products, seasonal homemade food items, and other goods that appeal to their local, primarily female, customers. Craft classes taught in the back of the shop help maintain customer interest in the pottery and other craft products, and also allow the store owner to keep his hand in the craft and produce a few pottery items of his own to sell in his store.

These three sites in Akita Prefecture help keep interest in local traditional Japanese pottery alive, in spite of the many mass-produced items available in the department stores. The two local kilns are able to sustain their business, appealing to both local visitors and tourists looking for items unique to Akita and to the specific kilns. The store located in a residential suburb of the capital city helps to sustain local interest in handmade pottery that is used in everyday life, even though many of the products come from other nearby prefectures. As the *mingei* movement had hoped, through the efforts of local Akita practitioners, residents and visitors to Akita alike have maintained an appreciation of folk crafts made for everyday use by local, 'unnamed' crafters.

## Acknowledgments

We thank all of the kiln and shop owners and workers who took the time to talk with us, and who allowed us to photograph their facilities and products. Cara Reedy appreciates the opportunity to participate in University of Delaware's study abroad program at Akita International University, when she first encountered the pottery kilns and shops.

## References Cited

Akagawa, Natsuko. 2015. *Heritage Conservation in Japan's Cultural Diplomacy: Heritage, National Identify and National Interest.* London and New York: Routledge.

Akagawa, Natsuko. 2016. 'Intangible heritage and embodiment: Japan's influence on global heritage discourse.' In *A Companion to Heritage Studies*, edited by William Logan, Máiréad Nic Craith, and Ullrich Kocke, 69-86. Chichester: John Wiley & Sons.

Arnold, Dean E. 2015. *The Evolution of Ceramic Production in a Maya Community.* Boulder: University Press of Colorado.

Bowers, D. Jared, and Corsane, Gerard. 2012. 'Revisiting Amerindian intangible cultural heritage in Guyana and its value for sustainable tourism.' In *Safeguarding Intangible Cultural Heritage*, edited by Michelle L. Stefano, Peter Davis, and Gerard Corsane, 201-212. Woodbridge (UK): Boydell Press.

Carter, Robert E. 2008. *The Japanese Arts and Self-cultivation.* Albany: State University of New York Press.

Crueger, Anneliese, Wulf Crueger, and Saeko Itô. 2004. *Modern Japanese Ceramics: Pathways to Innovation & Tradition.* New York: Lark.

Faulkner, Rupert. 2003. 'Cultural identity and Japanese studio ceramics.' In *Quiet Beauty: Fifty Centuries of Japanese Folk Ceramics from the Montgomery Collection*, edited by Robert Moes, 237-245. Alexandria (VA): Art Services International.

Fontein, Jan (ed.) 1982. *Living National Treasures of Japan.* Tokyo and Boston: Nippon Television Network Corporation and Museum of Fine Arts.

Graburn, Nelson H. H. 2004. 'Authentic Inuit art: Creation and exclusion in the Canadian North.' *Journal of Material Culture* 9 (2): 141-159.

Hamaka, Sheila, and Ayano Ohmi. 1999. *In Search of the Spirit: The Living National Treasures of Japan.* New York: Morrow.

Japan Folk Crafts Museum. 1991. *Mingei: Masterpieces of Japanese Folkcraft.* Tokyo: Kodansha International.

Kida, Takuya. 2012. 'Japanese crafts and cultural exchange with the USA in the 1950s: Soft power and John D. Rockefeller III during the Cold War.' *Journal of Design History* 25 (4): 379-399.

Kikuchi, Yuko. 1997. 'Hybridity and the Oriental Orientalism of *mingei* theory.' *Journal of Design History* 10(4): 343-334.

Komatsu, Ushio. 2017. 'よくある質問'. 楢岡焼web. 楢岡陶苑.' Accessed June 7, 2017. http://www.naraokayaki.com/

Kreps, Christina. 2012. 'Intangible threads: Curating the living heritage of Dayak Ikat weaving.' In *Safeguarding Intangible Cultural Heritage*, edited by Michelle L. Stefano, Peter Davis, and Gerard Corsane, 177-193. Woodbridge (UK): Boydell Press.

Kurabayashi, Yoshimasa. 1997. 'Features and recent developments of cultural heritage policy in Japan.' In *Economic Perspectives on Cultural Heritage*, edited by Michael Hutter, and Ilde Rizzo, 155-169. New York: St. Martin's Press, Inc.

Israr, Muhammad, Humayun Khan, Nafees Ahmad, Malik Muhammad Shafi, Sultan Baig, Mujeebur Rahman, and Niaz Muhammad. 2010. 'Role of local food and handicrafts in raising eco-tourism in the northern areas of Pakistan.' *Sarhad Journal of Agriculture* 16 (1): 119-124.

Mizuo, Hiroshi. 1981. *Folk Kilns I*. Tokyo: Kodansha International.

Moes, Robert. 2003. *Quiet Beauty: Fifty Centuries of Japanese Folk Ceramics from the Montgomery Collection*. Alexandria, VA: Art Services International.

Moeran, Brian. 1989. 'Bernard Leach and the Japanese folk craft movement: The formative years.' *Journal of Design History* 2/3: 139-144.

Moeran, Brian. 1997. *Folk Art Potters of Japan*. Honolulu: University of Hawai'i Press.

Muraoka, Kageo, and Kichiemon Okamura. 1973. *Folk Arts and Crafts of Japan*. New York and Tokyo: Weatherhill/Heibonsha.

Okamura, Kichiemon. 1981. *Folk Kilns II*. Tokyo: Kodansha International.

Pryor, Pamela Takiora Ingram. 1988. 'Tourism and traditional art and crafts in the Cook Islands.' *Pacific Arts Newsletter* 26: 3-8.

Reedy, Chandra L., Pamela B. Vandiver, Ting He, and Ying Xu. 2017. 'Talc-rich black Tibetan pottery of Derge County, Sichuan Province, China.' *MRS Advances.* 2 (35-36): 1943-1968.

Rhodes, Daniel. 1970. *Tamba Pottery: The Timeless Art of a Japanese Village*. Tokyo: Kodansha International.

Sanders, Herbert H., and Kenkichi Tomimoto 1967. *The World of Japanese Ceramics*. Tokyo and Palo Alto: Kodansha International.

Smith, Laurajane, and Natsuko Akagawa (eds) 2009. *Intangible Heritage*. London and New York: Routledge.

Szala-Meneoka, Karen, and Kara McIntosh. 1996. 'Craft development and development through crafts: Adaptive strategies of Labrador women in a changing fishery.' *Anthropologica* 38 (2): 247-270.

UNESCO. 2003. 'Convention for the Safeguarding of Intangible Cultural Heritage.' United Nations Educational, Scientific and Cultural Organization. Accessed June 12, 2017. https://ich.unesco.org/en/convention

UNESCO. 2007. 'What is Intangible Heritage?' United Nations Educational, Scientific and Cultural Organization. Accessed June 12, 2017. https://ich.unesco.org/en/what-is-intangible-heritage-00003

White, John Howell. 2004. 'The preservation of handicrafts in the southern highlands: Northern philanthropy and social idealists.' *Visual Arts Research* 30 (1): 44-52.

Wilson, Richard L. 1995. *Inside Japanese Ceramics: A Primer of Materials, Techniques, and Traditions*. New York and Tokyo: Weatherhill.

Yanagi, Soetsu (trans. Bernard Leach). 1972. *The Unknown Craftsman: A Japanese Insight into Beauty*. Tokyo: Kodansha International.

Xu, Yiyu (trans. Dorothy Ko). 2013. 'The knowledge system of the traditional Chinese craftsman.' *West 86th* 20 (2): 155-172.

Zhang, Tracy Y. 2012. 'The making of 'valuable' carpets in Lhasa.' *Journal of Material Culture* 17(1): 83-101.